SINGER

Children's Clothes, Toys & Gifts Step-by-Step

NON PAGA DORMIRE

CY DeCOSSE
INCORPORATED

A COWLES MAGAZINES COMPANY

SINGER

Children's Clothes, Toys & Gifts
Step-by-Step

Contents

Copyright © 1995
Cy DeCosse Incorporated
5900 Green Oak Drive
Minnetonka, Minnesota 55343
1-800-328-3895
All rights reserved
Printed in U.S.A.

Singer Children's Clothes, Toys & Gifts draws
pages from the individual titles of the
Singer Reference Library. Individual titles
are available from the publisher and in
bookstores and fabric stores:
*Clothing Care & Repair, Sewing Specialty
Fabrics, Sewing Activewear, Sewing for Children,
Decorative Machine Stitching, Creative Sewing
Ideas, More Creative Sewing Ideas, Quick &
Easy Sewing Projects, Sewing for the Holidays,
Quilt Projects & Garments*

Library of Congress
Cataloging-in-Publication Data

Singer children's clothes, toys & gifts
step-by-step.
  p. cm.
Includes index.
ISBN 0-86573-304-X (hardcover)
1. Children's clothing. 2. Machine
sewing. I. Cy DeCosse Incorporated.
TT635.S538 1995
646.4'06 — dc20   95-30810

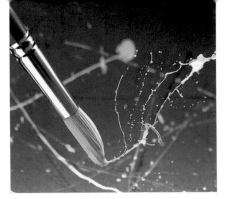

Published in the U.S.A. in 1995
and distributed in the U.S. by:
Cy DeCosse Incorporated
5900 Green Oak Drive
Minnetonka, MN 55343

CY DECOSSE INCORPORATED

A COWLES MAGAZINES COMPANY

Chairman/CEO: Bruce Barnet
Chairman Emeritus: Cy DeCosse
President/COO: Nino Tarantino
Executive V. P./Editor-in-Chief:
  William B. Jones

Created by: The Editors of Cy DeCosse
  Incorporated, in cooperation with
  the Sewing Education Department,
  Singer Sewing Company. Singer is a
  trademark of The Singer Company
  and is used under license.

Printed on American paper by:
  R. R. Donnelley & Sons Co. (1095)

How to Use This Book

Children's Clothes, Toys & Gifts will help you sew customized, professional-quality items. Whether you are sewing for infants, toddlers, or school-age children, you will find inspiring projects in this book.

To make the most efficient use of your time, become familiar with the information in the Getting Started section. Learn about up-to-date sewing equipment, notions, and techniques. Whenever appropriate, sewing techniques for the serger, or overlock machine, are included; however, when a serging method is shown, a conventional sewing machine method is also suggested, in case you do not have access to a serger. Also learn about important features in children's garments for safety, self-dressing, and customized style; and learn how to measure the child correctly to select an appropriate pattern.

The Infants section shows you how to plan and sew a basic layette. This section also includes complete instructions for sewing receiving blankets, hooded towels, bibs, crib sheets, and rompers; no purchased patterns are needed.

In Growing Up, you will find helpful tips for planning a child's wardrobe and discover ways to personalize the clothes. Because children's clothes are subjected to the stress and wear-and-tear of active play, they should be constructed for durability. You will learn how to strengthen and reinforce seams, add decorative patches, and build in grow room to prolong the life of the garment.

Comfortwear includes information on sportswear fabrics especially appropriate for children's clothing and on garment styles that maximize comfort. For activewear, learn how to select stretch fabrics with the built-in give necessary for a child's freedom of movement. For knitted shirts, we suggest special techniques for ribbed edges and shirt plackets. For pants and skirts, we show you how to make easy-to-sew elastic waistbands and mock fly fronts. This section also includes several techniques for custom details, such as piping and creative pockets, to personalize children's sportswear garments.

Sewing Outerwear discusses fabrics that provide warmth and protection from the elements. Learn the special methods needed for sewing nylon jackets constructed with an inner layer of insulation. Or sew an unlined jacket from fleece for a lightweight but warm garment, and make coordinating mittens, scarves, and other accessories from keep-you-cozy fleece.

So you can make special christening gowns and dresses for little girls, Dressing Up shows you the techniques of machine heirloom sewing and how to make perfect gathers and ruffles. For little boys, the section includes instructions for a dress-up reversible vest, bow tie, and suspenders.

The Personalizing section shows you how to paint on fabrics, sew appliqués, and use decorative machine stitching to create unique children's garments. This section also includes basic patchwork and color-blocking techniques that can inspire endless designs for children's wear.

The Repair section helps you extend the life of children's clothing with techniques for repairing tears, cuts, and holes. Learn how to repair clothing at the knee and elbow areas with patches that are both functional and decorative. Discover how to use ribbons and other trims to decoratively disguise tears in garments, turning the repair into a design feature. And learn how to replace a broken zipper.

Several gift ideas that help make events special for children are illustrated in Special Projects. These include Christmas stockings, Easter rabbits and baskets, Halloween party placemats and fabric ghosts, and birthday banners. And a puppy bath poncho makes every day special.

Then make a variety of children's toys that are easy to sew. Fun Toys to Sew contains nylon kites, teddy bears, ladybug and spider hand puppets, and playhouse tents.

Getting Started

Choosing Children's Clothing

Sewing children's clothes can be quite economical and need not be time-consuming. Because children's garments require less fabric than garments for adults, the fabric cost is usually minimal. You may be able to use fabric from other sewing projects to construct a garment, or part of a garment, for a young child.

Most children's clothing designs follow simple lines, have few pieces, and are easy to sew. They are a good starting point for a beginning sewer or for a sewer whose skills need updating.

Planning for Safety

Build safety into children's garments. Avoid loose strings or excess fabric that may get tangled, especially for infants. Beware of long skirts or gowns that may cause a child to trip, or very full sleeves that may catch on objects. Limit tie belts and drawstrings to short lengths, and securely fasten buttons and trims. Use fire-retardant fabrics for sleepwear.

Customizing Clothes for Children

Creative touches can make a garment special to a child. Use a child's crayon drawing as a guide to colors and shapes for a machine-embroidered design. Or let children color or paint fabric before you cut out the pattern. Some children may enjoy designing their clothes by drawing the garment they would like and then having you match the color and general style. Simple, original appliqués can reflect a favorite hobby or special toy.

Involve the child in selecting patterns, fabrics, and notions. For young children learning to identify colors, primary colors of red, yellow, and blue are popular. Look at colors of a favorite toy and the colors a child often chooses for painting or drawing. Consider the coloring of the child's hair, eyes, and skin; select colors that compliment them.

Features for Self-dressing

To encourage self-dressing, choose garments with loose-fitting necklines and waistlines and with manageable fasteners. Make closures easy to see and reach on the front or side of a garment. Hook and loop tape can be used for closures on most types of garments. Young children can easily unfasten simple, large, round buttons and snaps, but may have difficulty closing them with small hands. They also enjoy smooth-running zippers with large teeth and zipper pulls. Pull-on pants that have elastic waists are easier for young children to pull on and off. Children can be frustrated by trying to fasten hooks and eyes, tiny buttons, and ties.

Tips for Planning Garments for Growth and Comfort

Add ribbing cuffs to lower edges of sleeves or pants legs so you can turn up built-in room for growth.

Choose pants patterns in a style that can be cut off for shorts when outgrown in length.

Use elastic waists on generously sized pants or skirts for comfort during growth spurts.

Allow extra crotch and body length in one-piece garments to prevent them from becoming uncomfortable as the child grows.

Add elastic suspenders with adjustable closures.

Choose dress and jumper patterns with dropped waist or no waist for comfort and maximum length of wear.

Use knit fabrics for easier sewing and maximum stretch for growth and comfort.

Consider patterns with pleats, gathers, and wide shapes that allow for growth without riding up.

Select patterns with raglan, dolman, and dropped sleeves to offer room for growth and less restriction of movement.

Select oversized styles for comfort.

Selecting Patterns

All children are comfortable in loose-fitting garments, but their clothing requirements change as they grow. For infants, select one-piece garments, such as kimonos, that make it easy to dress the baby and change the diapers. Toddlers are also comfortable in one-piece garments, such as overalls, with a crotch opening. Two-piece styles with elastic waistbands are easy to get on and off and are practical for children who are being toilet-trained. Adjustable shoulder straps and straps that crisscross at the back, as well as elastic waistbands, help keep pants and skirts in place.

Look for basic, versatile styles. Coordinated pants, shirts, skirts, jackets, overalls, and sweatsuits can be worn year-round. Except for skirts, these garments can be worn by both boys and girls. Use a basic pattern to plan a mix-and-match wardrobe. Coordinate fabrics and notions, and save time by sewing several garments, using the same pattern.

Selecting a Pattern Size

Buy patterns according to the child's measurements, not the child's age or ready-to-wear size. Compare the child's measurements with the chart on the pattern or in a pattern catalog. Most pattern measurement charts are standardized; however, the fit of similar garments may vary, even though the same size pattern is used. The style of the garment, whether it is loose-fitting or close-fitting, and the amount of ease added for movement and comfort, affect the fit.

You may want to compare the pattern with a well-fitting garment to check the fit of the garment you intend to make. If the child is between two sizes, buy the larger size pattern. Multi-sized patterns can be used for several sizes. To preserve the original pattern, trace each size as it is used.

To reflect the changing shape of growing bodies, pattern sizes for different ages use different body measurements. Infants' patterns give the baby's length and weight. Toddlers' patterns give chest, waist, and approximate height measurements. The Toddlers' sizes are shorter in length than Children's sizes and have extra room for diapers. Children's sizes give measurements for chest, waist, hip, and approximate height. Up to a size 6, Children's patterns generally increase one size for each additional inch (2.5 cm) around the body.

Fitting

Most children's garments require minimal fitting. Even if some of the child's measurements differ slightly from those on the pattern, you may not need to make adjustments. For example, a garment with elastic at the waist may not need a waistline adjustment. Determine adjustments before cutting the fabric. Make the same amount of adjustment to adjoining pattern pieces, and preserve the grainline on the adjusted pattern. You can make some adjustments as you sew by using wider or narrower seam allowances.

Adjusting Pattern Length and Width

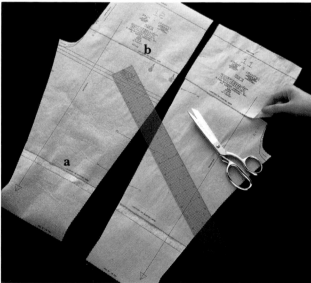

Lengthen (a) or shorten (b) pattern at adjustment lines. Spread or lap pattern pieces to desired adjustment; tape, preserving grainline. Blend the cutting and stitching lines.

Increase (a) or decrease (b) width up to ¼" (6 mm) on each side seam allowance for total adjustment up to 1" (2.5 cm). To increase or decrease width more than 1" (2.5 cm), use different pattern size. On bodices, you will need to adjust ease in sleeve to fit new armhole size.

Taking Measurements

To take a child's measurements, use a tape measure or brightly colored nonstretch ribbon held snugly, but not tightly. The child should wear underwear or diapers and stand in a natural position. For a very young or active child, you can measure a garment that fits well and compare it with the garment size on the pattern envelope. You will not need all measurements every time you sew.

Head. Measure around the fullest part of the head. This measurement is important for garments without neckline plackets.

Chest. Measure around the fullest part of the chest, just over the shoulder blades.

Waist. Toddlers often do not have a distinct waistline. To determine the natural waistline, tie a string around the midsection; have the child move and bend. The string will fall into place; measure over the string.

Hips. Measure around the fullest part of the hips.

Back waist length. Measure from the prominent bone at the neck to the natural waistline; you can locate the neckbone when the child's head is bent forward.

Arm-across-back length. With the child's arm extended straight out at the side, measure from the wrist across the shoulder to the middle of the neck. Place the sleeve pattern next to the garment back pattern, overlapping seam allowances; measure pattern from wrist to center back. You can now compare the body measurement with the pattern measurement.

Crotch depth. Tie a string around the waist. Have the child sit on a chair; measure at the side from the waist to the seat of the chair.

Finished dress or skirt length. Measure from a string at the waist to the desired hem length.

Finished pants length. Measure from a string at the waist to the anklebone.

Selecting Fabrics

Children's everyday garments need to withstand the wear and tear of active play and numerous launderings. For these clothes, select durable, comfortable, easy-care fabrics. For special-occasion clothing, use velvets, velveteens, and taffetas. For heirloom sewing, look for even-weave fabrics that are fine, soft, and drapable; they may be sheer, and with or without sheen. Although 100 percent cotton is durable and consistent with the look of antique garments, it does require ironing. The easy-care features of polyester/cotton blends appeal to some sewers. Use sheer fabrics, such as polyester/cotton Imperial® batiste and 100 percent cotton Swiss batiste.

Natural fibers are soft and nonabrasive. They offer breathability and moisture absorption, qualities lacking in pure synthetics; but natural fibers may require more care. Synthetic fibers, such as acrylic and polyester, are easy-care, but they do not breathe or absorb moisture. They stain easily, and with repeated launderings they eventually pill, yellow, and lose their softness. Blends of natural and synthetic fibers combine the best properties of each to produce soft, absorbent, wrinkle-free fabrics.

Fabric Types

Woven fabrics that are sheer and lightweight are suitable for blouses, shirts, dresses, and skirts. Firmly woven fabrics are most durable; choose them for pants, shirts, and jackets. Woven fabrics best suited for sewing children's clothing are: batiste, broadcloth, calico, chambray, chino, cotton Swiss batiste, denim, dotted Swiss, duck, gingham, madras, organdy, polyester/cotton Imperial batiste, polyester taffeta, poplin, sailcloth, seersucker, shirting, twill, and voile.

Knit fabrics are a good choice, because children are active and knits give as the body moves. When selecting knits, check the stretch of the fabric with the gauge on the pattern envelope. Knit fabrics include: cotton spandex, double knit, interlock, jersey, sweatshirt fleece, and thermal knit.

Fabrics with nap have a surface texture that feels soft or brushed, and may be either woven or knit. These fabrics include: brushed denim, corduroy, double-faced polyester bunting, flannel, French terry, piqué, stretch terry, terry cloth, velvet, velveteen, and velour.

Fabrics for children's clothing include: shirting (**1**), denim (**2**), velour (**3**), corduroy (**4**), terry cloth (**5**), interlock (**6**), jersey (**7**), dotted Swiss (**8**), Imperial batiste (**9**), taffeta (**10**).

8.

9

10

Selecting Specialty Trims

The finest specialty trims are 100 percent cotton or a blend with a high proportion of cotton. They feature a fine weave, and the designs are cleanly finished. Both edges of lace insertion (1) are straight. Lace edgings (2) have one straight edge and one scalloped edge.

Lace beading (3) has holes for threading ribbon. Eyelets and embroideries (4) may be embroidered in white or a color and are available as insertions, edgings, or beading. Entredeux (5) is used to separate trims and fabric and has seam allowances on both sides.

Selecting Elastic

Elastics vary in stretch and recovery characteristics. Look for elastics that retain their original width when stretched and that recover to their original length when applied to a garment. Those made from cotton and rubber are the most durable.

Knitted (1) and woven (2) elastics are most appropriate for stitching directly to the garment. Braided (3) and nonroll (4) elastic are suitable for casings. Transparent (5) elastic blends with any fabric color and is comfortable next to the skin.

Selecting Ribbing

The stretch and recovery of ribbing varies widely. The stretch is acceptable if a 4" (10 cm) piece stretches fully to about 7" (18 cm).

The finished width of ribbing is in proportion to the garment edge and size. Cut the ribbing twice the finished width plus ½" (1.3 cm) for two ¼" (6 mm) seam allowances. Trim the garment seam allowances to ¼" (6 mm) on edges where ribbing will be applied. Use the method below to cut ribbing to fit the edge of the garment. Or, for a closer fit at wrist, waistline, and pants leg, cut the ribbing to fit the body. It may then be necessary to gather the garment edge to fit the ribbing.

Tubular ribbing is 18" to 22" (46 to 56 cm) wide and is sold by the inch (2.5 cm). It is available in two weights. The lighter weight is suitable for use on T-shirt knits, sweatshirt fleece, velour, and lightweight woven fabrics. The heavier weight is used for outerwear or heavyweight fabrics. Do not preshrink ribbing; this distorts the ribbing and makes accurate layout and cutting difficult.

Guide to Cut Width of Ribbings (includes seam allowances)

Garment Edge	Infants'	Toddlers'	Children's
Short sleeve	2" (5 cm)	2½" (6.5 cm)	2½" (6.5 cm)
Standard crew neck	2½" (6.5 cm)	2½" (6.5 cm)	3" (7.5 cm)
Narrow crew neck	2" (5 cm)	2" (5 cm)	2½" (6.5 cm)
Prefinished collar	2½" (6.5 cm)	2¾" (7 cm)	3" (7.5 cm)
Waistband, wrists, pants legs	4¼" (10.8 cm)	5" (12.5 cm)	6½" (16.3 cm)
Pocket	2" (5 cm)	2" (5 cm)	2½" (6.5 cm)

How to Measure and Cut Ribbing

1) Measure pattern edge where ribbing is to be applied, standing tape measure on edge at seamline. For neck and waist edges, double this measurement.

2) Cut ribbing two-thirds the measured length of seamline and twice desired finished width; add ½" (1.3 cm) to length and width for seam allowances.

Selecting Equipment & Tools

A basic conventional sewing machine with a zigzag stitch works well for sewing children's clothing, although a computerized sewing machine can be helpful for adding embellishments. For small, hard-to-reach areas, such as knees and elbows, a free-arm sewing machine is useful. A serger, or overlock machine, does not replace a conventional machine, but it can cut sewing time considerably; it sews a seam at the same time it finishes and trims the edges.

Sewing machine accessories help make sewing for children more efficient. The ruffler attachment (1) saves time when you are sewing numerous ruffles or pleats. The pin-tuck foot (2) is used with twin needles (3) for making tucks of various sizes. Twin needles also work well for reinforcement stitches and hems. A general-purpose presser foot (4) and needle plate (5) are used with wing needles (6), which create holes in fabric to produce a decorative effect.

Ballpoint needles are used for sewing knits. Universal point needles are designed to be used with knits and woven fabrics. A fine needle, size 9 (65), is used for fine, lightweight fabrics.

A bodkin (7) is a long metal or plastic tool that is handy for threading elastic, ribbon, and cord through a casing. A rotary cutter (8) is available in two sizes and comes with a retractable blade for safety. The large rotary cutter quickly cuts several layers at a time and can be used for heavy fabrics. The small rotary cutter is used for single thicknesses, lightweight fabrics, and small curves. Use a rotary cutter with a cutting mat (9). Fastener pliers (10) are used for installing fasteners such as gripper snaps and eyelets.

A puff iron (11) is convenient to use when you are making machine heirloom clothing. It uses dry heat and irons delicate fabrics without scorching. A sleeve board is versatile for use in narrow seam areas, such as sleeves and pants legs.

Selecting Notions

You may want to stockpile assorted notions to make it easy to vary garments made from a single pattern.

Closures on children's garments may be decorative as well as functional. Snaps come in a variety of weights and colors. Novelty buttons add a special detail, but small or shaped buttons can make it difficult for young children to dress themselves. Hook and loop tape is an easier fastener for children to manage.

Zippers may also be decorative, especially when used in contrasting colors. Zippers with fine coils are available for use on small garments. Zipper coil, with separate zipper pulls, is available in rolls of 5½ yd. (5.05 m) or by the inch (2.5 cm). It allows you to make zippers of any length and eliminates the need for keeping various sizes of zippers on hand. Dye the zipper and zipper pull to match garments or to coordinate with them.

Hardware such as D-rings, snap hooks, plastic sliders, and overall buckles can be used for suspenders, belts, and adjustable straps. Tapes and trims include ribbons, bias and twill tapes, piping, and braid. Reflective tape can be applied as a safety measure to clothing worn outdoors after dark. Appliqués add a custom look.

Layout & Cutting

It is important to preshrink washable fabrics, trims, and notions before laying out patterns. Preshrinking prevents the garment from shrinking, and seams and trims from puckering. It also removes excess dye and chemical finishes. Do not preshrink ribbing; this distorts the ribbing and makes accurate layout and cutting difficult.

Preshrink and dry washable fabrics as recommended in the fabric care instructions. After preshrinking 100 percent cotton fabrics, it is important to launder them several times before cutting, because cotton fabrics continue to shrink during the first several launderings. Preshrink dark and vivid cottons separately, until colors are stabilized. To preshrink fabrics that require drycleaning, steam them evenly with a steam iron and allow them to dry thoroughly on a smooth, flat surface.

Some knits, especially lightweight cotton knits, may curl and ripple after preshrinking. Remove wrinkles from the fabric before laying out the pattern, making sure the lengthwise grain is straight. Press pattern pieces with a warm, dry iron.

Plaid, striped, and checked fabrics add variety to children's garments. When using one of these fabrics, select a pattern with few pieces to make it easier to match the design. Stand back and look at the fabric to determine the dominant part of the design. The easiest way to cut these fabrics is as a single layer. Cut out each pattern piece from the fabric, and turn the cut fabric piece over to use as a pattern so the design on the second piece will match the first piece.

Tips for Laying Out Plaid Fabrics

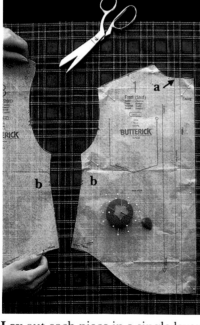

Lay out each piece in a single layer, beginning with front pattern piece. Use dominant part of design (**a**) for center front and center back. Match notches at side seams (**b**) of front and back.

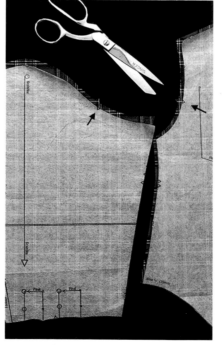

Center sleeve at same dominant part of design as center front. The design should match at the notches (arrows) of the sleeve front and armhole of garment front; notches at back may not match.

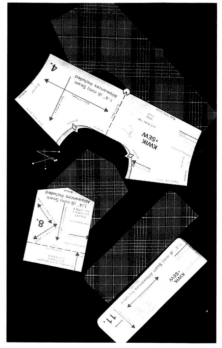

Position pockets, cuffs, yokes, and separate front bands on true bias to avoid time-consuming matching. Center a dominant design block in each pattern piece.

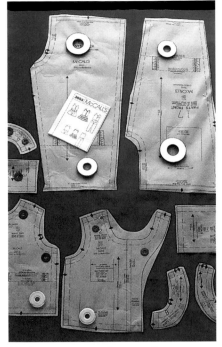

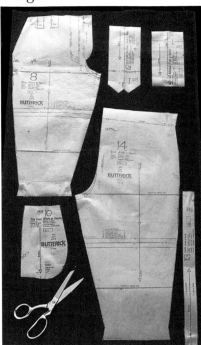

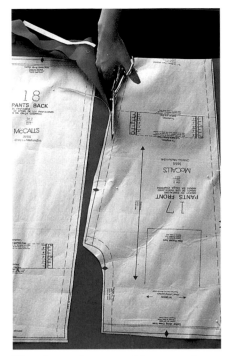

Refer to pattern layout diagram on guidesheet. Position pattern pieces, following grainline arrows and nap direction. Use weights to hold the pattern in place.

Lay out all pattern pieces on napped fabric with upper edge of pattern pieces toward same end of fabric. Corduroy and other napped fabrics wear better if sewn with the nap running down garment.

Use sharp shears and long strokes for smooth cutting. Do not trim excess pattern tissue before cutting fabric unless cutting thick fabrics such as corduroy and quilted fabric.

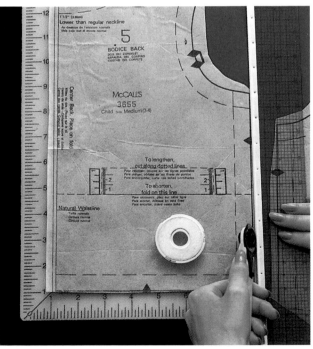

Use rotary cutter with protective mat, shifting mat to cut other pieces. Use metal-edged ruler for straight edges, placing blade side of rotary cutter next to ruler; trim off notches. Small rotary cutter may be used for tight curves or complex shapes.

Transfer all pattern markings after cutting. Make short clip no more than 1/8" (3 mm) into seam allowance to mark notches, dots, center front, center back, and ends of darts and pleats. To mark pockets, pin through pattern and fabric, lift pattern, and mark each fabric layer with chalk or washable marking pen.

Special Techniques for Plaids & Stripes

Plaid and striped fabrics require similar sewing techniques. Striped fabrics have bars of color running lengthwise or crosswise on the fabric. Plaids have color bars running lengthwise and crosswise.

Plaids and stripes need special pattern layouts to balance the arrangement of the color bars and to match the bars at important seams. Extra fabric is necessary for such a layout. The larger the plaid or stripe repeat, the more fabric is needed. The *repeat* of a plaid is the four-sided area that contains the complete design. The repeat of a stripe has two boundaries. For plaids, buy an additional repeat for each major pattern piece. For stripes, an extra ¼ yd. to ½ yd. (.25 to .50 m) is usually enough. Use the larger amount if the stripe is broad.

Add this allowance to the "with nap" fabric requirement if working with an uneven plaid or stripe. Patterns must be laid out on these one-way fabric designs in a single direction.

Determining Even & Uneven Plaids & Stripes

To decide whether a plaid is even or uneven, fold back one corner diagonally through the center of a repeat. If the color bars match diagonally, test the plaid one more way to make sure it is even. Fold a crease lengthwise and crosswise through the center of one repeat. If all quarters are identical, the plaid is even. If not, the plaid is uneven. A plaid can be uneven crosswise, lengthwise, or both. Some uneven plaids will pass the diagonal test but fail the lengthwise/crosswise test.

To decide whether a stripe is even or uneven, fold through the center of one repeat. If both halves are the same, the stripe is even. If not, it is uneven. Uneven stripes can be difficult to spot; sometimes the size and arrangement of the stripes are the same on both halves of one repeat, but the colors are different.

Selecting Patterns

The fewer seams and details a pattern has, the easier it is to use with plaids or stripes. Once you have had some experience handling these fabrics,

Identifying even and uneven plaids. An even plaid has lengthwise and crosswise color bars that match when the repeat is folded diagonally through the center (**1**). An uneven plaid may have differing color bars in one or more directions (**2**). Or an uneven plaid may have matching color bars but not form a mirror image when folded diagonally because the repeat is not square (**3**). This type of uneven plaid is the most difficult to identify.

however, you can place few limits on your pattern selection. In fact, when working with striped fabric, you may prefer a pattern with many details. By cutting sections such as yokes, cuffs, patch pockets, and applied bands crosswise, lengthwise, or on the true bias grain, you can run the stripes in contrasting directions to the stripes on the main body of the garment. This is an easy way to create a garment with a unique look.

Some pattern features to avoid when working with stripes and plaids are seams with eased areas, such as princess seams, and diagonal seams, which interrupt the straight lines of the color bars. Occasionally, a pattern has a warning, "not suitable for plaids and stripes," because the shape of the seams prevents an acceptable match.

Matching Plaids & Stripes

For pattern layout, position the pattern pieces so stripes or plaids match at major seams. Lay out the large pattern pieces first, beginning with the front. Use a "with nap" layout if working with an uneven plaid or stripe. Place the center front on the most noticeable stripe so the garment will look balanced. With even plaids, you have the option of placing the center front of pattern pieces through the center of a repeat.

Lay out adjoining pattern pieces so the stripe or plaid matches at the most noticeable seams. Use the notches as your guide, remembering to match the fabric design at the seamline, not the cutting line. It may not be realistic to match every seam in a garment. Attempt to match the design at the front, back, and side seams, and at the front notches where set-in sleeves join the armholes. When seams have eased areas or darts, the entire seam will not match. Begin to match the stripe or plaid below the eased area or dart.

Lay out small straight-edged pattern pieces such as yokes, cuffs, and bands so one dominant color bar runs along the finished edge or through the center. Position details, such as patch pockets and collars, so the striped or plaid fabric design flows uninterrupted from garment to detail. Or, to eliminate having to match these details, place them on the true bias.

Identifying even and uneven stripes. An even stripe has matching color bars on each side when the dominant stripe is folded through the center (**1**). An uneven stripe has different color bars in each half of the repeat. Striped fabrics can be uneven because of the one-way sequence of stripe colors (**2**). Stripes can also be uneven because of the one-way sequence of stripe colors *and* widths (**3**).

How to Lay Out Even Plaids

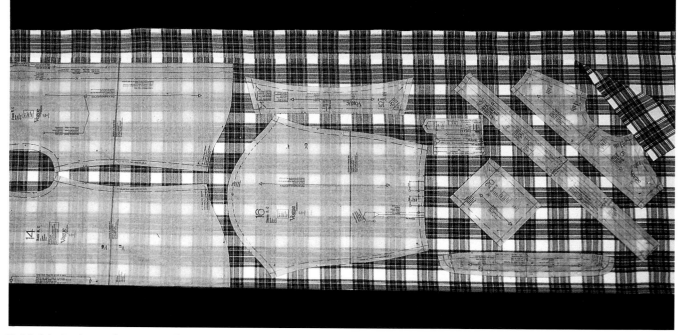

Fold fabric through center of repeat, lining up color bars to match on both fabric layers. Pin layers together to prevent shifting. Place most dominant color bar at center front and center back, or place centers in middle of plaid repeat. Lay out straight hemlines on complete, not partial, crosswise color bar. Lay out curved hemlines on least dominant color bar. Place yokes, pockets, and bands on the true bias.

How to Lay Out Uneven Plaids

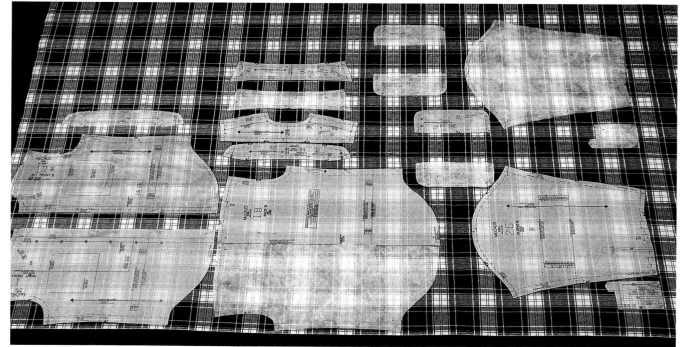

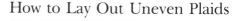

Lay out pattern on single layer of fabric, flipping pattern pieces over to cut right and left halves. Place most dominant color bar at center front and center back. Position hemlines as described above for even plaids. Optional layout method is folding fabric through dominant color bar and pinning all pattern pieces right side up. Place pattern pieces in one direction only, using "with nap" layout. Plaid will repeat around the garment instead of forming a mirror image on each side of the center front and center back seams.

How to Match Plaids

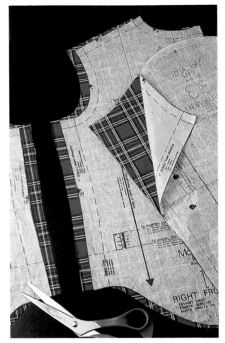

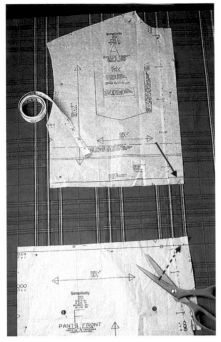

Match plaid at side seam notches of major front and back patterns. Lay out sleeve pattern so plaid matches at front armhole notch. Always match plaids at seamlines, not cutting lines.

Duplicate position of plaid on garment front when laying out front facing pattern. Match center back of upper collar to center back of garment. Plaids may not match where collar joins front facing, but will look balanced side to side.

Position bodice, top, or jacket pattern on plaid. Overlap skirt pattern at hemline or seamline, and transfer matching plaid line (arrow). Align skirt marking on same plaid line (broken arrow). For separates, make sure plaid on jacket hem matches at lap line on skirt.

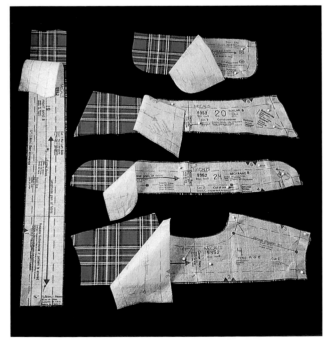

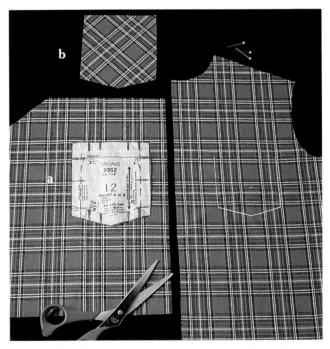

Align yoke, cuff, waistband, and other straight-edged pattern pieces so seamlines, not cutting lines, fall on complete color bar. If there is enough fabric, position these pieces on dominant color bar for attractive accents.

Trace plaid from garment section to patch pocket pattern to duplicate plaid placement when laying out pocket. Perfectly matched pocket (**a**) will blend into overall plaid. Pocket can also be cut on true bias grain (**b**) as accent.

How to Lay Out Even Stripes

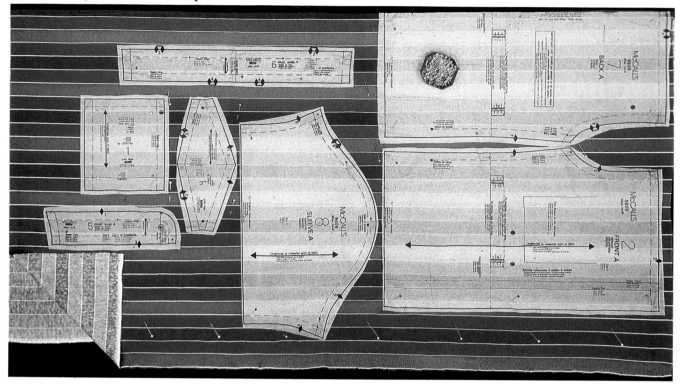

Fold fabric through center of repeat. Stripes should match perfectly on both layers. Pin to prevent fabric from shifting during layout. Cut details, such as pockets and applied bands, so stripes contrast with direction of main garment sections if desired.

How to Lay Out Uneven Stripes

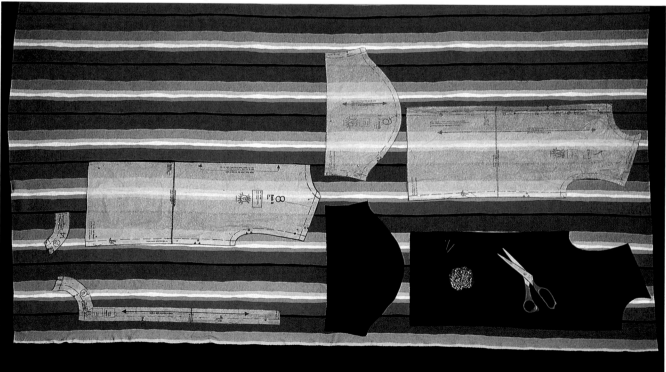

Lay out pattern on single layer of fabric, and flip pattern pieces over to cut right and left sides. For balanced look, place dominant stripe at center front and center back. Use "with nap" layout so stripes encircle garment. Position straight-edged pieces so complete, not partial, stripe falls along seamline.

How to Match Uneven Stripes at a Front Closing

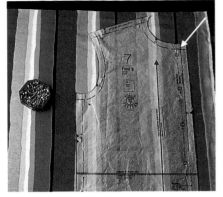

1) Pin pattern to single layer of fabric, placing pattern so center front (arrow) falls on dominant stripe. Squint or stand back from fabric to pick out this stripe if it is not immediately apparent.

2) Flip pattern over to cut out other side front. Position center front of pattern (arrow) on same dominant stripe as in step 1, left.

3) Sequence of stripes in repeat continues across both garment sections. Dominant stripe is in center front.

Keeping Plaids and Stripes Matched during Sewing

Pin. Place pins through edges of color bars. Color bars are easy to see on wrong side of fabric if design is woven. Be sure pins penetrate same edge of color bar on both fabric layers. Pin at frequent intervals. Stitch with Even Feed™ foot.

Double-faced basting tape. Place tape next to one seamline, on right side of fabric. Fold back seam allowance of adjoining garment section to match plaid or stripe. Stitch seam; then remove basting tape from seam allowance.

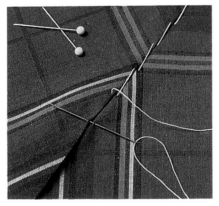

Slip-baste. 1) Press seam allowance under on one edge. Lap folded edge over seam allowance of adjoining section, matching stripes; pin at right angles to fold.

2) Bring needle up through three layers of fabric and out at fold on right side of garment. Take a tiny stitch below first stitch through single layer and through the fold.

3) Remove pins, and fold out seam allowance. From inside, machine-stitch through center of small stitches formed under folded edge. Remove basting.

Timesaving Techniques

You can save time by planning your sewing carefully. Use the same pattern to make several of the garments most commonly worn by the child, and purchase fabrics that can be sewn with the same thread color or invisible thread. If you plan coordinating colors, you can achieve a custom look by interchanging cuff and trim pieces among several garments.

Eliminating center front and center back seams saves cutting and construction time. Another timesaving technique is to select a pattern that has ¼" (6 mm) seam allowances, or trim the pattern seam allowances to ¼" (6 mm) as you cut. You can also save time by using weights instead of pins to hold fabric in place. Glue-stick or water-soluble basting glue can be used in place of pins and hand basting.

Stack three or four light to mediumweight fabrics of the same width to cut at one time. Cut front and back pieces on folds; do not cut any center front openings at this time. Use rotary cutter with guide arm to trim seam allowances to ¼" (6 mm) while cutting out garment.

Determine which garments will have ribbings, elastic, front openings, or trims. Cut ribbings and trims to correct size. Group the fabric for each garment with the corresponding notions and trims.

Group garments that use same thread color, so you can sew all at one time. Use continuous stitching wherever possible, stitching from seam to seam without stopping. Cut threads after all garments are stitched.

Organize work sessions according to type of activity. Do all straight-stitching at one time, as well as all pressing, seam finishing, and zigzagging or serging. Attach closures at end of sewing process.

Hems & Seams

Topstitched hems and seams can be decorative as well as functional. Use a matching or contrasting color thread that coordinates with other items of clothing.

Machine-stitched hems are fast and durable, and are a good alternative for ribbing at cuffs, waistlines, and pants legs on children's clothing.

Select seams and seam finishes based on the type of fabric. Also consider if the seam will show through the garment, if strength is required at the seam, and if the seam will be comfortable when it is next to the skin.

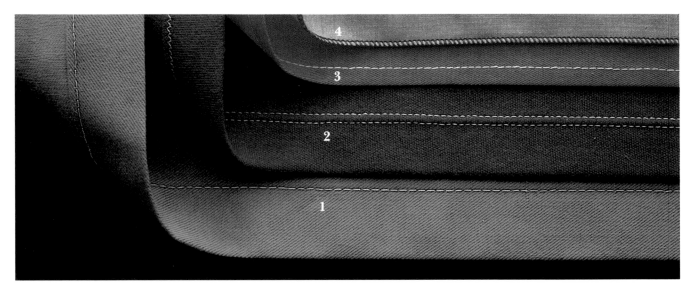

Hems. Topstitched hem (**1**) has one or more rows of topstitching near upper edge of a finished hem allowance. A twin-needle topstitched hem (**2**) is suitable for knits, because the bobbin thread zigzags on the wrong side and allows stitches to stretch. Stitch about ¼" (6 mm) below cut edge of hem allowance and trim close to stitching. For a narrow hem (**3**), trim hem allowance to ½" (1.3 cm); press to wrong side. Open hem, and fold raw edge to hemline crease. Fold again to make double-fold hem; topstitch one or two rows as desired. Use a rolled hem (**4**), sewn on a serger, for lightweight or sheer fabrics. Stitch with right side up; fabric rolls under to the wrong side.

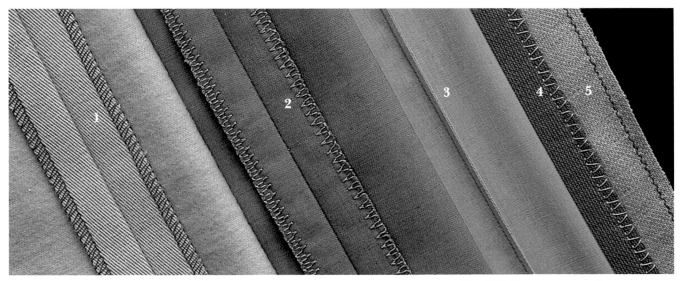

Seams and seam finishes. For plain seams, press open ⅝" (1.5 cm) seam allowances. Finish edges with overlock stitching (**1**) sewn on a serger, or with a three-step zigzag (**2**). A French seam (**3**) is neat and inconspicuous from the right side, but it is difficult to use on curves. For ¼" (6 mm) seam allowances on stretch fabrics, use an overedge stitch (**4**) or a narrow zigzag stitch (**5**); stretch seams slightly while stitching. Press narrow seams to one side.

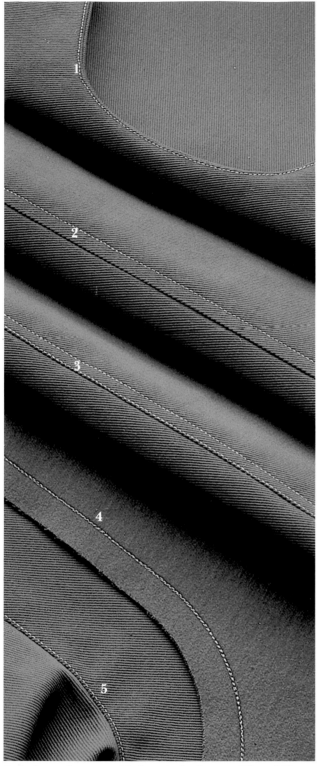

Reinforced seams. Understitched seam (**1**) stabilizes the seam by stitching seam allowances to the facing. Welt seam (**2**) has seam allowances pressed to one side and topstitched to garment. Mock flat-fell seam (**3**) has exposed seam allowances on the wrong side of the garment with topstitching and edgestitching. Double-stitching (**4**) is stitching sewn over previous stitching. Edgestitching (**5**) is stitching sewn on the right side of the garment, through both seam allowances, as close to the seamline as possible.

Overlock seams. 3-thread stitch (**1**) stretches with the fabric and can be used as a seam or edge finish, but it is not recommended for woven fabrics in areas of stress. 4-thread stitch with chainstitch (**2**) is strong and stable for woven fabrics, but it does not stretch on knit seams. 4/3-thread stitch (**3**) provides an additional line of stitching, has stretch, and can be used on knit fabrics. Flatlock seam (**4**) is less bulky and lies flat.

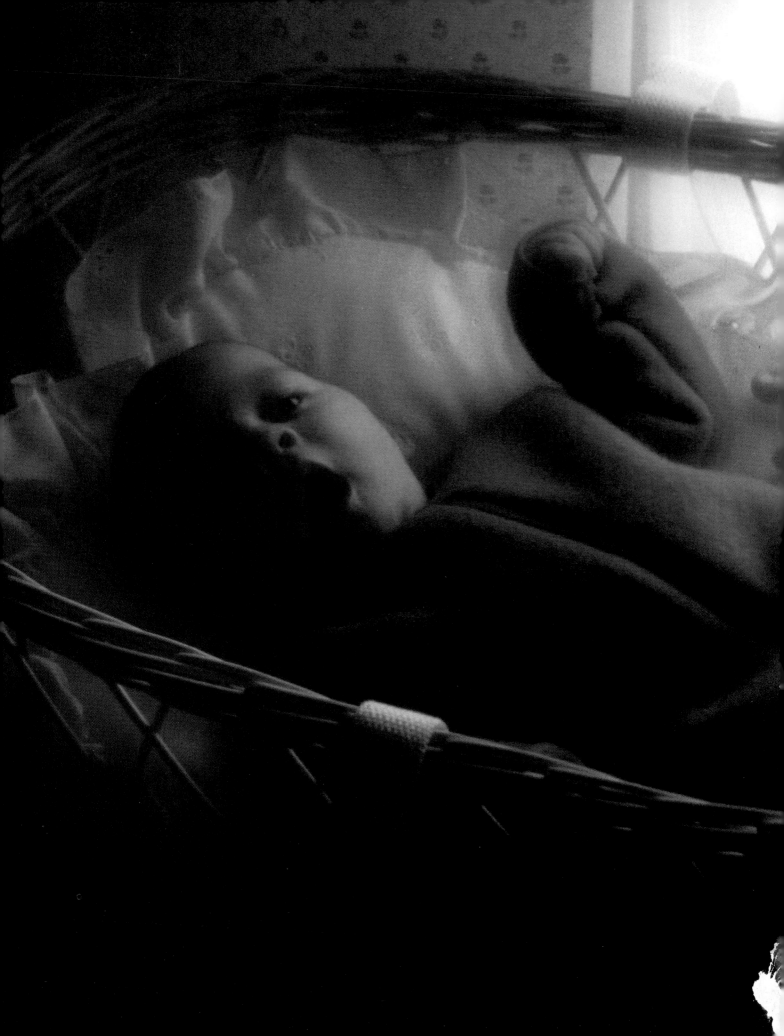

Infants

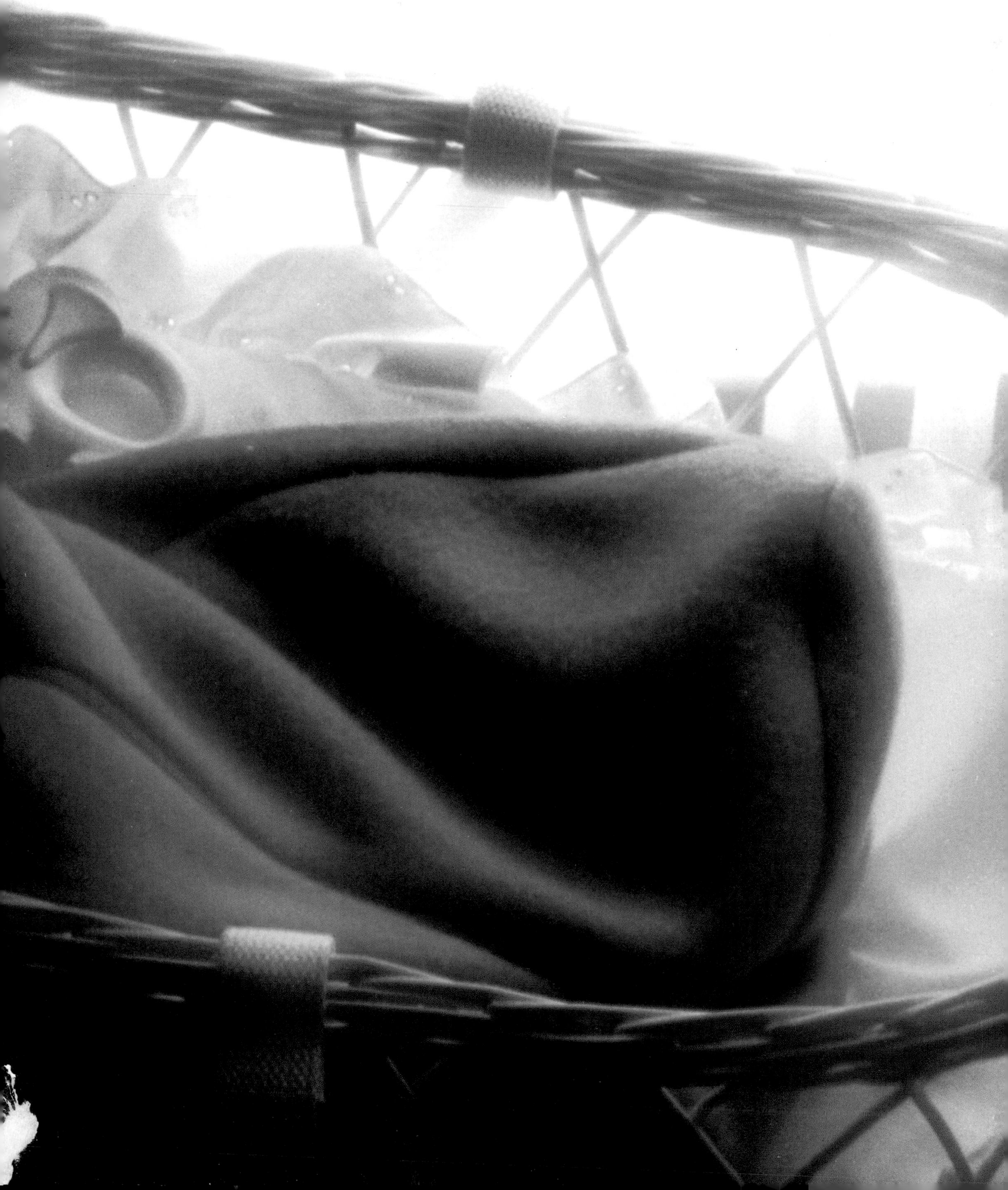

Sewing a Basic Layette

Many of the items in a basic layette, such as receiving blankets, hooded towels, bibs, kimonos, and buntings, are easy and practical to sew. Multi-sized layette patterns are available for making most of these items. For everyday wear, use simple, loose-fitting designs and high-quality fabrics that are easy to sew and launder.

Cotton or cotton-blend fabrics are good choices because cotton breathes, absorbs moisture, and is easy to launder. Infants are most comfortable in soft fabrics.

Stretch knits adapt well to movement, growth, and easy dressing. Woven fabrics such as flannel, seersucker, and broadcloth work well with the addition of ribbing at the neck, sleeves, and hem.

Government regulations require that garments designed for children's sleepwear meet flame-retardancy standards. Look for this information on the ends of fabric bolts. Cotton must be blended with synthetic fibers to accept this treatment.

If you select basic styles, you can use timesaving techniques that allow you to sew several garments in a short time. By choosing high-quality fabrics, you can sew garments superior to the average ready-to-wear items, and often at a more reasonable cost.

Receiving blankets and hooded towels are important to a layette. Several blankets or towels can be made at a time. Hooded towels can also be used as beach towels.

Bibs can easily be made by sewing ribbing and a neck closure to a hand towel. Older infants and toddlers enjoy large bibs with sleeves and pockets, which you can coordinate with several garments.

Kimonos of soft flannel or knits are comfortable for an infant during the first several months, and the open lower edge of the kimono allows for easy diapering. If the neck and armhole openings are large enough, the garment can also be used as a dress or T-shirt in later months. Buntings, adaptations of the kimono,

are closed at the lower edge for outerwear use and are often made of quilted fabrics, double-faced polyester bunting, or other soft, heavyweight fabrics.

Infant Accessories

Patterns are available for infant seat covers, pillows, diaper stackers, high chair pads, and other accessories. All of these can be customized by using coordinating colors, extra padding, warm fabrics, ruffles, and piping. Patterns may need to be adapted to the specific needs of the equipment; for example, tie and strap locations may need to be adjusted.

Receiving Blankets & Hooded Towels

Receiving blankets and hooded towels can be made large enough to accommodate the growth of the child. Choose soft, warm, and absorbent woven or knit fabrics. Select from flannel, interlock, jersey, thermal knit, terry cloth, and stretch terry. Two layers of lightweight fabric can be used with wrong sides together. Round all corners for easy edge application.

Cut a 36" (91.5 cm) square blanket or towel from 1 yd. (.95 m) of 45" or 60" (115 or 152.5 cm) fabric. When using 45" (115 cm) fabric, the mock binding and hood require an additional ¼ yd. (.25 m). Cut a 1½" (3.8 cm) binding strip on the lengthwise or crosswise grain, 2" (5 cm) longer than the distance around the item; piece, as necessary. Press binding in half, with wrong sides together.

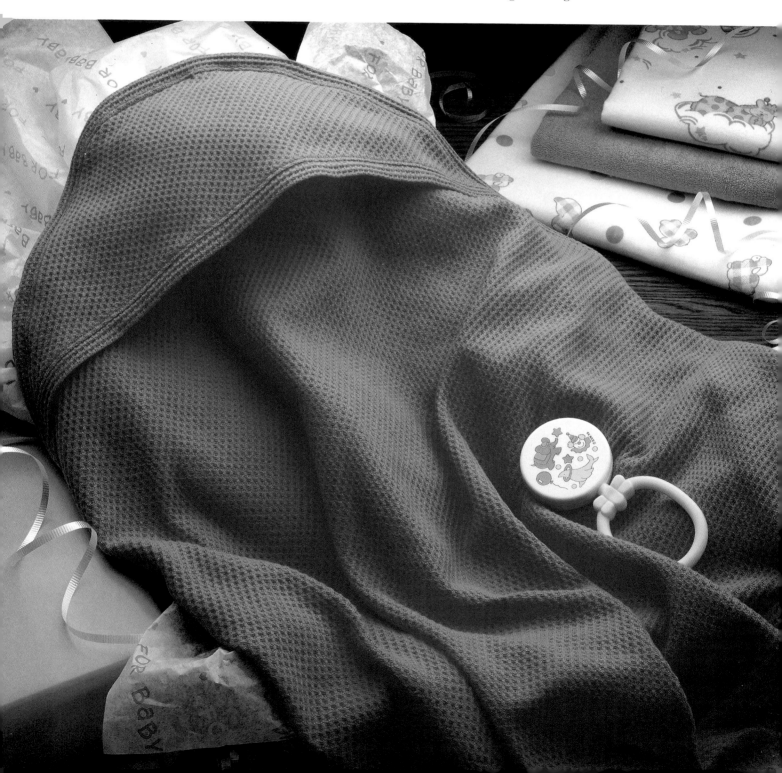

How to Finish Edges with a Mock Binding

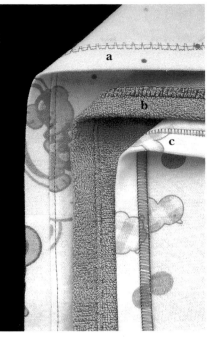

1) Use overedge stitch or serge binding to right side of fabric, starting 1½" (3.8 cm) from end of binding. Stitch to within 2" (5 cm) of start of binding, stretching fabric slightly at corners; do not stretch binding. (If flatlock stitch on serger is used, stitch *wrong* sides together.)

2) Fold 1" (2.5 cm) of binding to inside; lap around first end of binding. Continue stitching binding to fabric, stitching over previous stitches for 1" (2.5 cm) to secure the ends.

3) Turn seam allowance toward blanket or towel; topstitch through all layers of overedged **(a)** or serged **(b)** seam, to hold seam allowances flat. If flatlock **(c)** stitch is used, pull binding and fabric flat.

How to Sew a Hooded Towel

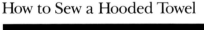

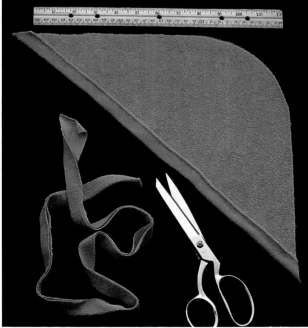

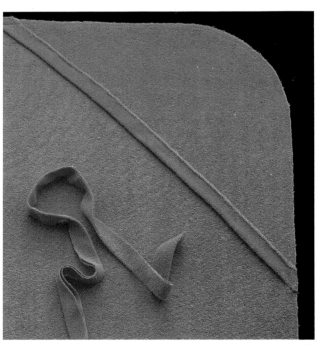

1) Cut a right triangle with two 12" (30.5 cm) sides from matching or contrasting fabric. Round right angle corner, and finish diagonal edge with mock binding, above.

2) Position wrong side of the hood to right side of the towel. Stitch triangle to one rounded corner of towel, ¼" (6 mm) from matched edges. Finish outside edges, above.

Bibs

Infant bibs are quick and easy to make. Create durable bibs from terry cloth or knit fabric or from fingertip towels, and customize the bibs with simple appliqué techniques and bias tape. Increase absorbency by using a double layer of fabric. Back a fabric bib with soft, pliable plastic to protect clothing; finish edges with wide double-fold bias tape. Or use a fingertip towel with prefinished edges.

Custom Bibs

Attach a toy or pacifier to a bib with a snap-on strip **(1)**. Stitch together the edges of a 12" (30.5 cm) strip of wide double-fold bias tape, and fold under the ends of the strip. Attach one end to the bib with the ball half of a gripper snap. Attach the socket half of the gripper snap to the other end of the tape. Slip the toy or pacifier onto the tape; snap securely to the bib.

A purchased squeaker can be inserted between the appliqué and bib **(2)** before you stitch the appliqué (page 213).

A fingertip towel makes an absorbent, washable bib. Fold the towel for double absorbency under the chin **(3),** and attach double-fold bias tape around the neck edge.

How to Make a Pullover Bib

1) Use fingertip towel. Cut 5" (12.5 cm) circle with center of circle one-third the distance from one end of the towel. Cut 3" (7.5cm) ribbing, with the length two-thirds the circumference. Stitch short ends to form circle, using ¼" (6 mm) seam allowance.

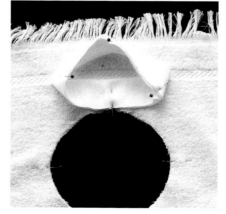

2) Fold ribbing in half, with wrong sides together. Divide ribbing and neck edge into fourths; pin-mark. Matching pins, and with seam at center back, pin ribbing to neck edge, with raw edges even. Stitch ¼" (6 mm) seam, stretching ribbing to fit neckline.

3) Fold seam allowance toward bib. Edgestitch to bib through all layers.

How to Make a Tie-on Bib

1) Press wide double-fold bias tape to follow curve of outer edge of bib. Glue-baste tape over raw edge of bib, positioning the wider tape edge on the wrong side; edgestitch in place.

2) Cut bias tape 30" (76 cm) longer than neck curve. Center bias tape over the neck edge; glue-baste. Edgestitch from one end of tie around neckline to other end. Bar tack bias tape at edge of bib (arrow) by zigzagging in place; tie knot at each end.

Alternative. Cut fingertip towel as for pullover bib, opposite. Fold so neck opening forms a half circle. Zigzag raw edges together with wide stitch. Apply bias tape for ties and neck finish, step 2, left.

Kimonos

Timesaving techniques enable you to cut and sew several kimonos at one time. Neckline openings for woven fabrics should be at least 1" to 2" (2.5 to 5 cm) larger than the infant's head. Openings for knit fabrics do not need to be as large, because knits will stretch to fit over the head.

Use the flat method of construction to sew infant-size garments; complete as much stitching as possible while the garment is flat. Access to parts of tiny garments becomes difficult once seams are completed. Apply all ribbing while one seam is still open.

How to Sew a Kimono with Ribbing (flat method)

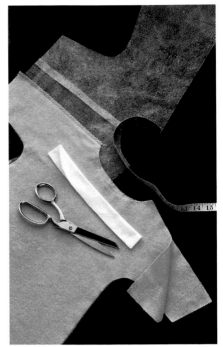

1) **Measure** and cut ribbing for neck, wrists, and lower edge (page 17); fold in half lengthwise. Straight-stitch or serge garment front and back together at one shoulder seam, right sides together.

2) **Divide** ribbing and neck edge into fourths; pin-mark. Pin the ribbing and the neck edge together at marks and ends. Overedge stitch or serge ¼" (6 mm) seam, stretching ribbing to fit neck edge as you sew.

3) **Straight-stitch** or serge other shoulder seam, right sides together; carefully match ribbing edge and ribbing seam. Finish the seam allowances, if necessary.

4) **Divide** ribbing and wrist edge in half; pin-mark. Pin and stitch as in step 2, above.

5) **Straight-stitch** or serge one underarm seam, with right sides together; carefully match ribbing edge and ribbing seam. Finish seam allowances, if necessary.

6) **Divide** ribbing and lower edge; pin and stitch as in step 2, above. Stitch remaining underarm seam as in step 5, left. Finish seam allowances, if necessary.

Customizing Kimonos

To add a placket, slash the front of the kimono and apply a continuous self-binding. Position the opening off-center so fasteners line up on the center front.

For a boy's garment, mark the placket opening to the right of center to lap left over right. For a girl's garment, mark the placket opening to the left of center to lap right over left. The photos that follow are for a girl's kimono. Mark a 6" (15 cm) opening 3/8" (1 cm) from the center front for a 3/4" (2 cm) finished placket width. Cut a binding strip 12" × 2" (30.5 × 5 cm) on the lengthwise grain. Press the binding strip in half lengthwise, wrong sides together. Open the strip, and press under 1/4" (6 mm) on one long edge.

For a kimono pattern without a cuff, add sleeve mitts to be folded over the baby's hands. Finish the kimono with a mandarin collar and gripper snaps.

How to Apply a Continuous Self-bound Placket

1) Mark the placket opening, and cut binding, above. Staystitch 1/4" (6 mm) from marked line, tapering to a point. Shorten stitches for 1/2" (1.3 cm) on each side of point, and take one short stitch at point. Slash along line to, but not through, point.

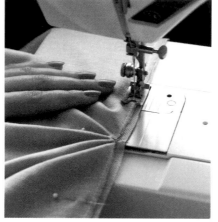

2) Hold placket opening straight; pin to unpressed edge of binding, right sides together. Stitch over staystitching with 1/4" (6 mm) seam allowance on binding; raw edges match only at seam ends. Add sleeve mitts, opposite. Stitch shoulder seams. Add collar, opposite.

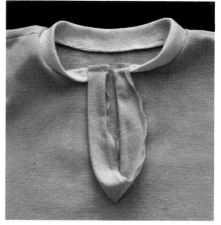

3) Place pressed edge of binding on seamline of overlap, *wrong* sides together; pin. For underlap, place pressed edge on seamline, *right* sides together; pin. Stitch overlap and underlap at neckline.

4) Fold the binding to inside of the garment, with fold on the seamline. Edgestitch binding over previous stitching; stitch to within 1" (2.5 cm) of neckline.

5) Pin overlap binding flat to inside of garment. Mark topstitching line on front side of overlap near the inside fold.

6) Topstitch through garment and binding, beginning at lower end of overlap (arrow); pivot at marked line, and stitch to neckline. Pivot; edgestitch around neckline through the garment and seam allowances, stretching slightly. Apply gripper snap at top of placket.

How to Attach a Mandarin Collar

1) Cut ribbing for collar 2" (5 cm) wide and 2" (5 cm) shorter than neck opening. Fold in half lengthwise. Mark center back. Apply placket as in steps 1 and 2, opposite. Fold front, matching shoulder seams; pin halfway between placket seams (arrows) to mark adjusted center fronts.

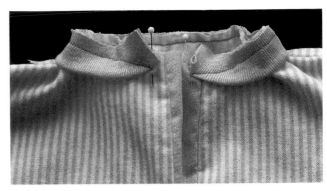

2) Pin collar to neck edge at center back, with right sides together and raw edges even. Place pin on folded edge of collar ¼" (6 mm) from each short end. Match pins to center fronts; pin securely. Stitch collar to neck edge, stretching collar to fit. Trim collar to match neck edge. Complete placket, steps 3 to 6, opposite.

How to Add Sleeve Mitts

1) Cut ribbing for sleeve mitt 6" (15 cm) long on lengthwise grain and 1" (2.5 cm) wider than width of sleeve. Fold ribbing in half crosswise to 3" (7.5 cm), and lay under end of sleeve. Trim to match shape of sleeve. Stitch folded ribbing to wrong side of sleeve back at lower edge, using ¼" (6 mm) seam and matching raw edges. Turn mitt to right side.

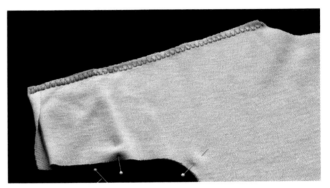

2) Pin kimono front to back at shoulder and underarm seams, right sides together. Fold hem allowance of sleeve front over finished sleeve back. Stitch shoulder and underarm seams.

3) Turn back hem allowance of sleeve front, encasing seam allowances. (Do not turn garment right side out.) Topstitch hem, stitching through sleeve back and mitt; use twin needle, if desired.

One-piece sleeve. Fold ribbing as in step 1, above. Cut mitt one-half the width of sleeve plus ¼" (6 mm). Stitch ¼" (6 mm) seam in one short end; turn seam to inside. Lay mitt on right side of back of sleeve, with seam at center; edgestitch short end at center. Stitch underarm seam. Turn hem allowance to wrong side. Topstitch hem as in step 3, left.

Buntings

A gusset applied at the lower edge of a kimono makes a bunting that covers the infant's feet and provides kicking room. For indoor use, make the bunting in the same fabric as that recommended for a kimono. For a warmer, outdoor bunting, use double-faced polyester fleece. To accommodate clothing worn under an outdoor bunting, use a kimono pattern one size larger than used for indoor buntings or kimonos.

Finish the neck of the bunting with a mandarin collar, or add a hood to the bunting if it is included in the pattern. For easy dressing, insert an 18" or 20" (46 or 51 cm) zipper. You may want to use zipper coil, which is available by the inch (2.5 cm) or in a 5½-yd. (5.05 m) package.

How to Make a Zipper Using Zipper Coil

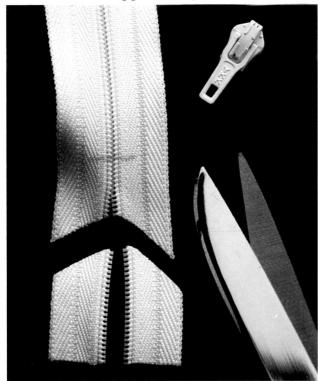

1) Cut zipper 2" (5 cm) longer than garment opening. Mark bar tack placement 1½" (3.8 cm) from lower end of zipper. Open zipper about 1" (2.5 cm). Cut a notch to within ½" (1.3 cm) of mark for bar tack.

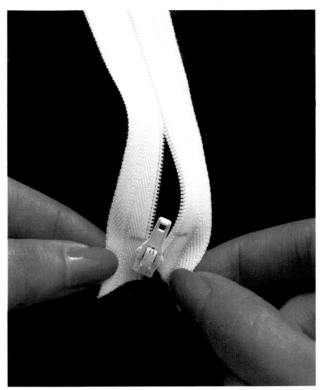

2) Insert one side of zipper coil into shaped end of zipper pull, with flat side of coil and tab of zipper pull facing up; insert other side, gently working coil into zipper pull.

3) Open coils above zipper pull. Partially close zipper. Bar tack by zigzagging in place over coil at placement mark to secure lower end of zipper.

4) Secure upper ends of coil with bar tacks ½" (1.3 cm) from ends. Zipper is ready to be applied to garment.

How to Insert a Zipper in a Bunting

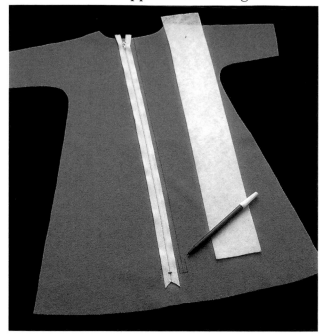

1) Mark line for zipper opening at center front from neck edge to zipper stop. Draw stitching box across lower end of line and ¼" (6 mm) on each side of line. Cut tear-away stabilizer 3" (7.5 cm) wide and 2" (5 cm) longer than zipper opening; glue-baste on wrong side of fabric under line for opening.

2) Staystitch across bottom line of stitching box; pivot at corner, and stitch to neck edge ¼" (6 mm) from marked line, using about 15 stitches per inch (2.5 cm). Repeat on other side of line, beginning at bottom line of stitching box.

3) Slash center line carefully to ¼" (6 mm) from bottom line; clip diagonally to, but not through, the lower corners.

4) Place one edge of zipper along edge of opening, right sides together, with zipper stop at bottom line of stitching box. With *garment side up,* stitch over previous stitching from zipper stop to neck edge, using zipper foot. Repeat for other edge, stitching from bottom to top.

5) Fold lower part of garment and stabilizer back at bottom of zipper, exposing the triangle of the stitching box and the end of the zipper tape. Double-stitch across triangle on the staystitching to secure triangle to zipper. Remove stabilizer.

How to Sew a Gusset in a Bunting

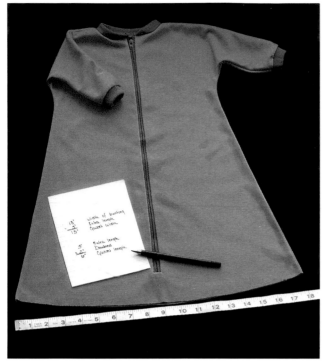

1) **Complete** bunting except for hem. The gusset adds 3" (7.5 cm) extra length to the bunting. For gusset width, subtract 3" (7.5 cm) from width of bunting at lower edge. The gusset length is 6" (15 cm), or double the extra length.

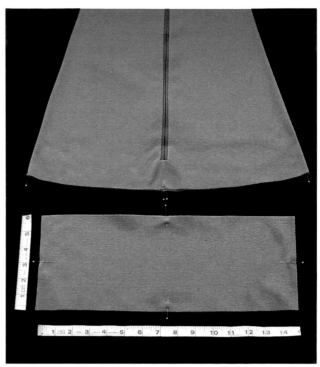

2) **Cut** a fabric rectangle for gusset according to the measurements, step 1, left. Divide edges of gusset and bunting into fourths; pin-mark.

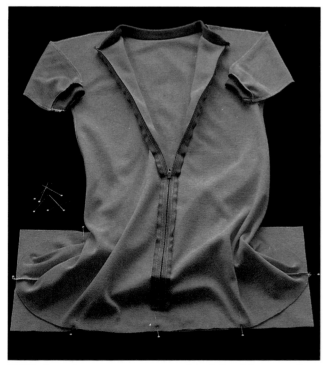

3) **Pin** bunting to gusset at marks, right sides together and raw edges even. Pin again halfway between pins, allowing bunting to curve naturally at corners.

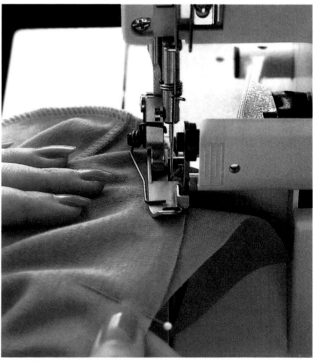

4) **Serge** or use three-step zigzag stitch for a ¼" (6 mm) seam around lower edge of bunting, using raw edge of bunting as a stitching guide. Serger knives will trim excess gusset fabric at corners; trim gusset before stitching if using three-step zigzag stitch.

Rompers from Secondhand Shirts

These rompers for infants and toddlers are easily made from secondhand or new shirts. Start with either a T-shirt or a button-front shirt in cotton flannel or shirting. For comfort, the rompers have a relaxed fit, and ribbing is used for the cuffs on the sleeves and legs.

For convenient diapering, the rompers fasten along the inseam with a zippered closure. When sewing a romper for an older child, you can eliminate the closure by simply sewing a seam instead.

For the correct fit of the romper, use the chart below to determine the original shirt size to use. Be sure that the original shirt is long enough to provide the desired measurements for the romper.

✂ Cutting Directions

Cut 3½" (9 cm) strips of ribbing on the crosswise grain. From the strips, cut two 5½" (14 cm) lengths for the cuffs on the sleeves and two 6" (15 cm) lengths for the leg openings.

Secondhand shirts can be made into rompers. A button-front shirt was used for the romper above, and a T-shirt for the romper opposite.

YOU WILL NEED

One T-shirt or button-front shirt, size as determined below.

3½" × 23" (9 × 58.5 cm) ribbing.

One zipper, 16" to 22" (40.5 to 56 cm) in length, depending on size of romper.

Conversion Chart for Sewing Rompers from Shirts

Finished Romper Size	Original Shirt Size	Shoulder to Ankle	Shoulder to Crotch	Chest Width	Back Neck to Wrist
6 to 9 mo.	Child's 6 or 8	22" to 23" (56 to 58.5 cm)	16" to 17" (40.5 to 43 cm)	11" to 12" (28 to 30.5 cm)	10" to 10½" (25.5 to 27.8 cm)
9 to 12 mo.	Child's 10 or 12	23" to 24" (58.5 to 61 cm)	17" to 18" (43 to 46 cm)	12" to 13" (30.5 to 33 cm)	11" to 11½" (28 to 29.3 cm)
12 to 18 mo.	Child's 12 or 14	25" to 27" (63.5 to 68.5 cm)	18" to 18½" (46 to 47.3 cm)	13" to 14" (33 to 35.5 cm)	12" to 13" (30.5 to 33 cm)
18 to 24 mo.	Child's 14 or 16	27" to 28" (68.5 to 71 cm)	19" to 20" (48.5 to 51 cm)	13" to 14" (33 to 35.5 cm)	13" to 14" (33 to 35.5 cm)
2 to 2½ yr.	Men's small or medium	28" to 30" (71 to 76 cm)	19" to 21" (48.5 to 53.5 cm)	13" to 14" (33 to 35.5 cm)	14" to 15" (35.5 to 38 cm)
3 yr.	Men's small or medium	29" to 31" (73.5 to 78.5 cm)	19" to 21" (48.5 to 53.5 cm)	14" to 15" (35.5 to 38 cm)	14" to 15" (35.5 to 38 cm)

How to Sew a Romper from a T-shirt

1) **Measure** shirt from top of ribbing at back neck to desired romper length, according to the chart on page 49. Cut off excess length evenly across shirt.

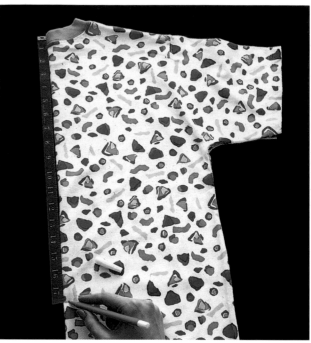

2) **Fold** shirt in half, matching sides. Measure from top of ribbing at back neck to desired crotch depth, according to the chart; mark, using a water-soluble marking pen.

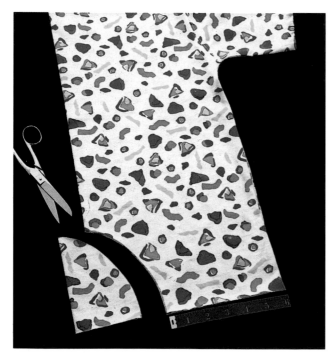

3) **Mark** a point on lower edge, 6" (15 cm) from side seam. Draw line from mark at lower edge to mark at crotch depth, curving line gradually at crotch. Cut away excess fabric through all layers.

4) **Measure** from center fold at back neck to desired sleeve length, according to chart; mark lower edge of sleeve to this length, perpendicular to upper fold. If sleeve is wider than 6" (15 cm), mark new width 6" (15 cm) from upper fold.

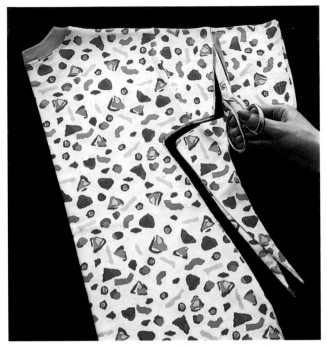

5) Draw new cutting line from mark at lower edge of sleeve, curving slightly toward chest and stopping at point of desired chest width.

6) Draw new side seam, rounding corner at desired chest width and angling side seam in a gradual curve to original shirt seam, as shown. Cut through all layers along marked lines for sleeve and side seams.

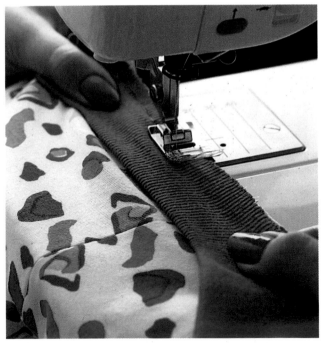

7) Turn garment inside out. On each side of romper, pin the raw edges together for sleeve and side seam; stitch in a continuous seam.

8) Fold one piece of leg ribbing in half lengthwise, *wrong* sides together. Divide ribbing and leg opening in half; pin-mark. Pin ribbing to leg opening, with raw edges even, matching pin marks and ends. Stitch in place ¼" (6 mm) from raw edges, stretching ribbing as you sew. Press seam allowances away from ribbing.

(Continued on next page)

9) Open the zipper. Pin one side of zipper to the back crotch opening, right sides together, with edge of zipper tape along raw edge and top zipper stop near fold of ribbing; fold back upper end of zipper tape. Stitch in place through the center of zipper tape.

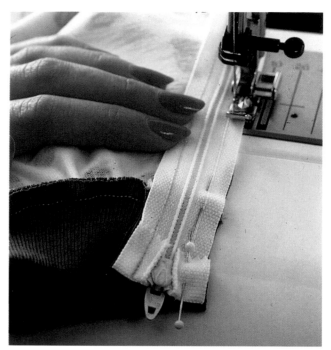

10) Close the zipper. Pin other side of zipper tape to front crotch opening, right sides together, aligning seams and ends of opening; fold back upper end of zipper tape. Stitch in place through the center of zipper tape.

11) Make new zipper stop, if zipper is too long, by stitching several times across the zipper teeth ½" (1.3 cm) from leg opening. Cut off excess zipper even with leg opening.

12) Stitch the short ends of the remaining piece of leg ribbing together in ¼" (6 mm) seam; press open. Fold ribbing in half lengthwise, *wrong* sides together. Divide leg opening and ribbing in half; pin-mark.

13) Pin ribbing to leg opening, with raw edges even, matching pin marks and centering ribbing seam on zipper tape. Stitch in place ¼" (6 mm) from raw edges, stretching ribbing as you sew.

14) Prepare ribbing for sleeves as in step 12. Pin ribbing to sleeve opening, with raw edges even, matching pin marks and seams. Stitch in place ¼" (6 mm) from raw edges, stretching ribbing as you sew. Press the seam allowances away from ribbing.

How to Sew a Romper from a Button-front Shirt

1) Button the shirt. Measure shirt from neckline seam, below collar, to desired romper length, according to the chart on page 49. Cut off excess length evenly across the shirt. Follow steps 2 and 3 on page 50, measuring for crotch depth from the neckline seam, below collar.

2) Follow steps 4 to 9; finish seams after step 7, using zigzag or overlock stitch. Baste fronts together across placket on lower edge. Apply zipper to crotch front as in step 10, stitching through all layers of basted placket. Complete garment as in steps 11 to 14.

Decorating the Nursery

When you plan the decor of a nursery, you may want to consider using neutral colors for wallpaper and paint. Save colorful decorating touches for the accessories, which can easily be changed or adapted as the child grows. Pastel colors are the traditional choice for a nursery, but do not overlook other choices, such as bold primary colors.

You can find many decorating ideas for nurseries in magazines, decorating books, and wallpaper and fabric stores. Select a theme to unify the nursery, and use your creative skills and sewing ability for projects such as appliqué, trapunto, or stenciling.

Patterns and kits are available for coverlets, bumper pads, diaper stackers, mobiles, wall hangings, infant seat pads, and toys. Sewing for the nursery can be even easier, using kits that include everything except the thread and filler. When using kits, there is no need for patterns, because the shapes are printed on the fabric. You may wish to embellish mobiles and wall hangings with buttons, ribbons, and pom-poms, and add fake fur to animal figures.

55

Nursery Accessories

Crib Kicker. Soft, stuffed, colorful shapes are joined with ribbon. Tie the crib kicker to the sides or end of the crib for the infant's enjoyment.

Mobile. Cut, sew, and stuff soft shapes. Tie them to a mobile hanger arm clamp. Attach the mobile to a crib or hang it from the ceiling over the changing table to entertain infants with color and motion.

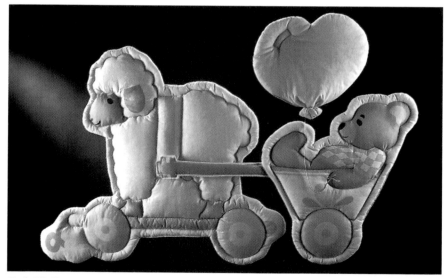

Soft Wall Hanging. Quilt a jumbo wall hanging by using a kit with preprinted fabric or by cutting a free-form shape around a printed design. Outline the design with machine quilting.

Diaper Stacker. Hang the diaper stacker in a convenient location. A heavy-duty hanger and cardboard bottom shape the fabric.

Crib Headboard and Side Bumper Pads. To make a crib safe and comfortable for infants, sew a padded headboard and bumper pads. Use 1" (2.5 cm) foam or polyester batting as padding. Make in separate pieces, and attach to crib with ties.

Fitted Crib Sheets

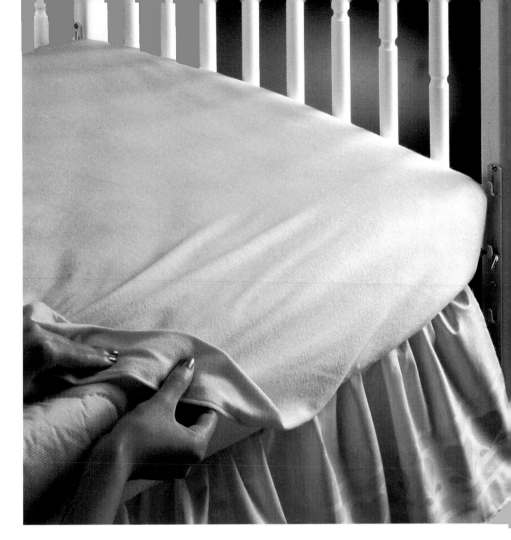

Fitted crib sheets can be coordinated with accessories such as bumper pads or coverlets. Interlock or jersey knit fabrics work best for comfort and stretchability.

Determine the fabric requirement for the size of your mattress. The fabric width equals the mattress width plus two times the depth plus 6" (15 cm) for seam allowances and fitted edge. The fabric length equals the mattress length plus two times the mattress depth plus 6" (15 cm). The square that is cut from each corner equals the mattress depth plus 3" (7.5 cm).

To fit a mattress of 27"×52"×5" (68.5×132×12.5 cm) for a six-year crib, cut a 43"×68" (109×173 cm) rectangle from 2 yd. (1.85 m) of 60" (152.5 cm) wide knit fabric. The width of the sheet should be on the crosswise grain or the grain with the greatest amount of stretch. Cut an 8" (20.5 cm) square from each corner.

How to Sew a Fitted Crib Sheet

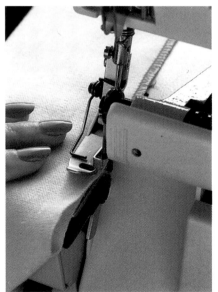

1) Cut square from each corner of sheet, as directed above. Fold sheet at each corner, with the right sides together and raw edges even. Stitch ¼" (6 mm) corner seam on a serger or use a narrow zigzag stitch on a conventional machine.

2) Cut two strips of ¼" (6 mm) wide elastic 3" (7.5 cm) less than width of mattress. On wrong side of sheet, pin center of elastic to center of each short end of sheet. Pin ends of elastic 6" (15 cm) beyond corner seams.

3) Serge or zigzag elastic to the raw edges, as in step 3, page 114. Continue stitching on edges between ends of elastic to finish all raw edges. Turn ¼" (6 mm) hem to wrong side of sheet, encasing elastic. Topstitch hem, stretching elastic.

Crib Coverlets

Prequilted panels make the construction of a crib coverlet easy. These printed panels are about 45" (115 cm) wide and 36" (91.5 cm) long. Prequilted fabrics may also be used. Fabric layers usually include a cotton/polyester top fabric that is quilted to polyester batting. The backing may be brushed nylon tricot or a coordinating print or solid fabric of the same fiber content as the top fabric. To finish the panel edges, use either a pregathered trim and single-fold bias tape or a coordinating ruffle with attached bias tape.

Purchase the trim 5" (12.5 cm) longer than the distance around the panel. For easy application of the trim, round all corners of the coverlet, using a dinner plate to form the curve. Stitch around the coverlet a scant ¼" (6 mm) from the edges to secure the cut quilting threads and to make it easier to apply the trim.

How to Apply Pregathered Trim and Bias Tape

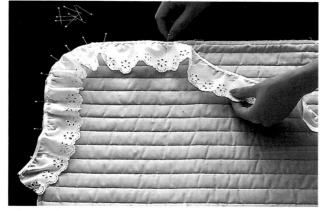

1) Pin trim on panel, with wrong side of trim facing underside of panel, beginning near one corner. Curve end of trim into seam allowance so ends overlap and finished edges taper to raw edge. Ease extra fullness into ruffle at corners, so ruffle lies flat when turned.

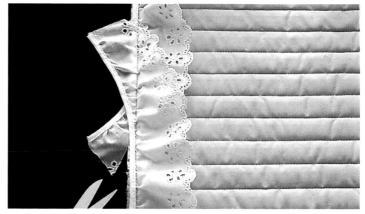

2) Stitch ¼" (6 mm) from raw edge (as shown) around panel to beginning of trim. Curve end of trim into seam allowance so ends overlap and finished edges taper to raw edge. Trim ends of pregathered trim even with panel edge.

How to Apply a Ruffle with Attached Bias Tape

1) Remove stitching for 1½" (3.8 cm) on bias tape. Trim excess ruffle even with bias tape. Press ½" (1.3 cm) of ruffle and both tapes to inside. Glue-baste tapes to both sides of ruffle.

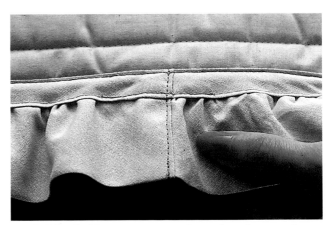

2) Insert edge of panel into bias tape, right sides up; pin. (Narrower bias tape or side with most attractive stitching is right side of trim.) Edgestitch tape to panel, beginning 1" (2.5 cm) from end of tape.

3) Stitch to within 2" (5 cm) from end. Cut excess trim, leaving ½" (1.3 cm); insert into the folded end of trim.

4) Finish stitching tape to panel, overlapping previous stitches. Stitch unstitched portion of other edge of tape, overlapping original stitching. Edgestitch ruffle and tape together at opening.

3) Open ½" (1.3 cm) single-fold bias tape; fold under ¼" (6 mm) at one end. Place tape foldline over trim, right sides together, on previous stitching; stitch in crease. Lap tape ½" (1.3 cm) over folded end to finish.

4) Turn tape to right side of panel, encasing raw edges of trim and panel. (It may be necessary to trim seam allowances.) Pin tape in place. Edgestitch free edge of tape to panel, matching needle thread color to tape, and bobbin thread to underside of panel.

Pieced Heart Quilts

This Pieced Heart quilt, used as a baby quilt or a wall hanging in a child's room, makes the perfect gift. Created from the Pieced Heart design (page 62) and assembled as on pages 64 to 67, the finished quilt measures about 34" × 50" (86.5 × 127 cm). The quilt consists of fifteen heart blocks separated by sashing strips with connecting squares. To create a lasting memento of a special occasion, such as a baby shower or a birthday, make a friendship quilt by having family members or friends sign the quilt along the sashing strips.

The pieces of the heart blocks are assembled to make two styles of blocks. The Pieced Heart baby quilt opposite has blocks of various colors. Each block is made from two heart fabrics and two background fabrics. The blocks for the Pieced Heart wall hanging above are made using four fabrics for the hearts and two fabrics for the background.

For a friendship quilt, the signatures may be obtained before or after the quilt top is stitched together. Use a permanent-ink marking pen for the signatures, testing the pen by writing on a scrap of the sashing fabric and washing the fabric several times to see if the ink bleeds or fades. If you are collecting signatures on the sashing strips before the quilt top is assembled, prevent the fabric from slipping during signing by placing the strips on a piece of fine-grit sandpaper or

taping them to a piece of cardboard. You may also want to record on a sashing strip who the signers are, when the quilt was made, and if it was made for a special occasion.

✂ Cutting Directions

From each background fabric, cut two 7¼" (18.7 cm) strips; from the strips, cut eight 7¼" (18.7 cm) background squares of each fabric.

Make the heart template and cut sixteen hearts as on page 63, steps 2 and 3. For the baby quilt, cut two hearts from each of the eight heart fabrics; for the wall hanging, cut four hearts from each of the four heart fabrics.

Cut seven 2½" (6.5 cm) strips from sashing fabric; these will be cut to size for the sashing strips on page 64, step 4. Cut twenty-four 2½" (6.5 cm) squares from the heart fabrics; these will be used for the connecting squares in the sashing.

Cut four 4½" (11.5 cm) strips from the border fabric; these will be cut to size for the border strips on page 65, step 9. Cut four 4½" (11.5 cm) squares from one or more heart fabrics, to use for the corner squares of the border. Cut five 2½" (6.5 cm) strips from the binding fabric.

YOU WILL NEED

For a wall hanging:

⅜ yd. (0.35 m) each of four fabrics, for hearts, connecting squares of sashing, and corner squares of border.

½ yd. (0.5 m) each of two fabrics, for background.

⅝ yd. (0.6 m) fabric, for sashing.

⅝ yd. (0.6 m) fabric, for border.

1½ yd. (1.4 m) fabric, for backing.

⅜ yd. (0.35 m) fabric, for binding.

Batting, about 38" × 54" (96.5 × 137 cm).

⅓ yd. (0.32 m) muslin, for fabric sleeve, to hang quilt.

Lattice, for hanging quilt.

For a baby quilt:

¼ yd. (0.25 m) each of eight fabrics, for hearts, connecting squares of sashing, and corner squares of border.

½ yd. (0.5 m) each of two fabrics, for background.

⅝ yd. (0.6 m) fabric, for sashing.

⅝ yd. (0.6 m) fabric, for border.

1½ yd. (1.4 m) fabric, for backing.

⅜ yd. (0.35 m) fabric, for binding.

Batting, about 38" × 54" (96.5 × 137 cm).

Pieced Heart design, used in an autographed wall hanging (opposite) or a pastel baby quilt (below), makes a perfect gift.

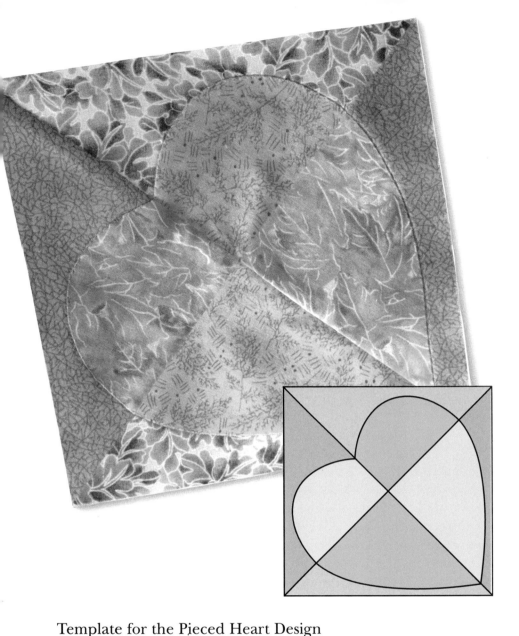

Pieced Heart Design

The quick piecing technique used to make the Pieced Heart quilt block actually yields two blocks. Two hearts are appliquéd to two background squares. Then the squares are cut and reassembled to make two 6" (15 cm) finished Pieced Heart blocks. Select two fabrics for the heart and two background fabrics that contrast.

A template made from cardboard or template material is used for shaping the heart appliqués. The hearts are applied to the background squares, using a technique called *blindstitch appliqué;* for this technique, stitch around the appliqués using the blind-hem stitch on the sewing machine. Set the machine for a short blindstitch, with the stitch width about $\frac{1}{16}$" (1.5 mm). For stitching that is almost invisible, use monofilament nylon thread in the needle and thread that matches the backing fabric in the bobbin. Stitch around the appliqué, catching the edge with the widest swing of the stitch.

Template for the Pieced Heart Design

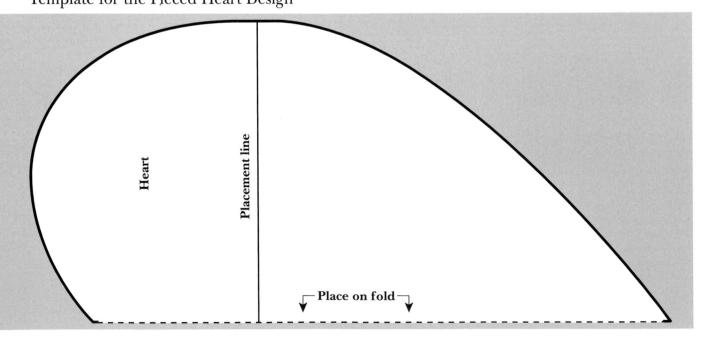

Heart

Placement line

⌐ **Place on fold** ¬

How to Sew a Pieced Heart Block

1) **Cut** one 7¼" (18.7 cm) square each from two background fabrics.

2) **Trace** template (opposite) onto paper. Fold paper on dotted line; cut on outer solid line. Trace heart onto cardboard; transfer placement line to template. Cut out template.

3) **Place** template on heart fabric on the straight of grain. Adding ¼" (6 mm) seam allowance, cut around heart. Clip inside corner almost to template. Repeat to cut remaining heart from second fabric.

4) **Spray** starch in small bowl; dab starch on section of seam allowance. Place template on wrong side of heart. With tip of iron, press seam allowance over edge of template; using dry iron, press until spray starch dries. Continue pressing around heart. Turn heart over; press right side up.

5) **Mark** each side of heart appliqué at the placement line, on seam allowance, using marking pencil. Fold background square diagonally in both directions; press foldlines. Center heart diagonally on square, aligning placement marks with a foldline; pin in place. Repeat for remaining heart and background square.

6) **Position** tear-away stabilizer, cut larger than heart, on wrong side of background square. Using blindstitch appliqué (opposite), stitch hearts to squares. Remove stabilizer. Cut squares diagonally in both directions.

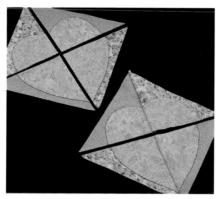

7) **Rearrange** triangles, alternating fabrics to make heart blocks. Using ¼" (6 mm) seams, stitch the upper heart triangles, right sides together; then stitch lower heart triangles together.

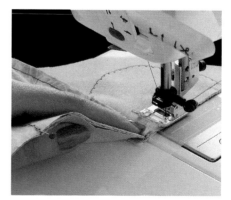

8) **Stitch** upper portion of heart to lower portion of heart, matching raw edges and finger-pressing seam allowances in opposite directions. Press block, pressing long seam allowances to one side.

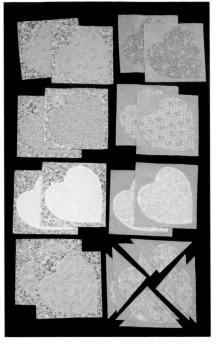

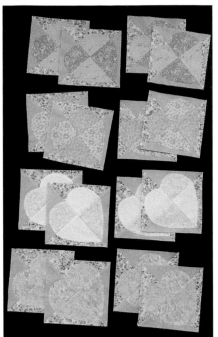

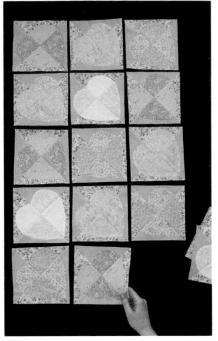

1) Prepare heart appliqués, stitch to background squares, and cut as on page 63, steps 3 to 6; stitch hearts from four fabrics to squares of one background fabric. Stitch hearts of remaining fabrics to squares of second background fabric.

2) Reassemble the triangles as on page 63, steps 7 and 8, to make 16 blocks as shown.

3) Arrange blocks as desired into five rows of three blocks; there is one extra block that will not be used for the quilt.

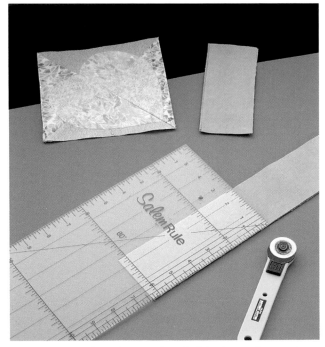

4) Measure sides of several quilt blocks to determine the shortest measurement; from the 2½" (6.5 cm) sashing strips, cut 38 strips to this length.

5) Stitch the sashing strips between blocks, right sides together, to form rows. Stitch strips to ends of rows. Press seam allowances toward sashing strips.

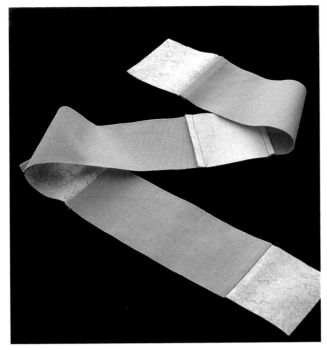

6) Stitch the remaining sashing strips alternately to the connecting squares to equal the length of the block-and-sashing row; there will be a connecting square at each end. Press seam allowances toward sashing strips.

7) Place one sashing unit along the lower edge of first block-and-sashing row, right sides together, matching seams. Pin along length, easing in any fullness; stitch. Repeat for remaining block-and-sashing rows.

8) Pin bottom of one row to top of a second row, as in step 7; stitch. Repeat to join remaining rows. Stitch sashing unit to upper edge of first row. Press seam allowances toward sashing units.

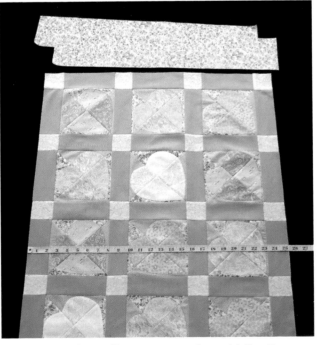

9) Measure the quilt top across the middle. From 4½" (11.5 cm) fabric strips, cut two border strips to this length. Measure the quilt top down the middle, from the top to the bottom; cut two border strips to this length.

(Continued on next page)

10) Pin upper border strip to upper edge of quilt top at center and ends, right sides together; pin along the length, easing any fullness. Stitch. Repeat at lower edge. Press seam allowances toward the border.

11) Stitch corner squares for border to ends of side border strips, right sides together. Finger-press seam allowances toward border strip.

12) Pin and stitch the pieced border strips to sides of quilt top, as in step 10, matching seamlines at corners. Press the seam allowances toward the border.

13) Cut backing fabric 4" (10 cm) wider and longer than quilt top. Layer and baste the quilt top, batting, and backing (pages 68 and 69). Quilt the wall hanging, using the stitch-in-the-ditch method (pages 70 and 71). Stitch in seamlines of sashing and borders; then stitch an X through each Pieced Heart block.

14) Apply binding as on pages 73 to 75, using 2½" (6.5 cm) strips.

How to Sew a Pieced Heart Wall Hanging

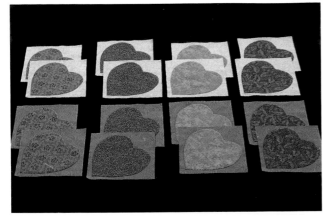

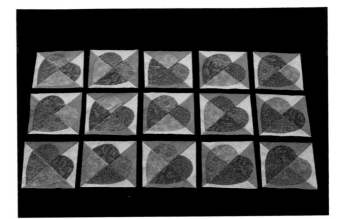

1) Prepare heart appliqués, stitch to background squares, and cut as on page 63, steps 3 to 6; stitch two hearts from each fabric to two squares of each background fabric.

2) Reassemble the triangles as on page 63, steps 7 and 8, to make 16 blocks; in step 7, alternate triangles randomly, using four heart fabrics in each block. Complete quilt as on pages 64 to 66, steps 3 to 14. Attach fabric sleeve (below).

How to Hang a Quilt Using a Fabric Sleeve

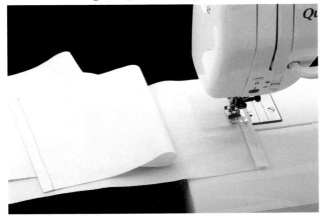

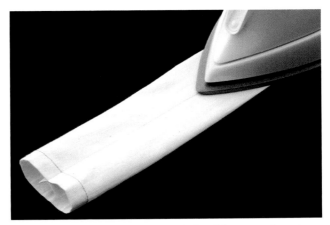

1) Cut a piece of washed, unbleached muslin 6" (15 cm) wide by the width of the quilt. Turn under and stitch ½" (1.3 cm) double-fold hems at short ends.

2) Stitch long edges of strip, right sides together, in ½" (1.3 cm) seam; press seam allowances open. Turn sleeve right side out; press flat, centering seam.

3) Pin the sleeve to the back of the quilt, close to the top edge and 1" (2.5 cm) from the ends. Hand-stitch sleeve to quilt along upper and lower edges; stitch through backing and into batting.

4) Hang the quilt by inserting strip of sealed wooden lattice, cut ½" (1.3 cm) shorter than the width of the quilt, through sleeve. Secure lattice to wall, placing screws or nails at ends of lattice.

Basting a Quilt

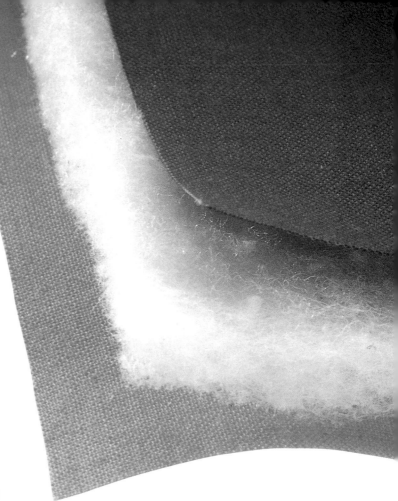

Basting is used to hold the quilt top, batting, and backing together while quilting. For ease in handling, the backing and batting should extend 2" to 4" (5 to 10 cm) beyond the edges of the quilt top on all sides.

Before layering and basting, press the quilt top and backing fabric and mark any quilting design lines. If you are using template quilting with plastic stencils, mark the quilting design lines; it is not necessary to mark the design lines when quilting with tear-away stencils.

Follow the manufacturer's recommendations for pretreating the batting. Some battings require rinsing or washing with soap before using them. If you are using polyester batting, unroll the batting and lay it flat for several hours to allow the wrinkles to smooth out.

Traditionally, quilts were basted using a needle and thread; however, for a faster method, safety-pin basting may be used instead. Lay the quilt flat on a hard surface, such as the floor or a large table, and baste the entire quilt about every 6" (15 cm). If basting with thread, use white cotton thread and a large milliners or darning needle. Use a running stitch about 1" (2.5 cm) long. If basting with safety pins, use rustproof pins.

How to Layer and Baste a Quilt

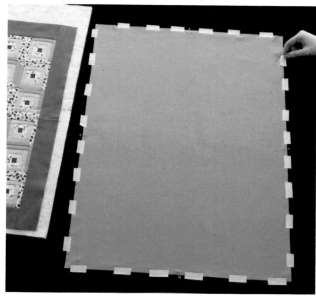

1) **Mark** center of each side of quilt top at raw edges with safety pins; repeat for batting and backing. Tape the backing, wrong side up, on work surface; begin at the center of each side and work toward the corners, stretching fabric slightly. Backing should be taut, but not stretched.

2) **Place** batting over backing, matching the pins on each side. Smooth, but do not stretch, working from center of quilt out to sides. Place quilt top right side up over the batting, matching the pins; smooth, but do not stretch.

3) Baste with safety pins or thread, from the center of quilt to pins on sides; if thread-basting, pull stitches snug so the layers will not shift, and backstitch at ends. Avoid basting on marked quilting lines or through seams. (Both basting methods are shown.)

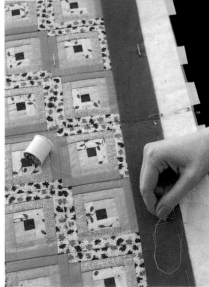

4) Baste one quarter-section with safety pins or thread, in parallel rows about 6" (15 cm) apart, working toward the raw edges. If thread-basting, also baste quarter-section in parallel rows in opposite direction. Repeat for remaining quarter-sections.

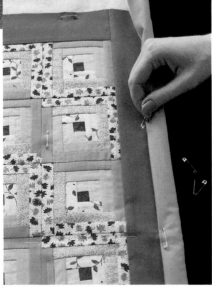

5) Remove tape from backing. Fold edges of backing over the batting and edges of quilt top to prevent raw edges of fabric from raveling and to prevent the batting from catching on needle and feed dogs during quilting. Pin-baste.

Quilting Techniques

For machine-guided quilting, such as stitch-in-the-ditch and channel quilting, it is helpful to stitch with an Even Feed® foot, or walking foot, if one is available; this type of presser foot helps to prevent puckering. Position your hands on either side of the presser foot and hold the fabric taut to prevent the layers from shifting. Stitch, using a stitch length of 10 to 12 stitches per inch (2.5 cm), and ease any excess fabric under the foot as you stitch. The presser foot and feed dogs guide the quilt through the machine.

For free-motion quilting, such as template, motif, and stipple quilting, remove the regular presser foot and attach a darning foot. Set the machine for a straight stitch, and use a straight-stitch needle plate; cover the feed dogs, or lower them. It is not necessary to adjust the stitch length setting on the machine, because the stitch length is determined by a combination of the movement of the quilt and the speed of the needle. Use your hands to guide the fabric as you stitch, applying gentle tension. With the presser foot lifter in the lowered position, stitch, moving the fabric with wrist and hand movements. Maintain a steady rhythm and speed as you stitch, to keep the stitch length uniform. When changing your hand positions, stop stitching, with the needle down in the fabric.

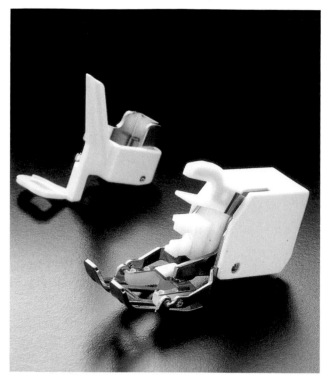

Presser feet recommended for quilting include the darning foot (left) and the Even-Feed or walking foot (right). An Even-Feed foot is used for machine-guided quilting. A darning foot is used for free-motion quilting.

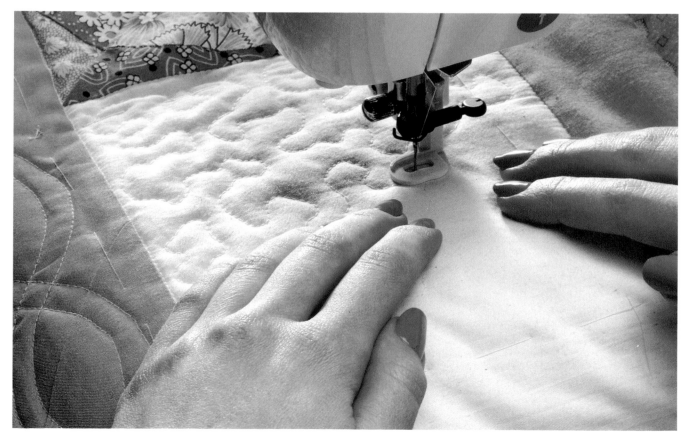

Quilting techniques, including both free-motion and machine-guided, are used to add dimension to a quilt.

How to Secure the Thread Tails

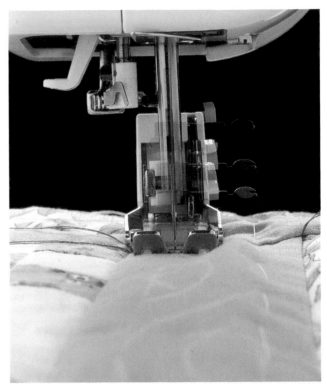

1) Draw up the bobbin thread to the quilt top, by turning flywheel by hand and stopping with needle at highest position. Pull on needle thread to bring the bobbin thread up through the fabric.

2) Stitch several short stitches to secure threads at the beginning of stitching line, gradually increasing stitch length for about ½" (1.3 cm), until it is desired length. Reverse procedure at end of stitching.

How to Quilt Using Machine-guided and Free-motion Techniques

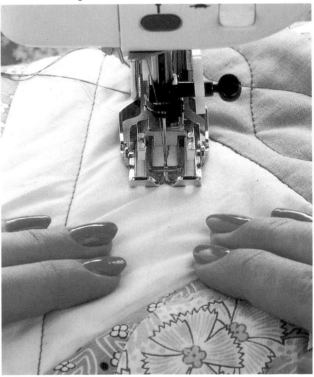

Stitch-in-the-ditch quilting. Stitch over the seamline, stitching in the well of the seam.

Channel quilting. Stitch parallel quilting lines, starting with inner marked line and working outward.

(Continued on next page)

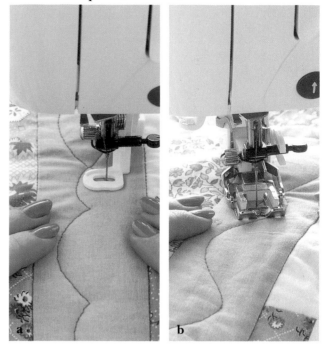

Single-motif template quilting with plastic stencils. Mark design, using marking pencil and plastic stencil. Stitch as much of design as possible in long, continuous lines, without stopping.

Continuous-motif template quilting with plastic stencils. Mark design, using marking pencil and stencil. Stitch motifs along one side to points where motifs connect **(a).** Or stitch one side of first motif, then opposite side of second motif, and repeat **(b).** Return to starting point; stitch motifs on opposite side.

Template quilting with tear-away stencils. Stitch either single motif or continuous motif, following the directional arrows on paper stencil. Tear away the paper stencil.

Stipple quilting. Stitch random, curving lines, beginning and ending at an edge and covering background evenly. Work in small sections; keep spaces between quilting lines close. Do not cross over lines.

Motif quilting. Determine longest continuous stitching line possible around desired motif. Stitch around motif without stopping; continue to next motif. Stitch any additional design lines as necessary.

Binding a Quilt

Double binding provides durable finished edges for quilts. The binding can be cut to match the border of the quilt, or it can be cut from a fabric that coordinates with the pieced quilt top.

Double binding, cut on the straight of grain, has two popular finished widths. Regular binding has a finished width of a scant ½" (1.3 cm), and narrow binding has a finished width of a scant ⅜" (1 cm). Regular binding is used for most quilts; cut the binding strips 2½" (6.5 cm) wide. Narrow binding is used for small quilts, such as wall hangings that are 36" (91.5 cm) or smaller; cut the binding strips 2" (5 cm) wide.

The directions for the quilts in this book specify either regular or narrow binding, and the required binding yardage is given. Binding strips are cut on the crosswise grain of the fabric and pieced to the necessary length.

How to Bind a Quilt with Double Binding

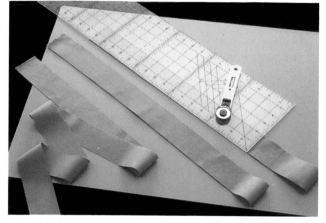

1) **Fold** the fabric in half on the lengthwise grain. On the crosswise grain, cut strips 2½" (6.5 cm) wide for regular binding or 2" (5 cm) wide for narrow binding.

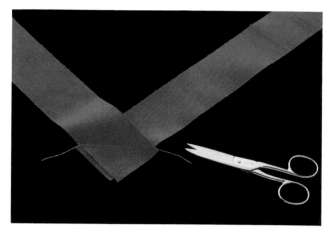

2) **Pin** strips, right sides together, at right angles, if it is necessary to piece binding strips; strips will form a V. Stitch diagonally across strips.

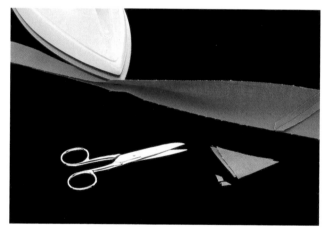

3) **Trim** seam allowances to ¼" (6 mm). Press seam open. Trim points even with edges. Press the binding strip in half lengthwise, wrong sides together.

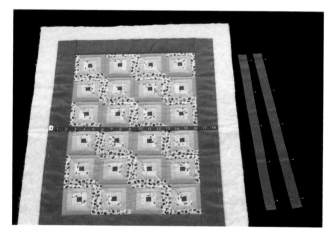

4) **Measure** quilt top across middle. Cut two binding strips equal to this measurement plus 2" (5 cm). Mark binding strips 1" (2.5 cm) from ends; divide area between pins in fourths, and pin-mark. Divide upper and lower edges of quilt in fourths; pin-mark.

5) **Place** the binding strip on upper edge of quilt top, matching the raw edges and pin marks; binding will extend 1" (2.5 cm) beyond quilt top at each end. Pin binding along length, easing in any fullness.

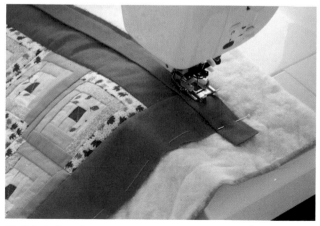

6) **Stitch** binding strip to the quilt, a scant ¼" (6 mm) from raw edges of binding.

7) **Trim** the excess batting and backing to a scant ½" (1.3 cm) from stitching for regular binding; trim to a scant ⅜" (1 cm) for narrow binding.

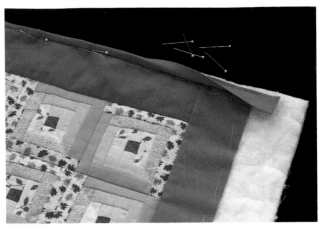

8) **Wrap** binding strip snugly around edge of quilt, covering stitching line on back of quilt; pin in the ditch of the seam.

9) **Stitch in the ditch** on right side of quilt, catching binding on back of quilt.

10) **Repeat** steps 5 to 9 for lower edge of quilt. Trim ends of upper and lower binding strips even with the edges of quilt top.

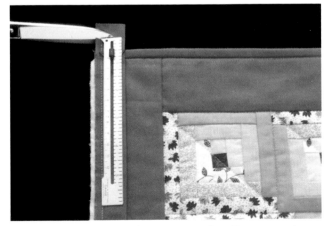

11) **Repeat** steps 4 to 7 for sides of quilt, measuring the quilt top down middle in step 4. Trim the ends of binding strips to extend ½" (1.3 cm) beyond the finished edges of quilt.

12) **Fold** binding along the stitching line. Fold ½" (1.3 cm) end of binding over finished edge; press in place. Wrap binding around edge, and stitch in the ditch as in steps 8 and 9. Slipstitch end.

Growing Up

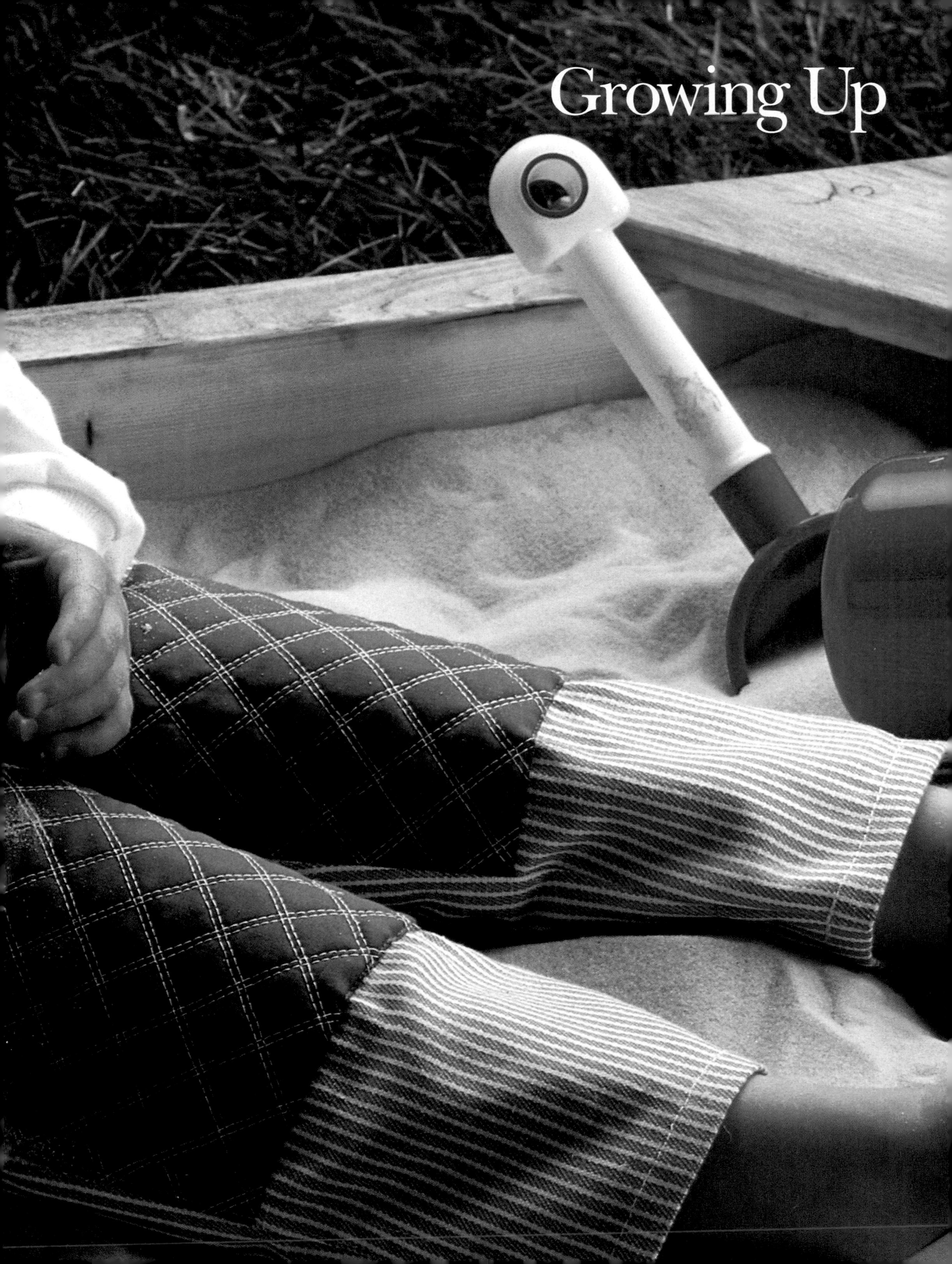

Wardrobe Planning

Plan a child's wardrobe before you begin to sew. If the garments you sew are coordinated, they are more versatile and will have a different look with each ensemble. The child can easily select garments to wear together. Planning a wardrobe does not mean, however, that all garments must be made at one time.

Begin wardrobe planning by considering colors. Notice which colors are in style in ready-to-wear garments and which colors the child likes. Many garments and colors are suitable for either sex, so large portions of a wardrobe can be used by boys and girls.

Decide which colors will be central to the wardrobe. For basic wardrobe items, select colors and fabrics that can be worn year-round. Take swatches of fabrics with you when you shop. Garments for children do not take large amounts of fabric, so stockpile remnants in the wardrobe colors. You may want to purchase trims in coordinating colors for future use.

Wardrobe Basics

The core garments of a child's wardrobe include shirts, pants, overalls, a jacket, and for girls, a skirt and jumper. For sewing these core items, you may want to select a simple pattern that contains directions for sewing several garments, and vary the fabrics, trims, and finishes.

You can use one basic pants pattern for sweatpants, jeans with rolled cuffs, shorts, and pants with a mock fly. From a T-shirt pattern, you can make a shirt with a rugby placket and a pullover shirt with a kangaroo pocket. From one skirt pattern, make a skirt with a mock fly and another with a ribbing waistband. A simple yoked dress can be a school dress or a party dress, depending on the fabric.

Personalizing

To personalize simple pattern shapes, use coordinating fabrics for color blocking. Mix woven fabrics with knits. Sew the body of a shirt with a neck placket from a woven fabric, and the sleeves from a knit. Use piping to highlight the neckline, armholes, side seams, or pocket seams. Repeat trims, such as appliqués or buttons on shirts, to coordinate with pants or skirts.

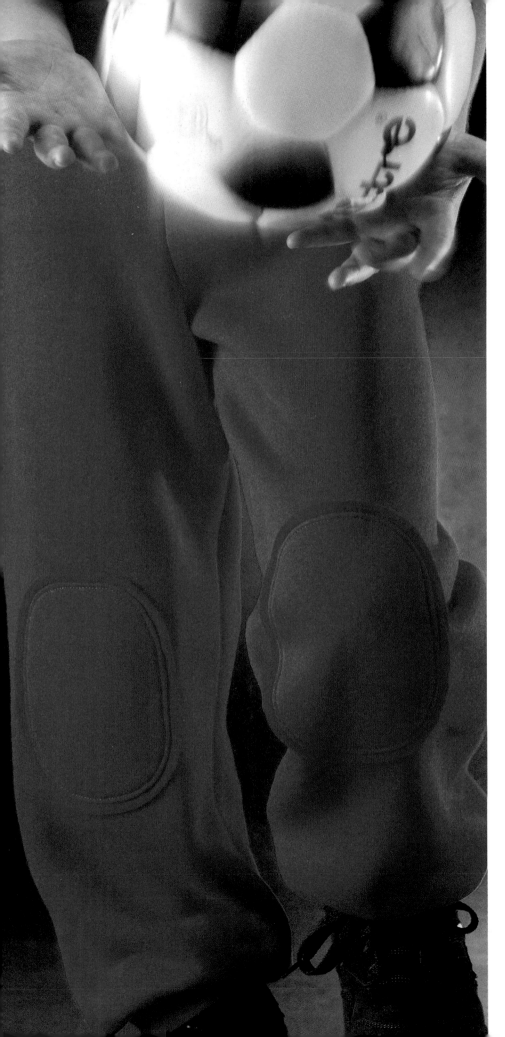

Adding Durability

Build in durability as you construct children's garments. Seams and knees are subject to the most stress during dressing and active play, but both areas can be strengthened easily as you sew the garment.

Seams are most vulnerable at the crotch, shoulder, neck, and armhole. Strengthen the crotch and armhole seams with double-stitched, mock flat-fell, or edgestitched seams (page 31). Reinforce shoulder and neckline seams with a decorative twin-needle seam finish (page 82), stitching before crossing with another seam. Machine-stitch hems for added strength in activewear (page 30).

The knee area wears out faster than any other part of a child's garment and is difficult to reach for repairs. Flat construction techniques allow you to reinforce knee areas as you construct the garment.

Patches

Tightly woven fabrics make the most durable patches. Interfaced, padded, or quilted patches give extra durability and protection at the knee, especially for crawling toddlers. Fuse the patch to the garment to make the application easier and to strengthen the patch.

Double-knee and decorative patches are cut according to the child's size. For infants, cut the patch 3½" × 4" (9 × 10 cm); for toddlers, 3¾" × 5" (9.5 × 12.5 cm); for children, 4½" × 6" (11.5 × 15 cm).

Round the corners of decorative patches to simplify application and to eliminate sharp corners that could catch and tear.

Extended pockets. An extended pocket (page 119) serves as both pocket and double knee, and is applied to the right side of a garment.

Double knees. Apply double-knee patches (page 82) to the right side or the wrong side of the garment. The double layer of fabric adds strength to the knee area. You may also pad the area with polyester fleece, and machine-quilt, for extra durability.

Decorative knee patches. For a decorative knee patch, use pinking shears to cut shapes from soft, nonraveling fleece. Glue-baste the patches in position, and topstitch to the garment. For a piped patch (page 83), select two coordinating fabrics for the patch and piping.

How to Reinforce Seams Using a Twin Needle

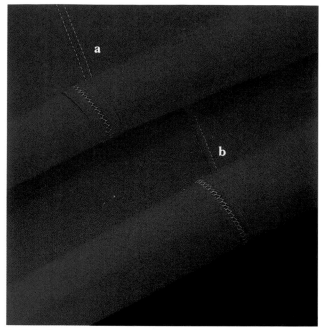

1) Stitch a plain seam. Press seam allowances to one side or open; trim to ¼" (6 mm). Insert twin needle in conventional sewing machine.

2) Stitch, centering seamline **(a)** between the two rows of stitching. For seam allowances pressed to one side **(b)**, you may prefer to stitch in the ditch with one needle as other needle stitches through garment and seam allowances.

How to Add Double-knee Patches

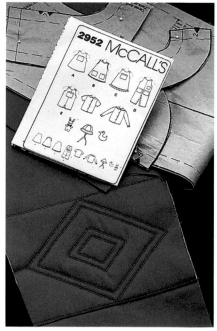

1) Cut two patches 6½" (16.3 cm) long and width of pattern at knee; press under ¼" (6 mm) on long edges. Mark placement lines on front of pants leg 3" (7.5 cm) above and below center of knee.

2) Cut polyester fleece to finished patch size; place on wrong side of patch, under ¼" (6 mm) seam allowances. Glue-baste patch in position over placement lines. Edgestitch long edges.

3) Machine-quilt patch to garment by topstitching through all layers, to provide extra strength. Construct garment according to pattern directions.

How to Add Decorative Knee Patches

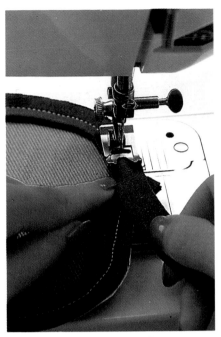

1) **Cut** two patches to size (page 80); round corners. Iron paper-backed fusible web to back of patches. Cut two strips of fabric for piping 1" × 24" (2.5 × 61 cm); cut on bias for woven fabrics or crosswise grain for knits.

2) **Press** strips in half lengthwise, wrong sides together. Stitch to right side of each patch, raw edges even, with ¼" (6 mm) seam allowance.

3) **Curve** ends of piping into seam allowance, so folded ends overlap and taper to raw edge. Trim piping even with raw edge of patch.

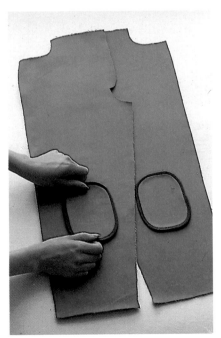

4) **Trim** seam allowance to ⅛" (3 mm). Press seam allowance to wrong side of patch, pulling piping out from patch. Remove paper backing from fusible web.

5) **Fuse** one patch to front of pants leg, parallel to hemline with center of patch slightly below center of knee. On the other pants leg, align second patch with first; fuse.

6) **Stitch** patch to garment, stitching in the ditch. Stitch again ⅛" (3 mm) from first stitching on patch. Finish pants according to pattern directions.

Adding Grow Room

Build in grow room when you construct children's clothing, to get the maximum amount of wear from the garments. Without this extra room, a child going through a rapid growth spurt may be unable to wear a garment that is well liked and in good condition. The easiest place to add grow room is at the lower edge or sleeve hem. Rolled-up cuffs can be gradually lowered as the child grows. To add a coordinated look, select a lining fabric to match a shirt or other part of the ensemble. Cut lining on the straight grain or bias; add interest with a plaid or stripe. When sewing a garment that has straps, add extra length to the straps, and use overall buckles for easy length adjustment.

Ribbing. Make ribbing twice the recommended finished width. Fold the ribbing up, and gradually unroll it to add length as the child grows. Add ribbing to outgrown sleeves or pants legs by opening the hem and using the hemline for the new stitching line.

Inserts and trims. Planning carefully for balanced finished proportions, cut off the lower edge of the garment. Cut an insert of coordinating fabric, lace, or eyelet 1" (2.5 cm) wider than desired length, to allow for ¼" (6 mm) seam allowances on insert and garment. Stitch upper edge of insert to garment, then stitch lower section of garment to insert. Trims with finished edges can be stitched to the right or wrong side of a garment at the hemline for added length.

How to Add Lined Cuffs

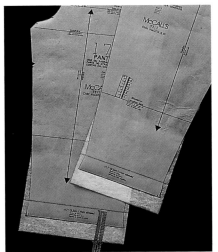

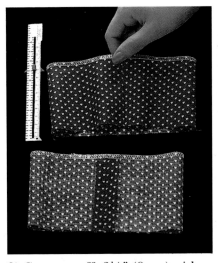

1) Adjust pattern at hem; lengthen hem allowance to 2½" (6.5 cm). Straighten side seams above the original hemline for 4" (10 cm) to eliminate taper. Cut out garment; assemble according to the pattern directions, but do not hem.

2) Cut two cuffs 3½" (9 cm) wide, and 1" (2.5 cm) longer than the circumference of finished sleeve or pants leg. Stitch the short ends of cuff, right sides together, using ½" (1.3 cm) seam; press open. Serge upper edge, or turn under ¼" (6 mm), and press.

3) Stitch cuff to garment, with right sides together and raw edges even, using ¼" (6 mm) seam; match cuff seam to inseam. Turn cuff at the stitching line, and press to wrong side of garment; topstitch at lower and upper edges. Fold the cuff to right side.

Comfortwear

Sewing Sportswear for Comfort

Rugby shirts, shorts, T-shirts, and pull-on pants are designed for active play, but they have also become all-purpose clothes for children. For comfort, these garments are often made from soft knit fabrics and have ribbing or elasticized edges.

Using a basic T-shirt pattern with a round neck, you can make children's knitted shirts in many styles, including pullovers with ribbed edges or prefinished collars. You may want to try one of the decorative ribbing techniques, add a contrasting neck placket, or trim the shirt with piping.

Exposed zippers can add detailing to a T-shirt or jacket. In garments from two-way stretch knits, such as dresses used for ice skating, special techniques are used for the zipper application as well as for the hems and cuffs.

Pull-on pants, shorts, and skirts are all easy to sew. To vary the patterns, try the alternative waistband techniques or add a mock fly detailing. For creative touches on children's clothing, you may want to add decorative pockets.

Ribbing

Ribbing is commonly used for children's activewear. It has lengthwise ribs and great crosswise stretch and recovery, enabling the ribbing to return to its original size and shape. Because of this stretch and recovery quality, ribbing may be used instead of a hem to finish necklines, wrists, ankles, armholes, and waistlines. Ribbed edges provide a snug but comfortable fit for pullover and pull-on garments.

Most ribbings are sold by the inch (centimeter), in tubular form. Polyester/cotton ribbings are a suitable choice for use with sweatshirt fleece, lightweight jersey, and T-shirt knits. The ribbing is cut smaller than the opening of the garment, taking advantage of its stretch quality, for a snug fit. For outerwear, nylon/spandex ribbing provides a firmer, stronger edge; these tubular ribbings are cut to the correct length for the garment. Because ribbing is folded crosswise to finish the outer edge, the cut width is equal to twice the finished width of the ribbing plus seam allowances.

For casual knit shirts, use a ribbing set for the collar and the sleeve edges; the set, which is usually striped in one or two additional colors, has prefinished outer edges, so it is applied as a single layer of ribbing, rather than folded in half.

Because the color selection of ribbing is somewhat limited, it may be difficult to match a knit garment fabric exactly. In this case, you may want to use a contrasting ribbing. Or you can cut self-fabric strips on the crosswise grain if you are using a knit that stretches at least 25 percent in this direction.

Ribbings vary in their amount of stretch, so it is best to estimate the length of the ribbing required either by pin-fitting it on the body or by measuring the garment edge. The finished width should be in proportion to the size of the garment edge. For example, waistline ribbings are cut wider than ribbings for necklines and sleeveless armholes.

Cut ribbing from a single thickness, or fold it crosswise and cut it doubled as it will be applied to the garment. Lightweight ribbings are easier to handle if folded and pressed lightly before cutting; be careful not to stretch the ribbing while pressing it.

Fabric Preparation

Preshrink fabrics, tapes, trims, and notions to prevent garments from shrinking, remove any chemical finishes and excess dyes, and keep seams and details from rippling. Preshrinking restores the original shape of knits and prevents twisted seams in the finished garment. Use the washing and drying methods recommended by the fabric's manufacturer. Do not preshrink ribbing; this distorts ribbing and makes it difficult to lay out and cut accurately.

After preshrinking, knits may ripple or look uneven along the selvages. To prepare the fabric for pattern layout, fold it along a lengthwise rib and smooth out any wrinkles. It is important to align the pattern sections on the straight grain of the fabric. If sections are cut off-grain, the finished garment will twist instead of hang properly.

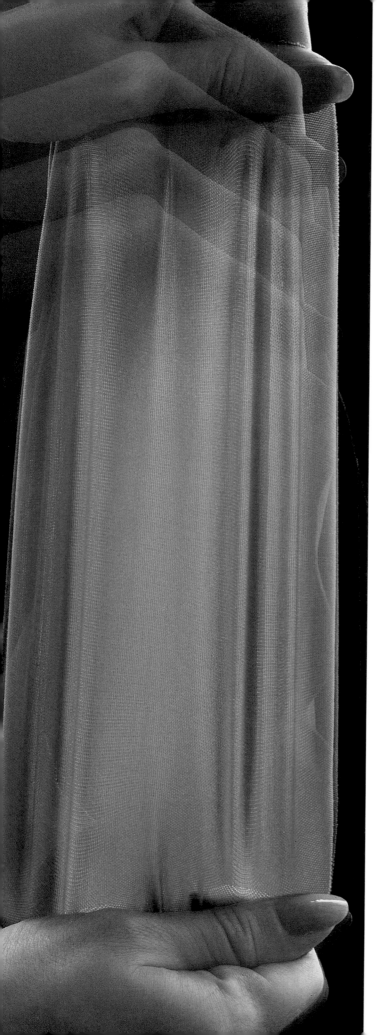

Fabrics for Action

When a child's activity requires a wide range of body motion, highly elastic knits offer a number of practical benefits. These fabrics stretch in both directions, crosswise and lengthwise, so they are called two-way or four-way stretch knits.

Spandex is a man-made elastic fiber that is blended with other natural or man-made fibers to give a knit garment added stretch and the ability to retain its shape. Garments made from such knits are flexible, comfortable, and nonrestricting. Two-way stretch knit garments are lightweight, easy to care for, and quick drying. Many solid colors, stripes, and prints are available for wardrobe variety and creative costumes.

Two-way stretch knits come in several fiber combinations, which have different performance characteristics and surface textures. Nylon/spandex knits have a distinctive shine and excellent shape retention. Originally used for swimwear, nylon/spandex knits are now also used for other strong, formfitting garments such as bicycle shorts, tights, and dancewear.

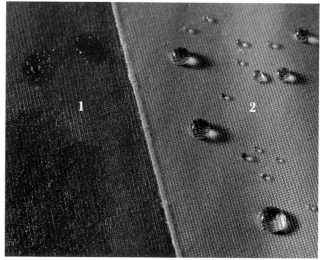

Absorbency. Cotton/polyester/spandex knits (**1**) have a matte surface and feel softer than nylon/spandex knits (**2**). They are more absorbent but do not dry as quickly and are slightly less durable. Although not as practical for swimwear, they can be used for many other activities, especially those enjoyed in hot weather, or for indoor play.

Fabrics for Comfort

Whether used for sport or leisure, garments such as sweatshirts, pull-on shorts or pants, and T-shirts are among the most versatile and comfortable items to sew. These loosely fitted styles can be layered over other garments or worn alone. When layered, they often serve as warm-ups over dance leotards or as cover-ups worn by the pool and on the way to the playground. Suitable fabrics include knits, wovens, and meshes.

Knits often used for these sportswear styles are sweatshirt fleece (**1**), velour (**2**), stretch terry (**3**), textured sweater knits (**4**), and double knits (**5**). Jersey (**6**) and interlock knits (**7**) are used for T-shirts and other pullover tops. Lightweight tricot (**8**) is often used for running shorts and sleeveless tank tops. Some of these knits have a one-direction stretch quality; others are stable and have little or no elasticity but get their comfort from loose, easy fit.

Woven fabrics recommended for casual garments include poplin (**9**), twill (**10**), and gabardine (**11**). Other sturdy mediumweight fabrics such as chino and plain weaves are also suitable.

Mesh knit fabrics (**12**), used as inserts, ventilate sportswear and provide an attractive contrast in texture. Various sizes of mesh are available in cotton, nylon, polyester, and blends.

As you select fabrics, notice the fiber content on the bolt-end label or hang tag. Fabrics made of all-cotton are likely to offer the most comfort because this fiber is absorbent and breathes. Follow care instructions closely because all-cotton fabrics may fade, shrink, and wrinkle unless special manufacturing finishes have been used.

Blends of cotton with polyester or acrylic fibers are easy to care for. They are more resistant to shrinkage and wrinkling than are fabrics made from pure cotton. These blends are less absorbent, which can be an advantage. The less moisture the fabric holds, the more quickly the garment dries when wet. But the higher the percentage of synthetic fiber, the less the fabric allows perspiration to evaporate.

Purely synthetic fabrics made from nylon, polyester, or acrylic fibers can be washed and dried by machine; they rarely require ironing. They are not absorbent, so they dry quickly. Colors are permanent; many of these fibers that tend to accumulate static electricity are treated to reduce static buildup.

Shirts

For a versatile shirt pattern, choose a loose-fitting, basic T-shirt style with a round neck. Using one pattern, you can make several shirts by varying the design with different neck, cuff, and hem finishes.

Fabric choices also add variety. Most loose-fitting T-shirt patterns may be sewn from lightweight knits and wovens for warm weather. Sweatshirt fleece or flannel make a warm shirt for cooler weather.

For easier sewing of a child's shirt, you may want to change the sewing sequence from the usual pattern directions. Do as much stitching as possible while the garment is flat. Pockets and appliqués are easier to apply before any seams are stitched. The flat method of ribbing application (page 41) is easier on Toddlers'

sizes, which have small neck and arm openings. The tubular ribbing application (page 94) is neater and may be preferred for Children's sizes.

Prefinished collars, cuffs, and waistbands are sold separately or in sets. They have a prefinished outer edge for a ready-to-wear look and are available in solid colors or in a variety of stripes and edge finishes. Prefinished collars, cuffs, and waistbands should be 1" to 3" (2.5 to 7.5 cm) smaller than the opening. If an appropriate child's size is unavailable, trim an adult size to fit. Use a prefinished collar for a T-shirt or for a shirt with a convertible collar. Use prefinished cuffs to finish a ribbed-top pocket.

How to Apply Prefinished Collar, Cuffs, and Waistband

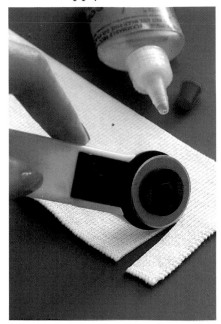

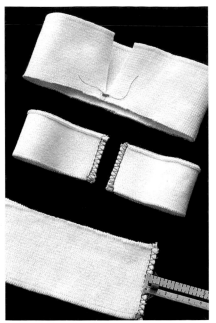

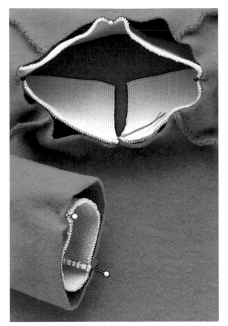

1) Trim short ends so collar, cuffs, and waistband are 1" to 3" (2.5 to 7.5 cm) shorter than garment edge; on collar, trim an equal amount from each end. Trim the width, if desired. Apply liquid fray preventer to short ends of collar.

2) Butt collar ends, and join with bar tack by zigzagging in place just inside neck seamline. Join short ends of cuff and waistband, using ¼" (6 mm) seam.

3) Divide collar, waistband, and garment edges into fourths; divide cuffs and sleeves in half. Place collar ends at center front, cuff seams at sleeve seams, and waistband seam at side seam. Attach as for ribbing, steps 2 and 3, page 94.

How to Apply a Prefinished Collar and Ribbing

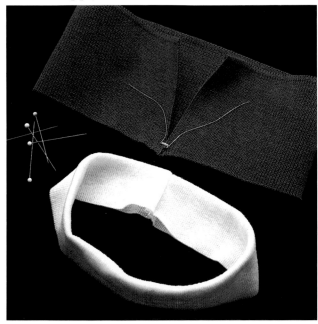

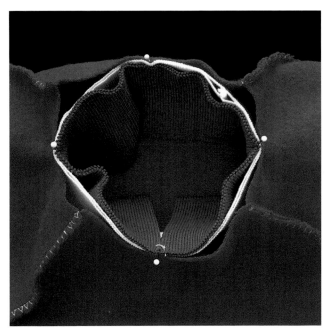

1) Trim prefinished collar, if necessary, as in step 1, above. Butt ends, and join with bar tack by zigzagging in place just inside neck seamline. Cut ribbing for narrow crew neck (page 17). Join ends, using ¼" (6 mm) seam; fold in half lengthwise, wrong sides together. Divide collar, ribbing, and neck edge into fourths; pin-mark.

2) Pin ribbing to right side of garment at neck edge, with pin-marks matching and raw edges even; position ribbing seam at back seam of raglan sleeve, at shoulder seam, or at center back. Pin collar over ribbing, with raw edges even. Place collar ends at center front. Stitch, stretching ribbing and collar to fit neck edge as in step 3, page 94.

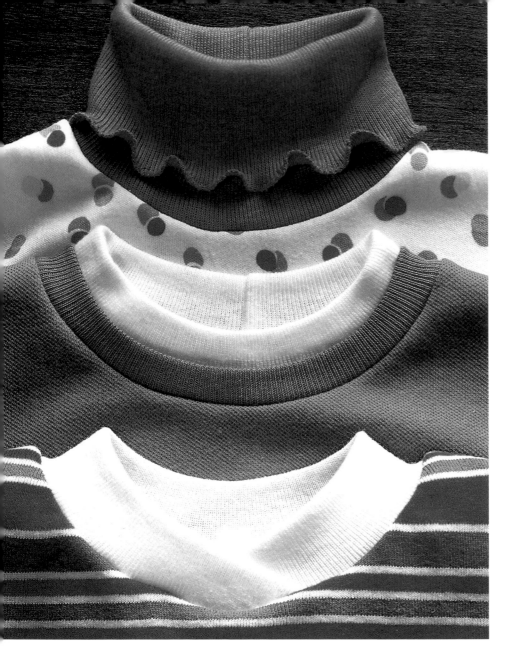

Ribbed Edges

Ribbing makes an attractive finish for necklines, cuffs, or waistlines on either knit or woven fabric. When using ribbing to finish a shirt made from woven fabric, check the size of the neck opening on the pattern to be sure the garment will fit over the child's head. Neck openings should be 1" to 2" (2.5 to 5 cm) larger than the child's head. It may be necessary to enlarge the opening or use a larger size pattern.

Ribbing does not have a right or a wrong side, so it can be folded with either side up. It can be applied using the flat method (page 41) or the tubular method, below. You can use the tubular method with large openings to produce a neater finish, because the seam that joins the ribbing into a circle is enclosed. Place the ribbing seam where it will be least visible.

For a double ribbing neck finish, combine two ribbings of different widths. For a lapped ribbing, cut a standard crew neck width, and lap the ends instead of joining them into a circle.

Lettuce edging can be used to finish the edge of the ribbing or knit fabric for a feminine look. Match the color of the thread to the fabric, or use a coordinating color thread.

How to Apply Ribbing Using the Tubular Method

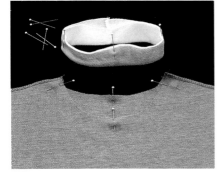

1) Cut ribbing two-thirds the length of neck opening; cut the width for standard crew neck (page 17). Join ribbing ends with ¼" (6 mm) seam. Fold the ribbing in half lengthwise. Divide ribbing and garment edges into fourths; pin-mark.

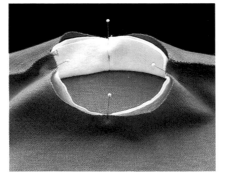

2) Position ribbing seam at center back or shoulder seam; pin ribbing to right side of garment, with raw edges even, matching pins.

3) Serge or use an overedge stitch (page 30) to apply ribbing to the garment, using ¼" (6 mm) seam; ribbing is on top and raw edges are even. Stretch ribbing between pins to fit garment.

How to Apply Double Ribbing

1) Cut two pieces of ribbing two-thirds the length of neck opening; cut one ribbing width for standard crew neck, and the other ribbing width for a narrow crew neck (page 17). Join short ends of each ribbing with ¼" (6 mm) seam.

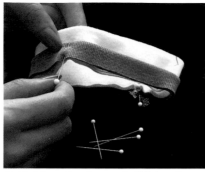

2) Fold each piece of ribbing in half lengthwise, with wrong sides together. Pin narrow ribbing over wide ribbing, with raw edges even and seams matching. Divide ribbing and garment edges into fourths, and pin-mark.

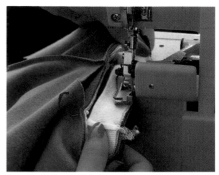

3) Position ribbing seams at center back or shoulder seam. Pin ribbings to right side of garment, matching pins, with wide ribbing on top and raw edges even. Stitch as for tubular method, step 3, opposite.

How to Apply Lapped Ribbing

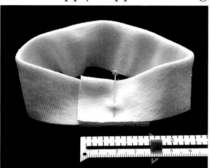

1) Cut ribbing two-thirds the length of neck opening plus 1½" (3.8 cm); cut width for standard crew neck (page 17). Fold in half lengthwise. Lap ends ¾" (2 cm); mark center of overlap with pin.

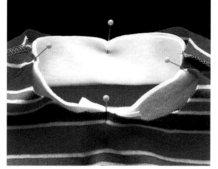

2) Divide ribbing and garment into fourths; pin-mark. Pin ribbing to right side of garment, with center of overlap at center front and raw edges even, matching pins.

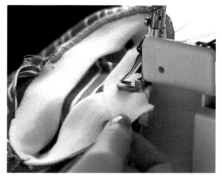

3) Curve ends of ribbing into seam allowance, so folded ends overlap and taper to raw edges. Stitch as for tubular method, step 3, opposite, starting at center back.

How to Finish Ribbing and Knits with Lettuce Edging

Conventional method. Zigzag closely spaced stitches over ribbing fold or folded edge of hem, placing fold at center of presser foot and stretching the fabric as you stitch. The more you stretch the fabric, the more ruffled the edge will be. For hems, trim the hem allowance close to stitching.

Serged method. Adjust serger for rolled hem setting according to manufacturer's directions. Stitch along ribbing fold or folded edge of hem, stretching fabric as you stitch. Do not cut the folded edge with the serger knives. The more you stretch the fabric, the more ruffled the edge will be. For hems, trim hem allowance close to stitching.

Shirt Plackets

Add a placket on a close-fitting neckline for easier dressing. Placket openings can be used on knit and woven garments. To add variety to a shirt or blouse, combine woven and knit fabrics for the garment and placket. You can also coordinate the garments in a wardrobe by using coordinating placket fabrics.

Add hook and eye tape to a front slash. For a neat look when the placket is open, finish neck edges with twill tape or bias binding. Bind the neck in a matching or coordinating color.

Snap tape can add a decorative touch. For heavy fabrics and knits, use snap tape instead of buttons and buttonholes. It is easy to apply, and children can master snaps quickly.

Stitch fastening tapes carefully to maintain alignment of fabric design. If snap, hook and eye, or twill tape is not available in the color you need, dye the tape to coordinate with the garment fabric. Preshrink all tapes before applying them to garments.

How to Apply Hook and Eye Tape to a Shirt Placket

1) Mark a 6" (15 cm) center front line. Beginning at the neck edge, staystitch ³⁄₈" (1 cm) from line. Pivot at lower end of placket, and stitch ³⁄₄" (2 cm) across; pivot again. Shorten stitches at the corners and across lower end. Continue stitching to neck edge.

2) Slash line to ¹⁄₄" (6 mm) from lower end; clip to corners, step 3, page 46. Press under the seam allowances at staystitching. Cut hook and eye tape ¹⁄₂" (1.3 cm) longer than opening. Center tape in opening, placing first hook 1" (2.5 cm) below raw edge. Glue-baste, and edgestitch using zipper foot.

3) Join shoulder seams. Trim the prefinished collar as in step 1, page 93. Stitch wrong side of collar to right side of garment at neck edge, with ends of collar at edges of tape. Bind neck seam with twill tape, as in steps 5 and 6, opposite.

How to Apply Snap Tape to a Full-length Shirt Opening

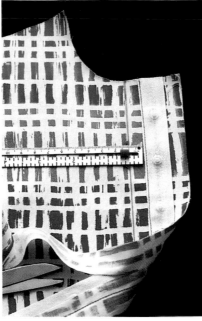

1) Cut the snap tape the length of the opening, with top and bottom snaps about 1" (2.5 cm) from raw edges. Press narrow double-fold hem to wrong side.

2) Mark center front on *right* side of *overlap*. Glue-baste tape to facing, with ball side up and tape edge ⅜" (1 cm) from center front. Edgestitch edge nearest center front, using zipper foot; at lower edge, turn under tape to match pressed hem. Trim facing to ¼" (6 mm).

3) Mark center front on *wrong* side of underlap. Glue-baste tape to facing, with socket side up and edge ⅜" (1 cm) from center front. Edgestitch edge nearest center front, using zipper foot; at lower edge, turn under tape to match pressed hem. Trim facing to ¼" (6 mm).

4) Turn ball side of tape to wrong side at stitched edge; turn socket side of tape to right side at stitched edge. Press lightly. Edgestitch free edges of snap tape to garment. Join shoulder seams. Trim prefinished collar as in step 1, page 93.

5) Attach collar as in step 3, opposite. Cut ¾" (2 cm) twill tape 1" (2.5 cm) longer than neck edge. With right sides together and edges even, stitch tape to neck edge over previous stitching. At ends, fold tape to wrong side.

6) Fold twill tape onto garment, encasing the seam allowances. Edgestitch twill tape to garment; backstitch at both ends.

Rugby Plackets

A rugby placket can be added to a basic T-shirt to duplicate a ready-to-wear look. For a girl's garment, mark the placket opening to the left of the center to lap right over left. For a boy's garment, mark the placket opening to the right of center to lap left over right. The center front is at the center of the closed placket. The photos that follow show a girl's shirt.

Face the placket with self-fabric or a coordinating fabric. Interface the placket piece with fusible interfacing. Roll the overlap facing slightly to the outside for a decorative edge.

1) Cut placket facing 4½" (11.5 cm) wide by length of opening plus 2" (5 cm); interface. Finish long edges by serging or by stitching with 3-step zigzag. Mark 5" to 6" (12.5 to 15 cm) slash line on right side of facing, 1½" (3.8 cm) from one long edge.

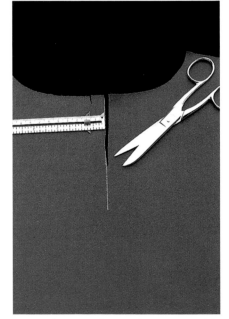

2) Mark center front of garment with clip. Mark 5" to 6" (12.5 to 15 cm) slash line, ⅝" (1.5 cm) to left of center front for girls, right of center front for boys. Cut slash.

3) Pin facing to garment, right sides together, with facing edge ½" (1.3 cm) above neck edge and marked slash line on facing directly under garment opening. Narrow side of facing is on right front for girls, left front for boys.

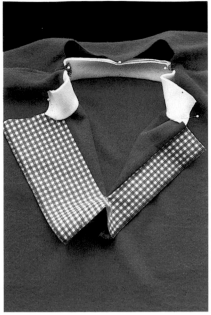

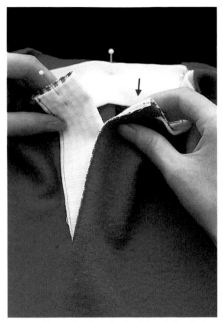

4) Stitch around slash on garment, ⅛" (3 mm) from raw edges, using 12 to 14 stitches per inch (2.5 cm). Shorten stitches near point; make two stitches across point. Cut facing at slash line; clip to stitching at point. Trim facing to match neckline curve.

5) Join shoulder seams. Turn facing to wrong side of garment. Pin collar to neckline, right sides together, so center backs match. Collar ends are ⅝" (1.5 cm) past seam of underlap and at center front mark of overlap.

6) Fold underlap in half, with right sides together. Fold overlap, right sides together, with placket seam about ⅛" (3 mm) from fold (arrow). Stitch neck seam; trim corners.

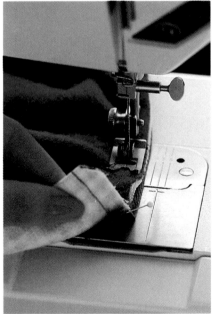

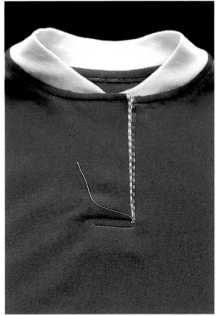

7) Cut ¾" (2 cm) twill tape for neck edge, so tape is long enough to overlap finished edge of each facing by ½" (1.3 cm). Pin tape over collar with right sides together and edges even; stitch over previous stitching. Turn facings to wrong side; turn tape over neck seam allowances, and pin to garment.

8) Stitch in the ditch (arrow) of underlap seam. Pin the overlap to the garment so about ⅛" (3 mm) of facing is visible at the fold; press. Stitch in the ditch of overlap seam, stitching from lower end to neckline; pivot, and topstitch ¼" (6 mm) from neck seam to secure tape.

9) Close placket; press. Stitch a rectangle ¼" (6 mm) long and the width of placket to secure all layers at lower end of placket. Make bar tack at point of slash by zigzagging in place. Trim excess facing below rectangle of stitching. Apply snaps, or buttons and buttonholes, at center front.

Piping

Piping adds a decorative touch at garment seams or edges. Use it on pockets, collars, side seams of pants and skirts, shirt yoke seams, and seams of raglan sleeves. Combine piping with color blocking (page 195) and topstitch for interesting effects.

Make piping from either woven or knit fabric. Cut woven fabric on the bias; cut knit fabric on the crosswise or lengthwise grain. Use fabric that is colorfast and requires care similar to that of the garment. Preshrink fabric and the cord or yarn used as the filler in the piping.

Before cutting the fabric strips for piping, decide whether the piping will be filled or flat. For a soft, yarn-filled piping or a firmer, cord-filled piping, the fabric width should be at least two seam allowances plus the circumference of the filler, plus ⅛" (3 mm). For a flat ⅛" (3 mm) piping, cut the width of the fabric strip at least two seam allowances plus ¼" (6 mm). The finished piping seam allowances should be the same width as those of the garment. When using ¼" (6 mm) seam allowances on the garment, it is easier to sew the piping with ⅝" (1.5 cm) seam allowances, and trim them later to match the garment.

How to Sew Piping

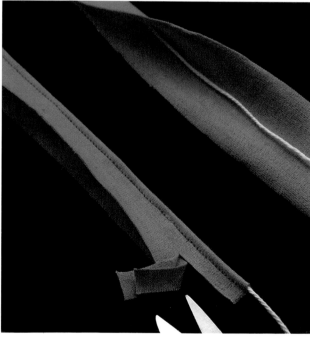

Filled piping. 1) Center cord or yarn on wrong side of fabric strip. Fold strip in half lengthwise, wrong sides together, enclosing cord. Stitch close to cord, using zipper foot; stretch woven fabric slightly as you sew. Trim seam allowances to match those of garment.

2) Pin piping to right side of garment, with raw edges even. Curve ends of piping into seam allowance at inconspicuous place, so ends overlap and piping tapers to raw edge. For enclosed seams, such as collar seams, taper piping into seam allowance at intersection of seams, step 2, page 180.

How to Prepare Bias Strips

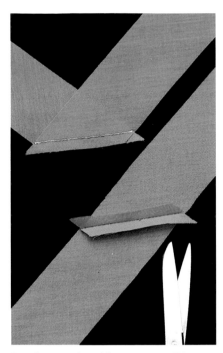

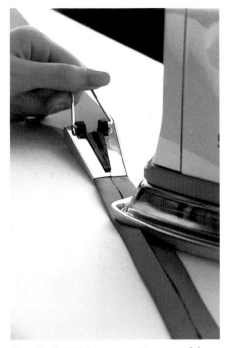

1) Fold fabric diagonally, so straight edge on crosswise grain is parallel to selvage. Cut on fold for first bias edge. Use ruler and rotary cutter to cut 2" (5 cm) strips.

2) Piece strips, if necessary. Pin strips in V shape, with right sides together and short ends aligned. Stitch ¼" (6 mm) seam; press seam open. Trim seam allowances even with bias strip.

Single-fold bias tape. Prepare bias strip, left. Trim one end to a point. Pull bias strip through bias tape maker; press folds to center as strip comes out end of tape maker.

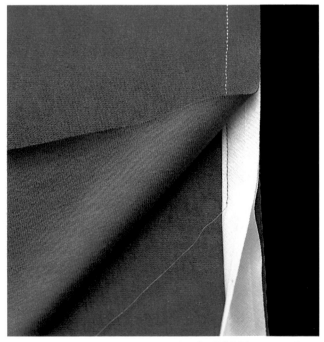

3) Stitch on seamline. Remove stitching in piping at ends; trim cord in seam allowance. Stitch garment seam over previous stitching line, with piping between right sides of garment pieces.

Flat piping. Use 1" (2.5 cm) single-fold bias tape for ⅛" (3 mm) finished piping and ⅝" (1.5 cm) seam allowances. Press tape open; fold in half lengthwise, and press. Pin piping to garment, and stitch seam as in steps 2 and 3, left.

Fold-over Braid

Fold-over braid is used to bind garment edges. It is especially suitable as a finishing technique for garments made from thick or bulky fabrics. Hems, seams, and facings can then be omitted, creating flatter and smoother edges.

Fold-over braid comes in folded and flat forms. Some braids are pressed so the edges do not meet. When applying the braid, place the wider side underneath the garment, and the narrower side on top. Flat fold-over braid has a raised thread or other folding guideline positioned slightly off-center throughout its length. When applying the braid, place the raw edge of the garment along this guideline, so the wider portion of the braid is underneath the garment. With some braids it is possible to stitch only once to secure both edges of the braid.

Considerable shrinkage can occur with these trims, so preshrinking is an important preliminary step. Preshrink by thorough steaming. Hold the iron just above the surface of the braid, and allow the steam to penetrate. Wait until the braid is cool and dry before handling it. To make braid easier to apply to curved edges such as necklines, preshape the braid to match curve, using the same steaming technique.

How to Apply Fold-over Braid

1) Open braid out flat. Pin braid to garment, wrong sides together, with fold of braid at cut edge. Stitch close to edge of braid.

2) Fold braid over to right side, enclosing cut edge; edgestitch from right side.

How to Join Ends of Fold-over Braid

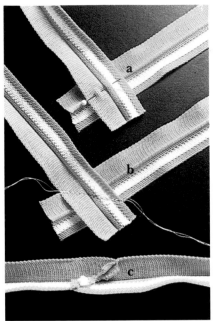

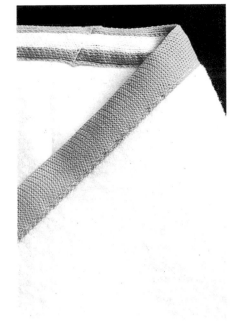

1) Mark seamline where ends of braid meet. Before cutting braid to proper length, add to each end a seam allowance equal to total width of braid.

2) Lap ends of braid at right angles, right sides together (**a**). Stitch diagonally across ends (**b**). Press seam open. Trim to ¼" (6 mm). Trim out V-shape to reduce bulk at foldline (**c**).

3) Apply braid to garment as in steps 1 and 2, opposite. Position braid seam next to garment seam, rather than on top of the seam, to reduce bulk. When braid is folded into finished position, diagonal seam staggers the bulky seam allowances for smooth edge.

How to Miter Corners of Fold-over Braid

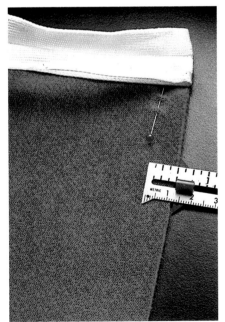

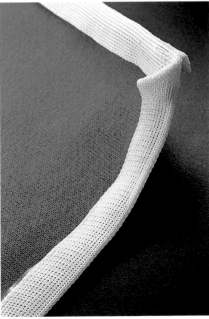

1) Baste edge of braid to right side of garment, using basting tape. At corner, fold braid back on itself, right sides together. Use pin to mark distance from corner equal to finished width of braid.

2) Fold braid diagonally at pin marker, bringing edge of braid into position along garment edge. Use basting tape to baste braid for short distance past corner.

3) Baste edge of braid on wrong side of garment around corner, making similar diagonal fold in braid. Aim miter in opposite direction from fold on right side of garment to reduce bulk.

Exposed Zippers

You can add color to a shirt by inserting a nonseparating zipper so that the teeth are exposed. Zippers are available in a variety of colors and may be combined with a facing, rolled to the right side to resemble piping. Facings may be made in a contrasting color or a coordinating print, plaid, or striped fabric.

An exposed zipper is inserted in a slash opening in the front of a shirt. Neckline seams finished with twill tape or bias binding are durable, and the tape covers the neckline seam, which will show if the zipper is open.

How to Insert an Exposed Zipper

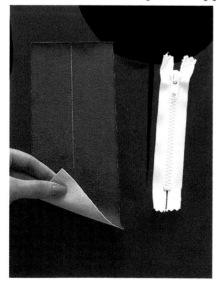

1) Mark center front of garment the length of zipper teeth, plus one seam allowance; slash. Cut facing 3½" (9 cm) wide and 2¼" (6 cm) longer than slash. Interface knit or lightweight facings; mark center line.

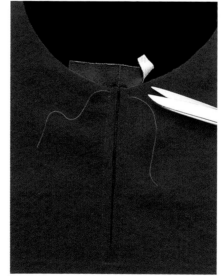

2) Pin facing to garment, right sides together, with ¾" (2 cm) above neck edge and marked line under slash. Stitch ¼" (6 mm) from slash, to ¼" (6 mm) below end of slash; pivot, and stitch ½" (1.3 cm). Pivot; stitch to neck edge. Trim excess facing at neck edge.

3) Cut facing on marked line; clip diagonally to corners. Serge or zigzag raw edges of facing. Turn facing to inside, rolling ⅛" (3 mm) of the facing to right side at slash line; press.

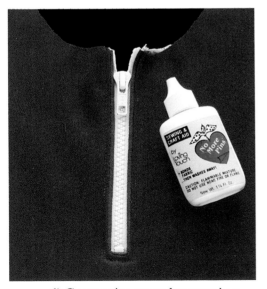

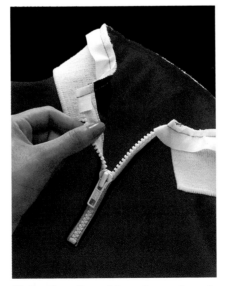

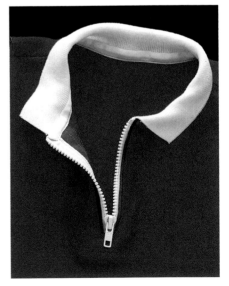

4) Center zipper under opening, with teeth exposed and zipper stop at lower end of opening; glue-baste. Topstitch, using zipper foot, ⅛" to ¼" (3 to 6 mm) from edge, through all layers. Stitch shoulder seams.

5) Apply collar with ends at edge of facing. Cut ¾" (2 cm) twill tape 1" (2.5 cm) longer than neck edge. Pin tape to neck edge, with right sides together and edges even; wrap ½" (1.3 cm) around zipper. Stitch over previous stitching at neck edge.

6) Fold the twill tape onto garment, enclosing the seam allowances. Edgestitch around outer edge of facing and lower edge of tape. Complete garment according to pattern directions.

Separating Zippers

Use exposed separating zippers as a decorative touch in children's sweatshirts or jackets made from warm, durable fabrics, such as corduroy, denim, sweatshirt fleece, and double-faced polyester bunting.

Before applying a zipper, complete the garment, including the collar and lower edge, according to pattern directions. Trim front opening seam allowances to ⅜"(1 cm), and trim the neck seam allowance to ¼" (6 mm). Finish neckline and zipper tapes with bias binding for a neat, decorative trim.

If the correct zipper size is not available, purchase a zipper longer than needed. The zipper can be trimmed to fit during application.

How to Apply a Separating Zipper

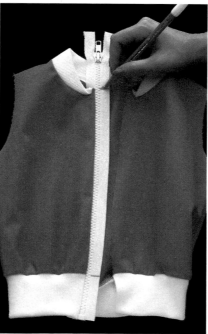

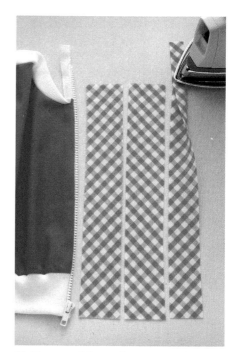

1) Trim neck and front opening seam allowances, above. Pin one side of open zipper to jacket edge, right sides together and edges even, with bottom stop at lower edge. Stitch next to zipper teeth from lower edge to neckline; leave excess zipper at neck edge.

2) Close zipper, and mark the alignment of seams or the fabric design. Open zipper. Matching marks on zipper to jacket, pin and stitch other side of zipper as in step 1.

3) Cut two bias strips (page 101), 2⅛" (5.3 cm) wide and 1" (2.5 cm) longer than zipper opening. Cut another bias strip, 1⅝" (4 cm) wide and length of neck edge. Press all strips in half lengthwise, wrong sides together.

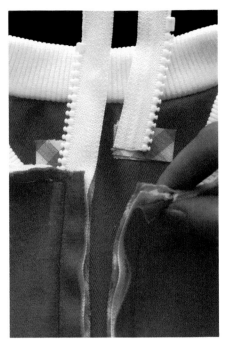

4) Place binding over zipper tape, with raw edges of binding and zipper even. Wrap ½" (1.3 cm) of binding tightly around zipper at lower end; leave ½" (1.3 cm) excess binding at neck edge. Stitch from lower edge over previous stitching.

5) Pivot, and stitch along the neck seamline to fold of binding. If zipper is longer than opening, turn handwheel by hand to stitch between zipper teeth.

6) Trim excess binding even with raw edge of neckline. Trim excess zipper one tooth beyond stitching line. Repeat binding application for other side.

7) Place binding over collar, with raw edges even. Extend the ends of the neckline binding ¼" (6 mm) onto the zipper binding; trim excess. Stitch the neckline binding over previous stitching.

8) Fold bindings to the wrong side. Baste bindings to garment on fold. Edgestitch folded edge of binding to jacket front, beginning at the lower edge. Pivot at fold of the neckline binding.

9) Continue stitching around the fold of neckline binding and down other front binding fold. Bar tack at bottom of zipper by zigzagging in place.

Zippers in Stretch Knits

Most two-way stretch knit garments are pull-on styles and do not need a zipper or other closure; however, when garments such as leotards or skating dresses have high, fitted necklines, a zipper is necessary.

The following method for inserting a zipper on stretch knit garments can be used at the center back or center front even if there is not a seam there. A layer of lightweight sew-in interfacing stabilizes the fabric in the zipper area for a smooth, even, nonbulky closure. Use a lightweight synthetic coil zipper for best results.

How to Insert a Zipper in a Stretch Knit Garment

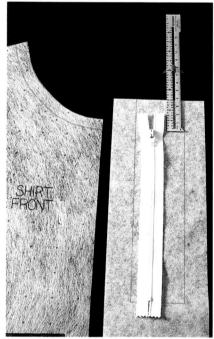

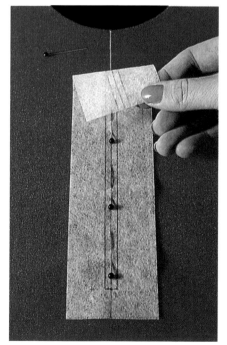

1) Determine the length of zipper opening by measuring the zipper between bottom and top stops, then adding pattern seam allowance. Cut lightweight nonwoven sew-in interfacing 2" (5 cm) wide and 1" (2.5 cm) longer than zipper.

2) Mark total length of zipper opening in center of interfacing. Draw a stitching box ¼" (6 mm) wide with marked length through center of box. Mark zipper opening on right side of garment.

3) Pin interfacing to right side of garment, centering stitching box where zipper will be inserted. Match interfacing center mark to zipper marking on garment.

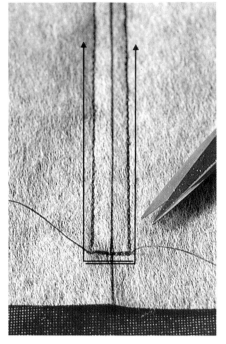

4) Stitch across bottom of box, pivot, and stitch up one side of box. Use short stitch, about 15 per inch (2 mm stitch setting). Repeat on other side, stitching in direction of arrows. To prevent stitches from piling up, do not backstitch.

5) Slash through center of stitching box, clipping diagonally to each corner. Do not cut into stitches. Turn interfacing to wrong side. Press with cool iron, rolling seam to wrong side.

6) Use basting tape to baste zipper behind opening. Position bottom stop of zipper exactly at bottom of opening; place sides of opening next to zipper teeth.

7) Lift garment up, and fold one side over to expose zipper tape and interfacing. Stitch across triangle at bottom of zipper tape, pivot, then stitch up exposed side. Stitch over previous stitching.

8) Fold other side of garment back to expose remaining side of zipper tape and interfacing. Again, stitch across bottom of zipper tape, pivot, and stitch up exposed side, stitching over previous stitching.

9) Trim interfacing close to edges of zipper tape. In completed insertion, zipper teeth are exposed and no stitches show from the right side.

Hems in Stretch Knits

Hems for actionwear are quick and easy to sew because knit fabrics do not ravel. Use a cut edge, edgestitching, lettuce edging, or mock-cuff hem.

Cut edge is the quickest and easiest hem of all. Because this no-sew method of cutting the edge at the hemline produces a single-layer finish, it eliminates bulk and encourages a graceful flow of fabric on full skirts or ruffles.

Edgestitching makes a neat, narrow hem for wrap knit skirts or the lower edge of tights that do not

have elastic. It does not add the weight of a deep hem or interfere with the stretch of the knit fabric.

Lettuce edging, shown above, gives a decorative three-dimensional look to skating skirts and other garments with ruffles or fullness. This hem can be stitched with an overlock or narrow zigzag stitch.

Mock-cuff hem is similar to a blindstitched hem but gives the look of a cuff, even though it is actually a turned-up hem stitched on the inside. The mock cuff is ideal for straight edges. Like lettuce edging, it can be stitched with an overlock or narrow zigzag stitch.

Four Ways to Hem Stretch Knits

Cut edge. Trim garment neatly on hemline. Use sharp shears and cut with long, firm strokes. When edge becomes worn, trim a slight amount to renew the fresh look. Clean-cut edge works best on firm knits, which will not fray.

Edgestitching. Turn under hem allowance, and edgestitch; then on inside of garment, trim excess hem allowance close to edgestitching. Use short straight stitch for this neat, narrow hem, and do not stretch fabric as you sew.

Lettuce edge. Trim garment on hemline. Use a closely spaced zigzag stitch over the cut edge of fabric, positioning edge at center of foot. Stretch hem as you sew; the more you stretch the fabric, the more ruffled the edge will be.

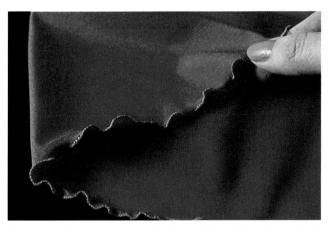

Lettuce edge on an overlock machine. Use the rolled hem setting. Stretch hem as you sew; the more you stretch the fabric, the more ruffled the edge will be.

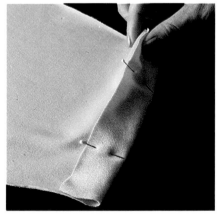

Mock-cuff hem. 1) Fold hem up; then fold hem back toward right side of garment into position for blind hemming.

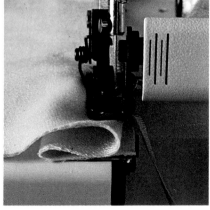

2) Stitch just to the left of the top fold, using an overlock stitch or narrow zigzag. Remove pins as you come to them.

3) Open hem out. Do not press flat; slight roll between garment and hem gives appearance of an attached cuff.

Pants & Skirts

Pants and skirts are basic items in a child's wardrobe. The easiest pants and skirts to sew are those with elasticized waistbands.

For skirts and pants made of heavyweight fabrics, such as denim, corduroy, and sweatshirt fleece, use lightweight knit or woven fabric as a decorative, less bulky waistband. Good choices for a waistband are ribbing or knit fabric used with a sweatshirt fleece or corduroy garment, or bias-cut plaid flannel or shirting with a denim garment.

The directions that follow are for a pattern with a cut-on waistband. Cut the pattern apart below the waist foldline, ¼" (6 mm) less than the width of the elastic; the ¼" (6 mm) will be the garment seam allowance. Cut a waistband that is twice the width of the elastic plus ½" (1.3 cm) for two seam allowances. For woven fabrics, the length of the waistband should equal the waist measurement of the garment plus ½" (1.3 cm). For stretch knit fabrics or ribbings, cut the waistband 4" (10 cm) shorter than waist measurement of the garment.

Select elastic carefully; the amount of stretch and recovery varies with the type of elastic, the method of insertion, and the weight of the fabric (page 16). To determine the minimum length needed for a waistline, stretch the elastic around the widest part of the hips. Determine the maximum length by comfort. As a general rule, elastic will be 2" to 3" (5 to 7.5 cm) shorter than the waist measurement. Heavy fabric hinders elastic recovery; you may want to cut the elastic 1½" (3.8 cm) shorter than usual. Topstitch through the waistband and elastic to keep the elastic from twisting. Multiple rows of topstitching may be added, if desired.

How to Add a Coordinating Elasticized Waistband

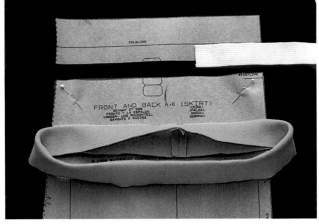

1) Cut pattern and waistband as directed, opposite. Join short ends of waistband with right sides together and using ¼" (6 mm) seam allowance; press open. Fold waistband in half lengthwise, wrong sides together. Complete garment except for applying waistband.

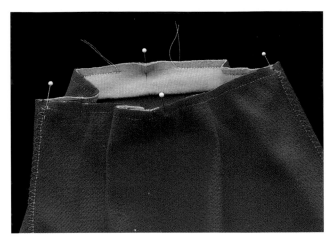

2) Divide waistband and garment into fourths; pin-mark. With seam at center back, pin both layers of waistband to right side of garment at pins; stitch ¼" (6 mm) seam, stretching knit waistband as you sew. Leave 2" (5 cm) opening at center back.

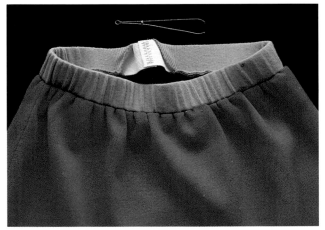

3) Cut elastic desired length plus 1" (2.5 cm). Insert into waistband, using a bodkin; lap ends ½" (1.3 cm). Stitch together securely.

4) Stitch opening closed, inserting loop of ribbon to identify garment back; stitch over previous stitching. Finish seam allowances, if necessary.

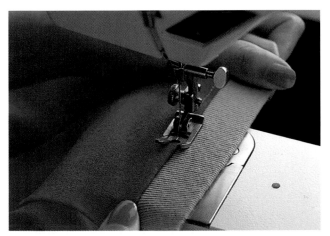

5) Press seam allowances toward garment. Topstitch through garment and seam allowances from right side.

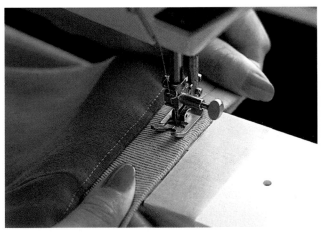

6) Topstitch waistband. Position presser foot at center of waistband. Mark guideline on machine with tape. Stitch waistband, stretching elastic as you sew.

Elastic Waistbands & Mock Fly

Apply elastic to the waistbands of pants or skirts. Use the stitched-on method for a comfortable finish that will not allow the elastic to roll or twist. For this method, use elastic with good stretch and recovery (page 16), so the waistband retains its fit. When stitching, stretch the elastic in front of the presser foot while holding the elastic taut behind the presser foot.

When using a pants or skirt pattern with a cut-on fly and elastic in the back waistband, you can save time by stitching a mock fly instead of inserting a zipper. You will need to eliminate the center front opening of the waistband pattern.

How to Apply Elastic to a Waistband

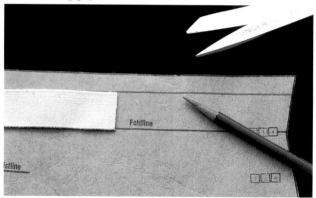

1) **Mark** new cutting line, above the foldline of the pattern, the width of the elastic. Cut and sew garment according to pattern directions, but do not apply elastic.

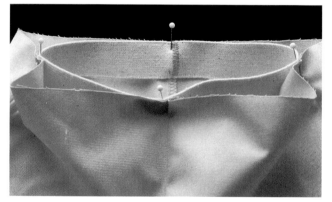

2) **Cut** elastic to fit snugly around hips; butt ends of elastic, and join with zigzag stitch. Divide elastic and garment edges into fourths; pin-mark. Pin elastic to wrong side of garment, with pins matching and edges even.

3) **Zigzag** or serge elastic to garment, stretching elastic between pins to fit garment; avoid cutting elastic when serging. Stretch elastic in front of presser foot, and hold taut from the back; do not pull fabric under the presser foot.

4) **Fold** elastic to inside, encasing elastic. Stitch in the ditch (arrow) from the right side at all seams. Topstitch at lower edge of elastic, stretching elastic to fit. Topstitch again ¼" (6 mm) inside first stitching; stretch elastic as you sew.

How to Sew a Mock Fly

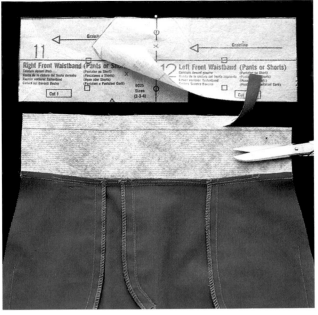

1) Stitch center front seam, right sides together; pivot at lower end of fly to stitch around outside of fly. Trim and finish seam; clip, and press. Press fly toward left front; topstitch fly through all layers at pattern marking.

2) Lap the front waistband patterns at center. Cut adjusted band; apply fusible interfacing. Stitch the waistband to garment front, right sides together; trim seam allowance, and press toward waistband. Trim seam allowance on other long edge to ⅛" (3 mm); finish by serging or using 3-step zigzag stitch.

How to Apply Elastic to a Back Waistband

1) Adjust pattern back at upper edge, as in step 1, opposite. Stitch and finish center back seam. Cut elastic 3" to 4" (7.5 to 10 cm) shorter than upper edge of pattern. With elastic on wrong side of garment and upper edges even, stitch ends to side seam allowances. Pin center of elastic to center back.

2) Attach elastic; fold to inside and topstitch as in steps 3 and 4, opposite. Pin side seams, right sides together. Turn front waistband over the back waistband at side seams; stitch seam.

3) Turn front waistband to inside, encasing ends of elastic. Clip back seam allowance below waistband; press seam open. Edgestitch around front waistband.

Pockets

Children like pockets, which can be both functional and decorative. Consider the pocket placement and size. Place pockets where the child can easily reach them, and make them large enough to hold objects.

Most styles and shapes of pockets can be used on shirts, jackets, pants, and skirts. Test the shape and size by using a template cut to finished size. Be creative with pocket placement, shape, and trim. Pockets are easier to attach before garment seams are stitched.

Add a kangaroo pocket to shirts and sweatshirts. A kangaroo pocket is a large patch pocket that has side openings. Sew this pocket into the side seams and waistline, and trim the upper edge with piping.

Ribbed-top pockets can be coordinated with knit collars and cuffs. To maintain the original pocket size, shorten the pocket by an amount equal to the finished width of the ribbing.

How to Sew a Kangaroo Pocket

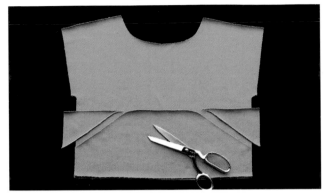

1) Cut pocket the same width as garment and half the garment length from neck edge at center front to lower edge. Cut hand openings at an angle from midpocket on the sides to one-third the width at the upper edge; round the corners at upper edge.

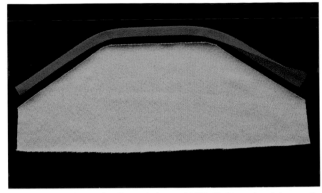

2) Cut fabric strip for piping, 1¼" (3.2 cm) wide and the length of upper edge of pocket; cut on crosswise grain for knits or on bias for wovens. Fold strip in half lengthwise, wrong sides together; press.

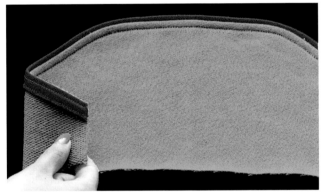

3) Stitch piping to right side of pocket at upper edge, raw edges even, using ⅜" (1 cm) seam. Press seam allowances to wrong side of pocket, with the piping turned up; topstitch the upper edge of pocket ¼" (6 mm) from seam.

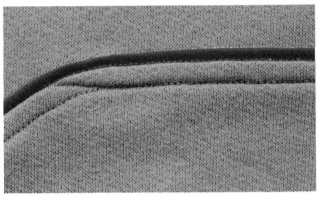

4) Glue-baste pocket on garment, matching side seams and lower edge. Topstitch upper edge of pocket, stitching over previous topstitching; do not stitch hand openings closed. Reinforce by stitching in ditch of piping seam; backstitch to strengthen ends.

How to Sew a Ribbed-top Pocket

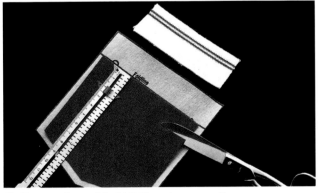

1) Cut pocket with ⅜" (1 cm) seam allowances at sides and lower edge. Trim pocket ¾" (2 cm) below finished upper edge. When using prefinished cuff, cut cuff ½" (1.3 cm) shorter than pocket width and 1¼" (3.2 cm) wide. When using ribbing, cut ribbing ½" (1.3 cm) shorter than pocket width and 2½" (6.5 cm) wide; fold in half lengthwise.

2) Stitch prefinished cuff or ribbing to upper edge of pocket, right sides together, using ¼" (6 mm) seam allowance; stretch cuff or ribbing to fit. Press seam toward pocket; press ⅜" (1 cm) to inside on lower and side edges of pocket. Finish as for basic patch pocket, step 3, page 121.

In-seam Pockets

Sew flat, nonbulky in-seam pockets in garment side seams for a ready-to-wear look. Adapt a pattern that has a two-piece pocket by cutting a single pocket piece from self-fabric. In-seam pockets may be either curved or rectangular.

An extended pocket (pictured on page 81) is applied to the outside of the pants and serves as a pocket and as a knee reinforcement. For a decorative touch, topstitch the extended pocket in a coordinating color thread.

How to Sew One-piece In-seam Pockets

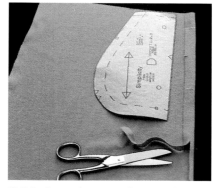

1) Mark pocket opening on side seam allowance of garment front; press to wrong side. Trim seam allowance to ¼" (6 mm).

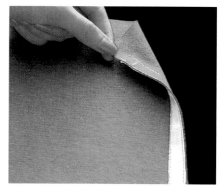

2) Cut ½" (1.3 cm) twill tape 1" (2.5 cm) longer than pocket opening. Pin tape over trimmed seam allowance at pocket opening, with tape edge next to the fold; stitch through all layers on both edges of twill tape.

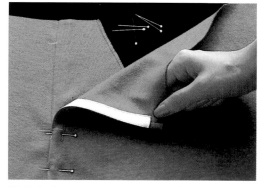

3) Stitch pocket to garment back at side seamline, with right sides together; finish pocket and seam edges. Press seam allowances toward pocket. Lap the garment front over the back side seam allowance, with taped edge even with seamline.

How to Sew Extended Pockets for Pants

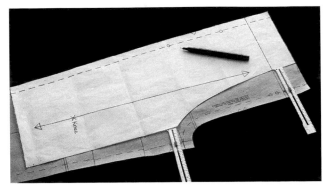

1) Place tissue on front pattern piece. Draw new pocket shape on tissue; begin at upper edge, 2" (5 cm) from center front, and curve to a point at crotch, 1¼" (3.2 cm) from inseam. Draw line from this point, parallel to grainline, to 4" (10 cm) below center of knee; draw line across to side seam. Transfer grainline and pocket opening marks.

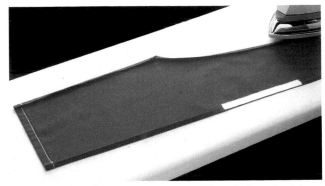

2) Cut pocket from new pattern. Topstitch a double ½" (1.3 cm) hem at the lower edge. Mark and finish edge of pocket opening as for one-piece in-seam pocket, steps 1 and 2, opposite. Press under a ¼" (6 mm) seam allowance on edges opposite pocket opening; clip curves.

3) Stitch pants front to pants back at side seam. Finish seam allowances; press toward the pants front. Glue-baste pocket over pants front, with the taped edge at seamline. Stitch pocket opening edge as in step 4, below. Topstitch edges opposite pocket opening.

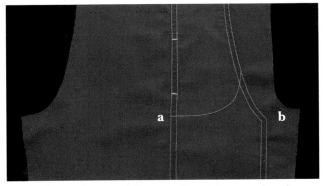

4) Mark a point on side seamline (**a**) opposite the crotch (**b**). Curve line from this point to inner edge of pocket. Topstitch on this line to finish pocket. Repeat steps for other pocket.

4) Topstitch through all layers above and below pocket opening to match stitching lines on twill tape. Make a bar tack by zigzagging at each end of pocket opening.

5) Pin and straight-stitch the loose edges of pocket to garment front. Repeat steps for other pocket.

6) Complete garment according to pattern directions. Catch upper edge of pocket in waistline seam.

Patch Pockets

Patch pockets can become a design element of the garment if they are made from a coordinating fabric. You may want to cut pockets from plaid fabric on the bias or from striped fabric on the crosswise grain when the garment is cut on the lengthwise grain. Pockets with straight edges are easier to sew. When adding trim to a pocket, apply it before stitching the pocket to the garment.

Create your own patch pockets of any size or shape, or use the pocket piece provided with the pattern. Check the size and placement of a pocket on the garment by cutting a pocket shape from paper; do not include seam or hem allowances. Mark the pocket placement on the garment with pins or washable marking pen. When creating your own pocket pattern, add seam allowances at the sides and lower edge, and a hem allowance at the upper edge.

A gathered or pleated patch pocket may be made by enlarging a patch pocket pattern. Because of the gathers or pleats, these pockets are more decorative and hold more than standard patch pockets.

How to Make a Basic Patch Pocket

1) Determine finished pocket size; add ⅜" (1 cm) to sides and lower edge, and 1⅜" (3.5 cm) at upper edge. Cut pocket. Press upper raw edge under ⅜" (1 cm), then 1" (2.5 cm); stitch.

2) Place a 2" (5 cm) cardboard template at corner on seamlines. Press ⅜" (1 cm) seam allowances over template; open, and fold diagonally across corner to miter. Refold on pressed lines; press.

3) Glue-baste pocket in place on garment. Edgestitch sides and lower edge. Topstitch ¼" (6 mm) from previous stitching. To bar tack, zigzag at upper corners.

How to Make a Gathered or Pleated Patch Pocket

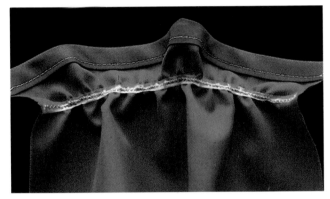

Gathered pocket. 1) Cut pocket 4" (10 cm) wider than basic patch pocket as in step 1, above. Finish upper edge with double-fold bias tape as in step 1, page 39.

2) Cut ¼" (6 mm) elastic 4" (10 cm) shorter than width of pocket; stitch to pocket 1⅜" (3.5 cm) below upper edge as in steps 1 and 2, page 172.

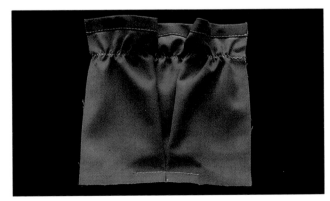

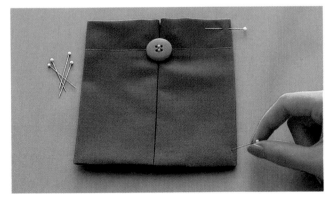

3) Press two 1" (2.5 cm) tucks to center at lower edge of pocket; staystitch. Press seam allowances, and attach pocket as for basic patch pocket, steps 2 and 3, above.

Pleated pocket. Cut pocket 4" (10 cm) wider than basic patch pocket, and finish upper edge as in step 1, above. Press two 1" (2.5 cm) pleats to center of pocket. Center and attach button 1" (2.5 cm) from upper edge, to secure pleats. Press seam allowances, and attach pocket as for basic patch pocket, steps 2 and 3, above.

121

Creative Pockets

Design your own creative pockets to enhance the style of a garment, making the pockets any shape or size desired. To add even more interest, sew the pockets from contrasting fabric.

Window Pockets

A window pocket (opposite) is inventive and easy to sew, and can be used for either lined or unlined garments. The pocket can be varied by changing the size or shape. Contrasting fabric may be used for the pocket piece, to emphasize the pocket opening.

Foldover Pockets

On lined foldover pockets, the top of the pocket folds back to make a contrasting flap. Plan the shape of the pocket to complement the fabric or garment design. The pocket shapes on the garments above mimic the designs in the print fabric and the shape of the neckline. Or the pocket can repeat the shape of other garment details; for example, the notched pocket at right may be used for a garment with notched lapels.

How to Sew a Window Pocket

1) Draw desired size and shape of pocket on paper, drawing pocket opening and placement lines for topstitching.

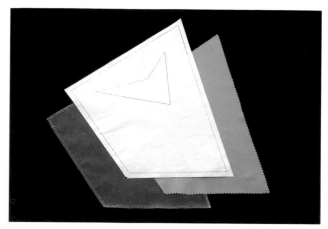

2) Make a tissue pattern, drawing cutting lines ⅜" (1 cm) outside topstitching lines. Cut one piece from lining, wrong side up. Cut another piece from matching or contrasting fabric, right side up; this piece will show at pocket opening. Finish edges.

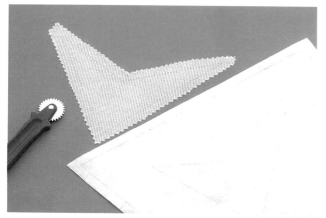

3) Mark mirror image of pocket opening on right side of fusible interfacing. Cut fusible interfacing ½" (1.3 cm) larger than pocket opening, using pinking shears. Fuse interfacing to wrong side of garment section at desired position.

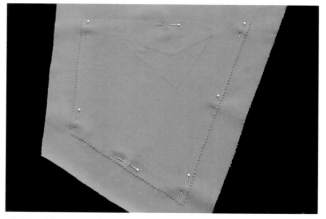

4) Position pocket lining on garment, right sides together; pin in place. Stitch through all layers, from wrong side, following marked lines for pocket opening.

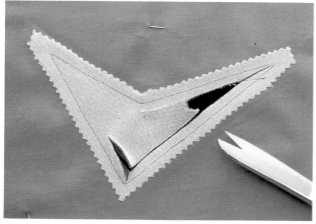

5) Trim fabric layers ¼" (6 mm) inside stitching lines; clip as necessary.

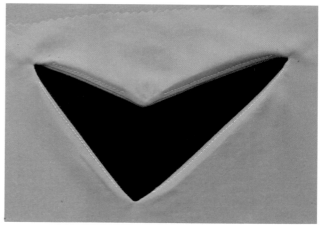

6) Turn pocket lining to wrong side of garment; press. Understitch edge of opening to prevent lining from showing on right side.

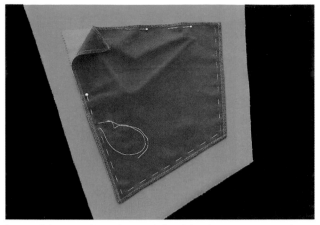

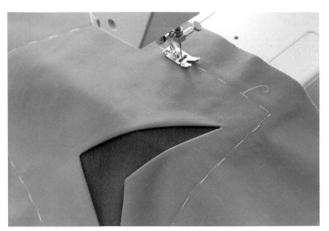

7) Position pocket piece, right side down, over pocket lining; baste from wrong side ⅜" (1 cm) from edges of pocket piece.

8) Topstitch around pocket from right side, along basting stitches. Remove basting.

How to Sew a Foldover Pocket

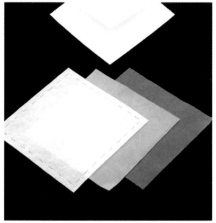

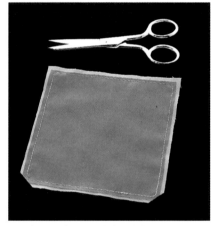

1) Design pocket, and cut the shape from paper in actual size; fold flap to check design. Make pattern from tissue, adding seam allowances. Cut one piece from each of two fabrics.

2) Place pieces right sides together, and pin. Stitch around edges; do not leave an opening. Trim corners and seam allowances; clip curves.

3) Cut small slash in lining close to lower edge. Turn pocket right side out, through slash.

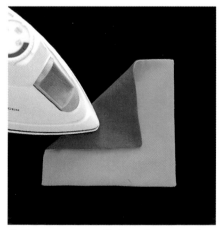

4) Press seam so lining does not show on lower pocket and outer fabric does not show on flap. Press flap.

5) Fuse slashed opening closed, using piece of fusible interfacing.

6) Pin pocket to garment; topstitch in place, backstitching at each end of pocket opening.

Closures

For children's activewear select closures that are decorative, functional, and easy to handle. To prevent tearing, interface closure areas that use buttons, snaps, hooks and eyes, and hook and loop tape.

Apply gripper snaps to shirt plackets, waistbands, and jacket openings. Mark snap placement carefully, and double-check the markings before applying the snaps; removal is difficult and may leave a hole in the garment. Two kinds of tools are available for attaching gripper snaps: the attaching tool and the fastener pliers. The attaching tool requires hammering and should be used only on a solid surface. Strike firmly, rather than tapping lightly. The pliers can be used for most sizes of snaps. Snaps and pliers must be made by the same manufacturer.

Use buttons with buttonholes or button loops to decorate garments. Button loops may be made from strips of knit or woven fabric. Cut knit fabric loops on the lengthwise grain; cut woven fabric loops on the bias grain.

Hook and loop tape is available in circles, squares, or strips, and is easy for children to use. For a shirt opening, use circles or squares. For a waistband, use a strip of tape at least an inch (2.5 cm) long. Self-basting hook and loop tape is backed with an adhesive. Position the tape, and press it on with a finger before stitching. Close hook and loop tape before laundering to prevent lint accumulation on the tape and snags in other garments.

Tips for Applying Closures

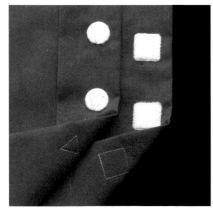

Hook and loop tape. For squares and strips, edgestitch, overlapping stitching at ends. For circles, stitch triangles. Cover stitching on right side with appliqué or button, if desired. Adhesive from self-basting tape can coat the needle; clean needle with alcohol.

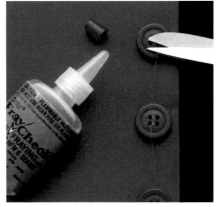

Buttons, sew-on snaps, and hooks. Attach button foot; cover or lower feed dogs. Adjust zigzag stitch width for distance between holes; stitch, ending with several stitches in one hole to anchor. Attach all closures with continuous thread; clip threads, and apply liquid fray preventer.

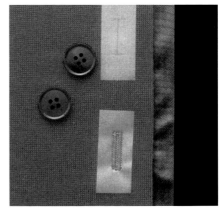

Buttonholes. Use water-soluble stabilizer under the buttonholes when sewing knit fabrics. Position transparent tape over buttonholes; mark buttonhole length on tape. To prevent puckers, set stitch length longer than for woven fabrics. Stitch over tape, parallel to ribs of knit.

How to Apply Button Loops

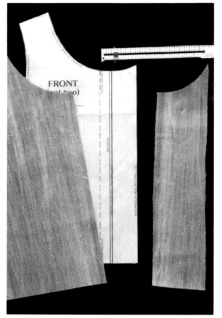

1) Trim pattern front lengthwise ⅝" (1.5 cm) from center front; cut garment fronts. Cut facings 2⅝" (6.8 cm) wide and the length of garment; trim facings to match shape of garment at neck edge.

2) Cut fabric strip 1" (2.5 cm) wide for loops; strip length equals length of loop, step 3, right, times number of loops needed. Add 2" to 3" (5 to 7.5 cm). Trim one end to a point; insert into bias tape maker. Press raw edges to meet at center.

3) Fold strip in half lengthwise; edgestitch, stretching strip as you sew. Cut strip into pieces, each twice the button diameter plus 1⅜" (3.5 cm). Fold pieces in half; baste loops to center front, matching raw edges. Stitch shoulder seams; attach collar.

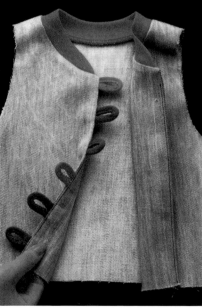

4) Stitch facing to garment, with right sides together and with loops between facing and garment; use ⅝" (1.5 cm) seam. For bulky fabrics, trim seam allowances. Turn facing to wrong side of garment; press.

5) Understitch on right side of facing, close to seamline, through facing and both seam allowances. Stitch other facing to front of garment; understitch.

6) Topstitch garment ¼" (6 mm) from the front and neck edges. Complete garment. Butt center fronts of finished garment; mark button placement at center of loops. Attach buttons.

Sewing Outerwear

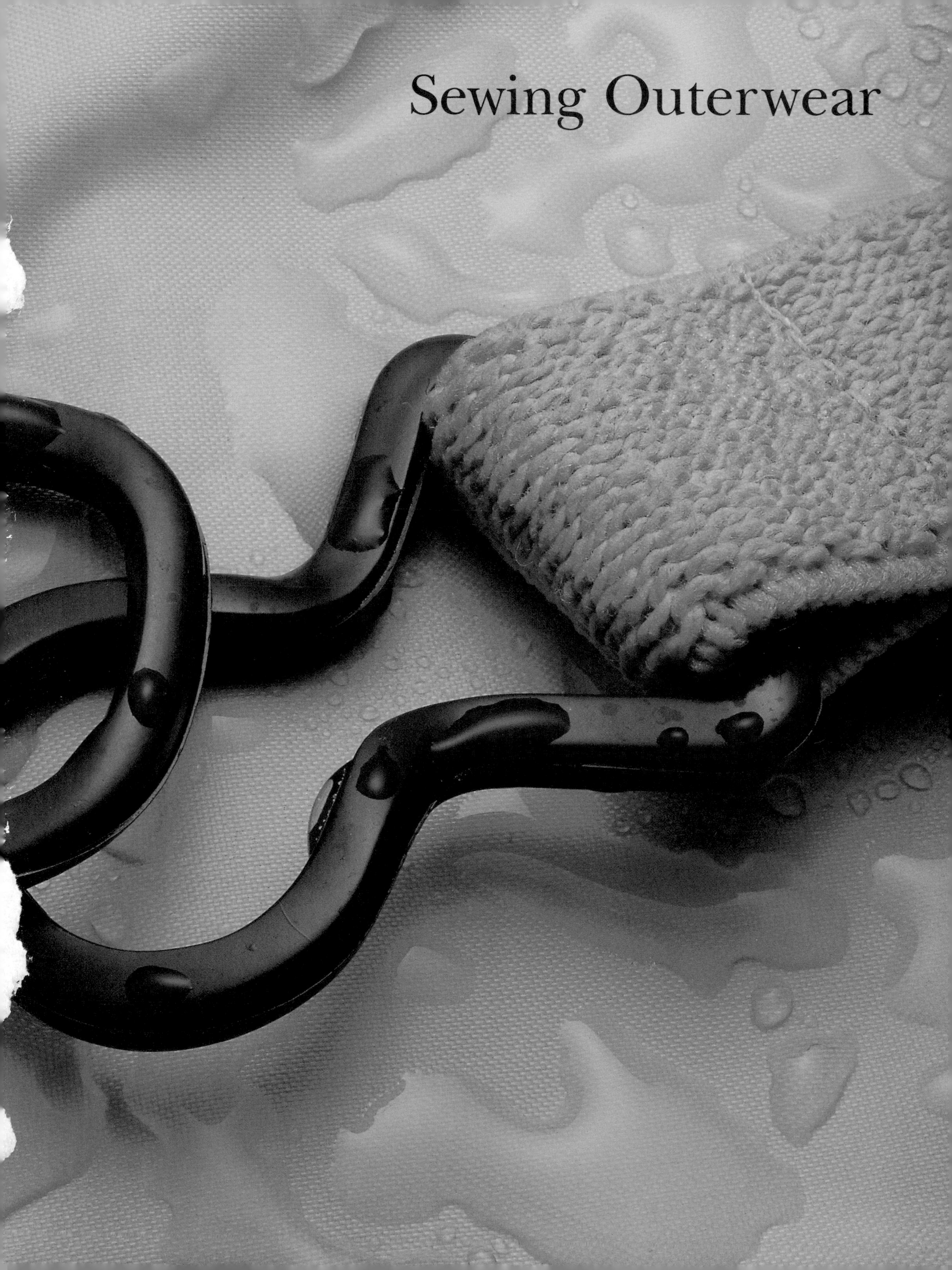

Fabrics for Warmth & Protection

Outdoor activities expose children to the climate and to sudden changes in the weather. Select outerwear fabrics to provide efficient protection from wind, rain, or snow without adding undue weight or bulk. Some of these fabrics may be sold in local fabric stores; however, many are available through mail-order firms that make sports fabrics their specialty.

The following terms describe the practical benefits that outerwear fabrics can contribute to the garments you sew:

Breathable fabrics are porous to let perspiration evaporate, an important factor for comfort.

Easy-care fabrics can be machine washed and dried without ironing or other special pampering. Some fabrics dry quickly.

Insulation proof, down proof, and fiber proof are equivalent terms describing a fabric that is so tightly woven that high-loft insulations, such as polyester fiberfill or down, will not pass through the weave. Fabrics without this quality can allow fibers to migrate through the weave to the outside of a garment; this is called *bearding*.

Strength is important; fragile fabrics will not withstand rugged outdoor abuse. A fabric may be strong because it is made from a durable fiber such as nylon, or its strength may come from a weave that is fine and tight.

Waterproof fabrics are coated or laminated so that moisture can neither enter nor penetrate the fabric. Although waterproof fabrics offer the ultimate protection from water, they are not breathable. Wearing comfort is sacrificed unless the garment is very loosely fitted or ventilated in some way.

Water repellent fabrics resist penetration by water. Water initially beads on the fabric surface but can pass through the fabric during prolonged exposure. Because water repellent fabrics are more porous than those that are waterproof, they are generally more breathable and more comfortable to wear.

Windproof fabrics will not allow air to pass through the fabric, either because of a chemical treatment applied during the manufacturing process or because the fabric has a fine, very tight weave.

Wind resistant fabrics keep much of the wind from passing through the weave. They are less efficient than windproof fabrics but may offer enough protection if you dress the child in layers.

Warm Fabrics

Quilted fabrics, or prequilts, are made with one or two outer fabric layers stitched to a puffy batting. When sewing outerwear, look for quilted fabrics with a nylon taffeta face. Those quilted in a diamond pattern (1) are used most often as linings for jackets, snow pants, and vests. Those quilted in a channel pattern of parallel rows (2) are most often used for jackets and vests that are lined with lightweight woven nylon. The filler for most quilted fabrics is polyester fiberfill, which is easy to care for.

Polyester bunting, such as fleece (3), retains insulating properties when wet, dries rapidly, and is breathable. This double-faced fabric is easy to sew because it will not ravel. It can be used by itself for unlined jackets, or as a lining to add warmth.

Waterproof & Water Repellent Fabrics

Woven nylon fabrics that have more than one ounce (25 g) of polyurethane *coating* per square yard (0.95 m) offer complete protection from water. These fabrics can be used for parkas, windbreaker jackets, ponchos, and pullover shells. Among the fabrics that may be coated are ripstop nylon, which

has a grid design in its weave, and nylon taffeta, which has a smooth weave and surface sheen.

Belonging in a separate category are *laminated* fabrics, which consist of a waterproof material bonded to another fabric. A durable outer fabric, such as poplin, may be laminated to a nylon tricot on the lining side. This combination makes a strong, lightweight fabric that is breathable, yet waterproof.

Water repellant fabrics are often a more comfortable alternative to waterproof fabrics. Some of the most popular water repellant fabrics are also wind resistant, lightweight, and durable. These include nylon taffeta (4), ripstop nylon (5), and Taslan® nylon (6); bi-blend (7) of nylon/cotton fiber content; tri-blend (8), a comfortable blend of nylon, polyester, and cotton fibers; and densely woven polyester/nylon blends.

Several polyester/cotton blend poplins have been chemically treated for water and stain resistance. These poplins are known for their durability and appealing hand. The finish wears off after repeated launderings, but there are products that can be applied to refresh the water and stain repellency.

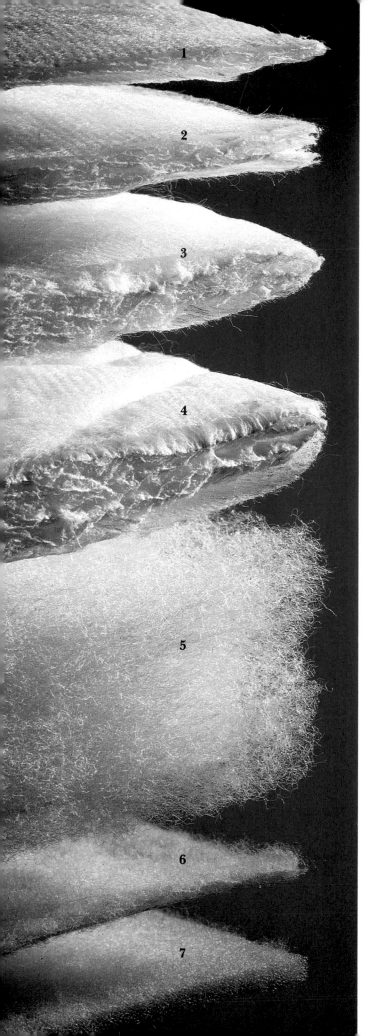

Insulations, Linings & Interfacings

The inner layers of a garment may include insulation, lining, and interfacing. In sportswear garments, insulations provide warmth; linings finish the inside of a garment, prevent show-through, ventilate, or add an extra layer for warmth; and interfacings reinforce and stabilize closure areas.

For the inner layers of sportswear, use fabrics that are compatible with the outer fabric; easy care is important. The inner fabric should also meet the needs of the garment. Some patterns, for example, are designed for a nonbulky insulation; others include insulation loft as part of the fashion design.

Thermal insulations trap body heat in tiny air pockets or hollow spaces to keep you warm in low temperatures. For warmth, the insulation is sewn into a garment between the outer fabric and the lining. These insulations are available in three types: thin, high-loft, and needlepunch. All three types are easy to care for but are heat-sensitive, so they should never be pressed with a hot iron.

Thin insulations are available in various weights. Very thin insulation (1) of 1.3 oz./sq. yd. (44 g/sq. m) is used for lightweight sportswear in milder climates or for indoor loungewear that requires extra warmth. Midweight insulations of 3.2 oz./sq. yd. (2) and 4.9 oz./sq. yd. (3) (110 and 165 g/sq. m) are suited for active play. Heavyweight insulation (4) of 6.5 oz./sq. yd. (330 g/sq. m) is used for vests, jackets, mittens, slippers, and garments for nonactive outdoor exposure.

High-loft insulations (5) are made from synthetic fibers to resemble down, a natural thermal insulator. The highest loft is the most down-like; the more firmly bonded is the most versatile.

Needlepunch insulations (6) resemble the texture of a blanket. Stretch needlepunch (7) has a foam base and is suitable for use with stretch knits.

Thin insulations keep you warm without adding bulk, allowing greater freedom of motion than high-loft and needlepunch. The most widely used contain olefin and polyester microfibers. Thin insulations are ideal for skiwear or other outdoor sportswear that has fitted styling or a soft, draped look; the more fitted the pattern, the more effective the insulation will be. Because thin insulations do not absorb water, they are especially suitable for raingear or for use in a damp climate.

High-loft insulations have qualities similar to down, but they are more affordable, easier to care for, and easier to handle than down. They are quilted or stitched into seams to prevent shifting. High-loft polyester insulations stay warm even when wet.

Needlepunch is made of a polyester fiber base that has been punched with many tiny needles; each needle hole creates an air pocket that helps keep you warm. Needlepunch is less bulky than high-loft insulation and requires no quilting to stabilize it.

Instead of adding thermal insulation to a garment, you can save time by using a prequilted lining. Because prequilted linings add bulk, use a pattern that is one size larger than usual if the pattern is not designed for a quilted lining. This prevents the fit from becoming too tight.

Garments made from stretch knits are never lined, with the exception of swimwear, which may have a crotch lining or a full-front lining. Self-fabric can be used for a front lining as long as there is no printed or knitted design that will show through the fabric when it is wet. Parkas, vests, and similar outerwear items are lined to make the garment easy to slip on and off, to finish the inside of the garment neatly, to make the garment more water repellent, and to save time spent on raw edge finishes. Usually these garments are lined to the edge, a shortcut sewing technique.

In active sportswear, interfacings are used sparingly. When interfacings are required, their primary function is to strengthen the outer fabric, making the garment more durable. One common place an interfacing is used is underneath a closure, such as a gripper snap or button. Do not use fusible interfacings, because most sportswear fabrics are damaged by a hot iron and steam pressing.

Linings and Interfacings

Choose appropriate linings and interfacings. For swimsuits, tricot (**1**) can be used for the crotch lining; two-way stretch knit lining fabric (**2**) can be used for the crotch or full-front lining. Lightweight woven nylon (**3**) is a popular lining fabric, especially when nylon fabric has also been used to sew the outer shell. A prequilted lining (**4**) adds the insulation and lining in one step. Polyester bunting (**5**) is a less bulky alternative to a prequilted lining. To reinforce closures, use sew-in interfacings, either woven (**6**) or nonwoven (**7**).

Insulated Outerwear

The triple layers of an insulated garment require different fabrics for the outer shell, the insulation, and the lining. The outer shell receives the most wear and is exposed to the weather. Use a tightly woven, durable fabric that offers protection from wind and water, such as coated or uncoated nylon ripstop or nylon taffeta; tri-blend, a mixture of three fibers, usually cotton, polyester, and nylon; or bi-blend, a mixture of two fibers, usually nylon combined with either cotton or polyester.

The insulation that keeps you warm is the middle fabric layer. Insulating fabrics available for sewing are described on pages 132 and 133.

The lining primarily hides raw edges and protects the insulation from abrasion. It should be lightweight to avoid adding bulk to the jacket. It should also be slick so it slides easily over other clothing. Care requirements of a lining should match those of the outer shell. Lightweight, slippery nylon is an ideal lining for jackets with nylon or nylon blend outer shells.

Layout and Cutting Techniques

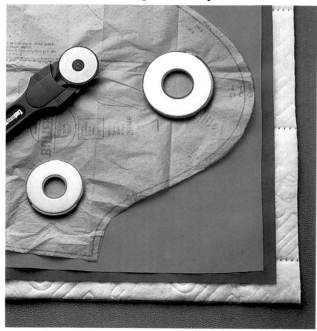

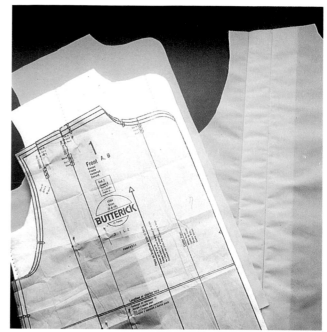

Stack lining, insulation, and shell fabric for layout and cutting. Use weights to hold the pattern in place. Cut all three layers at once with rotary cutter or sharp shears. Flip pattern pieces over to cut the right and left-hand sides.

Reduce bulk by folding details such as tucks, gathers, or pleats out of pattern to cut lining and insulation. Cut shell separately, using complete pattern. To prevent raveling, sear nylon fabrics immediately after cutting.

How to Handle Insulated Fabrics

1) Machine-baste insulation sections to wrong side of shell sections ¼" (6 mm) from edges. Use Even Feed™ foot, or hold layers taut in front of and behind presser foot. Do not use serging or overcasting; the extra thread makes seam allowances unnecessarily bulky.

2) Handle insulation and outer shell fabrics as one layer. To stitch, pin right sides of shell together, and use Even Feed™ foot or taut sewing to prevent uneven feeding. Do not pull fabric under the needle. Use as many pins as necessary to hold in place.

3) Topstitch set-in sleeves, raglan sleeves, and shoulder seams. Finger press seam to one side; from right side, stitch close to seam. This reinforces and strengthens the seam. It may be necessary to trim corners and grade seams before topstitching.

Insulated Jackets

An insulated jacket is rather time-consuming to sew, but the results are well worth the effort. Special sewing techniques are used for attaching the lining and handling the bulk of the insulation.

Cut the upper collar from the shell fabric and insulation, and the undercollar from lining fabric to reduce bulk. Cut in-seam pockets from the shell fabric only, because the jacket lining will cover the raw edges.

Check the sleeve length during the try-on fitting of the lining. This is the most common fitting adjustment required. If the sleeves will be finished with ribbing cuffs, fit the sleeves to the first knuckle of the index finger, for wearing ease and room for growth.

1) **Construct** jacket lining; to reinforce seams, press to one side and topstitch close to seamline. Stitch jacket upper collar to lining. Try on the lining to check the fit. This is the easiest time to make any necessary changes.

2) **Add** stripes, if desired (pages 198 to 201), to outer fabric. Machine-baste shell and insulation sections together (page 136).

3) **Insert** pockets according to pattern before joining jacket sections. Stitching on flat sections is easier than on shaped garment.

4) **Stitch** jacket shoulder and sleeve seams. Edgestitch seams for additional strength. Stitch underarm and side seams.

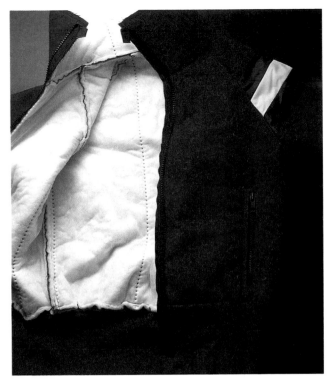

5) Cut ribbing for cuffs (page 17); attach, using tubular method (page 94). After stitching in place, do not turn them out. They should be in this position to attach lining.

6) Attach undercollar to jacket. Stitch one side of waistband to lower edge. Insert zipper according to pattern instructions; on jacket shown, lower end of zipper extends to finished length of jacket.

How to Line an Insulated Jacket

1) Match shell and lining sleeve seams, being careful not to twist lining sleeves. Pin lining to shell, turning back raw edge of lining to match edge of cuff. Right side of lining is facing cuff; cuff is between shell and lining.

2) Stitch around each sleeve opening on top of cuff seam stitching. The lining is not inside the jacket for this stitching.

3) Finished cuff seam has lining attached to shell with cuff sandwiched between. This method provides a sturdy machine finish and eliminates hand stitching.

(Continued on next page)

4) Turn the outer shell and lining wrong side out. Position shell and lining with right sides together. Pin free edge of waistband to lining, right sides together. Stitch in ¼" (6 mm) seam, stretching ribbing to fit as you sew.

5) Pin upper collar of lining and undercollar of shell together with right sides facing. Pin lining to front edges of shell, folding waistband up and zipper teeth in toward right side of shell.

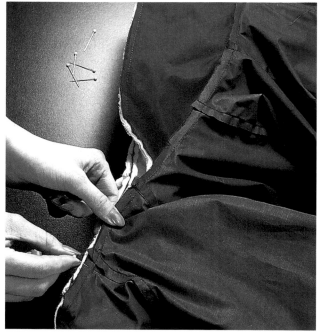

6) Stitch front edges and outer edge of collar to lining; leave 8" (20.5 cm) of seam unstitched at the center of one front edge to provide opening for turning jacket right side out. Backstitch to reinforce ends of opening.

7) Push collar down between shell and lining to pin neckline seam allowances together, matching center back of shell neckline to center back of lining. Stitch seam allowances together, beginning slightly before one shoulder seam and stitching slightly beyond other shoulder seam. Stitching helps collar roll properly and tacks lining permanently to shell.

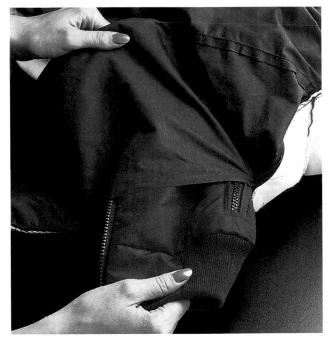

8) **Push** waistband up between shell and lining to pin waistband seam allowances together, matching center and back of shell to center back of lining. Stitch seam allowances together to tack shell permanently to lining, stretching as you sew. Begin and end stitching near zipper at front closing.

9) **Turn** jacket right side out through opening at front zipper closing. Pull small portions of jacket through opening, working slowly to avoid tearing fabric at top and bottom of opening.

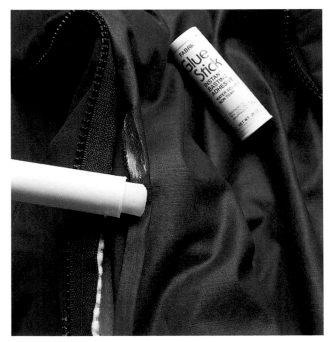

10) **Turn** seam allowance of lining under at front opening. Use glue stick, pins, or hand basting to attach folded seam allowance to zipper tape.

11) **Topstitch** collar and front of jacket ¼" to ⅜" (6 mm to 1 cm) from zipper seam and collar edges. Topstitching keeps lining neatly in place and prevents it from becoming caught in zipper closure.

Sewing Fleece

Fleece, such as Polartec®, is a popular outerwear fabric because it provides warmth without bulk or weight, is machine washable, and is easy to sew. Fleece will not ravel, so the raw edges of seams do not require finishing. Because fleece has a brushed surface texture, use a "with nap" pattern layout so the color looks uniform in the finished garment.

Although fleece can be used for warm unlined jackets, tops, and pull-on pants, it is not waterproof or windproof. For the best protection from the weather, wear a windproof or water repellent shell over a fleece garment. Or use fleece as a lining for a jacket, vest, or raincoat.

To minimize pilling, turn garments inside out when washing them. Pilling does not affect the insulating quality of fleece.

Finish edges of fleece garments with ribbing, serging, or contrasting binding. Cut binding from nylon/spandex two-way stretch knit to create an attractive contrast in texture. Stretch the knit binding as you sew it to the garment and the edge stretches like an elasticized binding. Hems, casings, and other self-fabric finishes are too bulky.

Serging techniques work well on fleece and shorten sewing time by automatically trimming seam allowances to reduce bulk. The slightly wider seam sewn by a four-thread serger is practical for the thickness of fleece, although the narrower seam sewn by a three-thread serger is also acceptable. On a conventional sewing machine, simply straight-stitch seams. To reduce bulk, trim seam allowances to ¼" (6 mm) after sewing. The raw edges will not ravel.

How to Bind an Edge with Two-way Stretch Knit

1) Trim hem or seam allowance off garment edge. Cut 2" (5 cm) wide binding crosswise from nylon/spandex two-way stretch knit, equal to three-fourths the measurement of garment edge.

2) Stitch short ends of binding together in ¼" (6 mm) seam, right sides together. If binding waistline of zip-front jacket, omit this seam. Fold binding in half lengthwise. Divide garment edge and binding into fourths, and mark with pins.

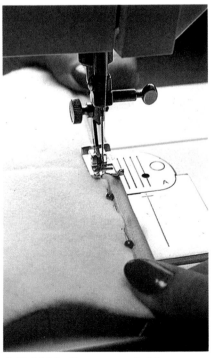

3) Pin binding to right side of garment, with raw edges even and pin markers matching. Stitch ¼" (6 mm) seam, using long straight stitch and stretching binding to fit edge as you sew.

4) Fold binding over stitching to wrong side of garment. From right side, edgestitch binding along fold, stretching binding as you sew.

5) Finished bound edges on fleece sleeves and hem stretch like an elasticized binding.

Quick & Easy Fleece Accessories

Fleece can be used to create outdoor winter accessories for the entire family. Because the fleece is available in a selection of bright colors, these items make fun fashion accents. Mix and match an assortment of scarves, neckwarmers, and headwarmers, each made from a single piece of fabric. To complete the accessory wardrobe, make easy-to-sew mittens, custom-fitted to each person's hand measurements. Synthetic suede can be added to the palms of the mittens, if desired, for a better grip.

✂ Cutting Directions

For an adult's scarf, cut one 12" × 60" (30.5 × 152.5 cm) strip of fleece crosswise on the fabric; or, for a child's scarf, cut one 10" (25.5 cm) strip.

To determine the lengths of the fabric strips for the neckwarmer and headband, measure the circumference of your head, using a tape measure. For an adult's neckwarmer, cut one 10" (25.5 cm) strip of fleece crosswise on the fabric, with the length of the strip ½" (1.3 cm) shorter than your head size; or, for a child's size, cut one 8" (20.5 cm) strip.

For an adult's or child's headband, make a pattern as on page 147, steps 1 and 2. Cut one piece of fleece crosswise on the fabric, using the pattern.

For an adult's mittens, make a pattern as on page 148, steps 1 to 3. Using the pattern as a guide, cut the fabric, elastic, and suede as in steps 4 to 6. For a child's mittens, follow the easy variations on page 149.

YOU WILL NEED

⅓" yd. (0.32 m) fleece, 60" (152.5 cm) wide, for scarf.

⅜ yd. (0.35 m) fleece, for adult's neckwarmer, or ¼ yd. (0.25 m) for child's neckwarmer.

⅛ yd. (0.15 m) fleece, for headwarmer.

⅓ yd. (0.32 m) fleece, for mittens.

¼ yd. (0.25 m) elastic, ⅜" (1 cm) wide, for mittens.

Synthetic suede, two 2 × 5" (5 × 12.5 cm) scraps, optional for mittens.

How to Sew a Fleece Scarf

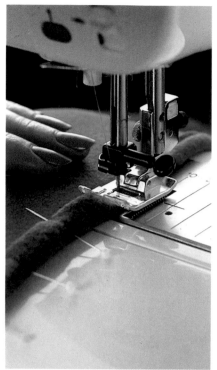

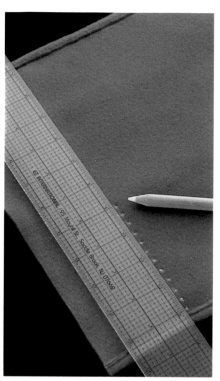

1) Cut fleece as on page 144. Fold ⅜" (1 cm) to wrong side on long edges of fabric strip for scarf; stitch close to raw edges.

2) Lay a ruler across one narrow end of scarf, 3" (7.5 cm) from raw edge. Using chalk pencil, mark fabric at ⅜" (1 cm) intervals, beginning at inner edge of side hems.

3) Move ruler to raw edge; mark as in step 2. Cut slashes from outer marks to inner marks, making the fringe. Repeat at other end of scarf.

How to Sew a Fleece Neckwarmer

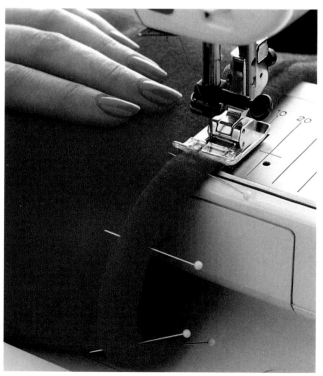

1) Cut fleece as on page 144. Stitch narrow ends of fabric strip together in ¼" (6 mm) seam.

2) Fold ⅜" (1 cm) to wrong side on the long edges; stitch close to raw edges.

146

How to Sew a Fleece Headband

1) Draw rectangle on piece of paper, 4½" (11.5 cm) wide, with length of rectangle equal to one-half of measurement around head minus ¼" (6 mm). Label one end as the foldline. Draw dotted lines 1" (2.5 cm) from each short end; on these lines, mark points ¾" (2 cm) from long edges.

2) Draw dotted line through center. On each long side, mark lines, starting at the marked points and tapering to side of rectangle at center. Draw solid lines straight from marked points to short ends. Cut the pattern for headband on solid lines.

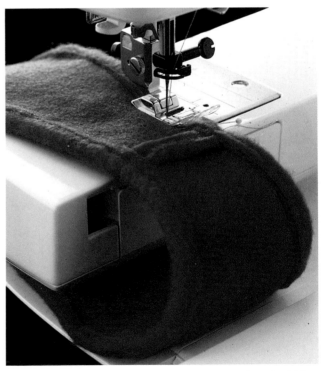

3) Fold fleece lengthwise; using pattern, cut fleece, with foldline of pattern on fold of fabric.

4) Stitch narrow ends of fabric strip together in ¼" (6 mm) seam. Fold ⅜" (1 cm) to wrong side on long edges; stitch close to raw edges.

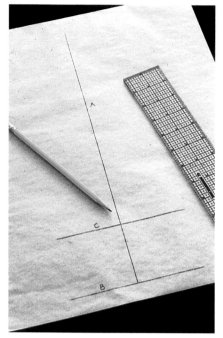

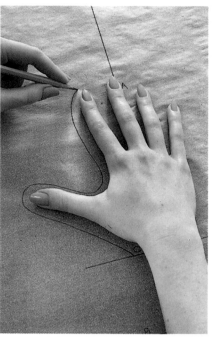

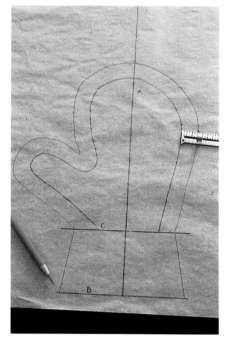

1) Draw a line on tracing paper, about 15" (38 cm) long. Draw 6" (15 cm) line at end of first line and another 3" (7.5 cm) from the same end; lines should be perpendicular to and centered on first line. Label the lines A, B, and C as shown.

2) Place hand on tracing paper, with middle finger on Line A and with wrist centered on Line C. Fingers should be slightly spread, with thumb extended out to the side, as shown. Draw around hand, beginning and ending at Line C.

3) Draw cutting lines ¾" (2 cm) outside the hand markings, to allow for ease and seam allowances. Extend cutting lines from Line C to Line B, angling lines so Line B measures 1" (2.5 cm) wider than Line C, between cutting lines.

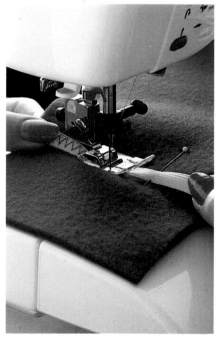

4) Fold fleece right sides together; cut four mitten pieces from fleece, with crosswise direction of fabric across palm. Using chalk, mark Line C on wrong side of two opposite mitten pieces.

5) Cut two lengths of elastic, each 1" (2.5 cm) shorter than Line C. Stretch one length to fit Line C on wrong side of mitten piece; stitch, using zigzag stitch. Repeat for the opposite mitten piece.

6) Cut two 2" (5 cm) strips of synthetic suede, if desired, with width of strips equal to width of mitten above thumb.

7) Apply synthetic suede pieces to elasticized mitten pieces, using a glue stick; position strip parallel to Lines B and C. Edgestitch in place on long edges.

8) Pin the elasticized pieces to the remaining pieces, right sides together, matching Lines B and C. Stitch ¼" (6 mm) seam around mittens, leaving ends open. Clip corner at thumb.

9) Turn the mittens right side out. Fold under a ½" (1.3 cm) hem allowance at the mitten openings. Stitch hems, using zigzag stitch.

How to Sew Child's Fleece Mittens

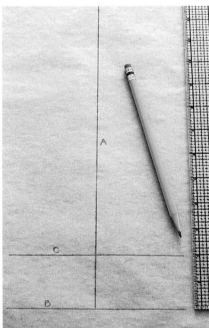

1) Follow step 1, opposite, for making mitten pattern, except draw Line C about 2" (5 cm) from Line B.

2) Follow steps 2 and 3, opposite, except in step 3, extend cutting lines so Line B measures ¾" (2 cm) wider than Line C.

3) Sew mittens as in steps 4 to 9, using narrower strips of synthetic suede, if desired.

149

Gripper-tread fabric is used for nonslip soles on booties.

Fleece Booties

Cozy, roomy booties made from fleece, such as Polartec®, are great for a quick warm-up after a day of outdoor winter play or for sitting around the house on chilly evenings. With the instructions that follow, you can make fleece booties for adults and children. For nonslip soles, a special gripper-tread fabric is used.

✂ Cutting Directions

Make the patterns for the booties as in steps 1 to 7, below. For each pair of booties, cut two upper pieces from the outer fabric. From the lining, cut two

upper pieces and two soles. From the gripper-tread fabric, cut two soles. From the cording, cut two ties, each 16" (40.5 cm) long.

YOU WILL NEED

¼ yd. (0.25 m) **fleece,** for outer fabric.

¼ yd. (0.25 m) **fleece,** for lining.

¼ yd. (0.25 m) **gripper-tread fabric,** for soles.

1 yd. (0.95 m) **cording,** for tie.

How to Sew Fleece Booties

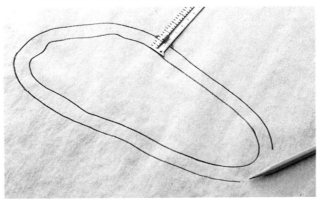

1) Make pattern for bootie sole by drawing around foot onto piece of tracing paper; draw cutting line ½" (1.3 cm) outside the foot marking, to allow for ease and seam allowances. Round the pattern in the toe area.

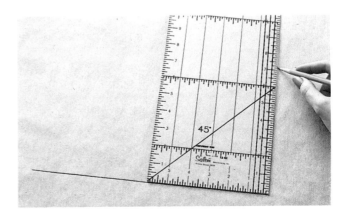

2) Make pattern for upper piece by drawing a straight line for lower edge, 1" (2.5 cm) longer than the sole pattern. For back foldline, draw perpendicular line at one end of lower edge, 7¼" (18.7 cm) long for adult size or 6" (15 cm) long for child size.

(Continued on next page)

3) Draw a line for top opening of bootie, parallel to lower edge and starting at the upper end of the back foldline; draw this line 6¼" (15.7 cm) long for adult size or 5" (12.5 cm) long for child size.

4) Draw line at toe end, perpendicular to lower edge, 3" (7.5 cm) long for adult size or 2½" (6.5 cm) for child size. Mark a point 1¾" (4.5 cm) down from upper end of line for adult size or 1½" (3.8 cm) from end for child size. Draw line from upper end of this line toward back foldline, 1¼" (3.2 cm) for all sizes.

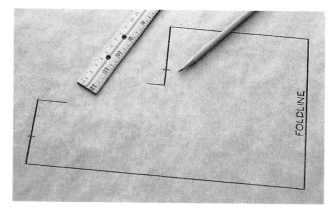

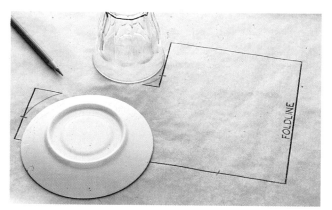

5) Draw a line down from the end of top opening, 3" (7.5 cm) long for adult size or 2¼" (6 cm) for child size. Mark a point ¾" (2 cm) up from bottom of this line for adult size or ⅝" (1 cm) for child size. Draw horizontal line from bottom of this line toward toe end, same length as line from marked point.

6) Round the corner at toe as shown, using saucer. Round the corner at top of foot as shown, using a water glass.

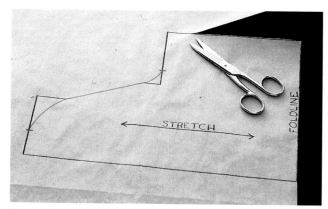

7) Draw straight line between toe curve and upper curve. Cut out pattern, following curved lines on front. Mark the direction of greatest fabric stretch, parallel to lower edge.

8) Cut out fabric as on page 151. Stitch ¼" (6 mm) center front seam in upper piece from outer fabric, right sides together. Repeat for remaining outer bootie and for bootie linings. Press seams open.

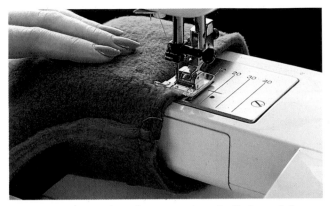

9) Pin one outer bootie to one bootie lining, right sides together, matching center front seams. Stitch ¼" (6 mm) seam around top opening. Repeat for other bootie. Press seams open.

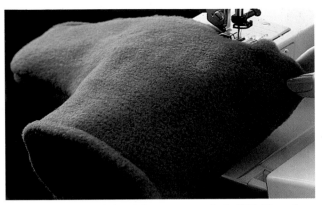

10) Turn bootie right side out; topstitch ⅜" (1 cm) from top opening seam. Baste the lower edges of outer fabric and lining together, within ¼" (6 mm) seam allowances.

11) Center cording for tie over front seam, at upper curve. Stitch to bootie, using short zigzag stitches; begin and end 1" (2.5 cm) on either side of front seam. Knot ends of cording; tie into bow.

12) Place one outer sole and one sole lining wrong sides together. Baste a scant ¼" (6 mm) from outer edge. Repeat for remaining outer sole and lining.

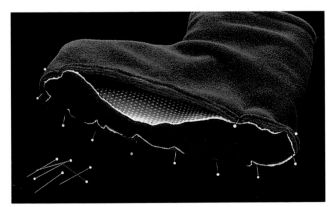

13) Turn bootie lining side out. Pin sole to bootie, outer sides together, centering sole at front seamline and center back; ease in excess fullness. Stitch ¼" (6 mm) seam, with sole side down.

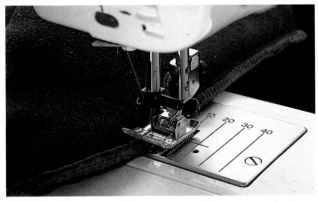

14) Trim the seam allowance on the outer sole to ⅛" (3 mm). Zigzag or overlock the seam allowances together around bootie. Turn bootie right side out.

Dressing Up

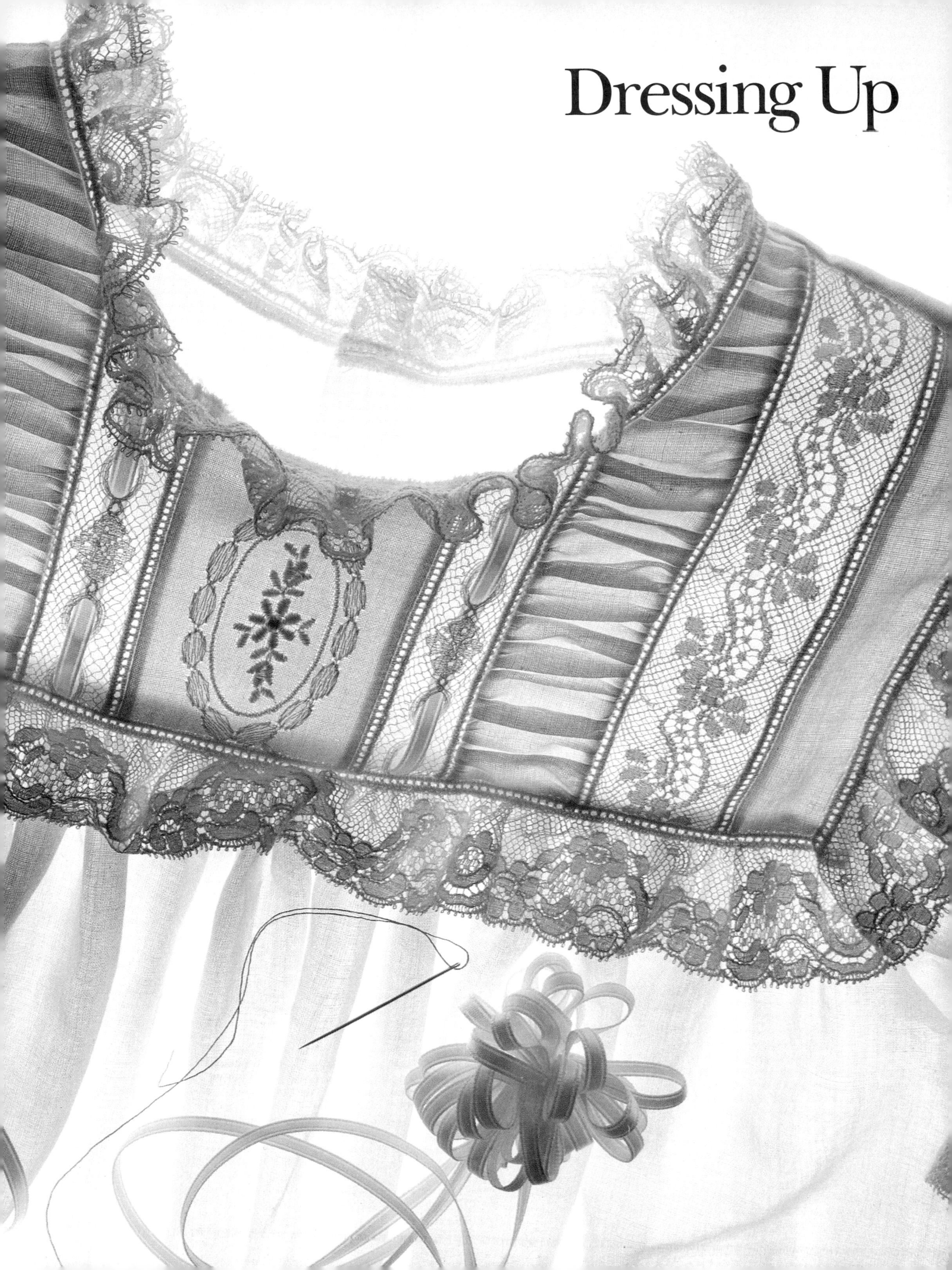

Machine Heirloom Sewing

Heirloom sewing adapts French hand sewing to machine methods. Although an heirloom project still takes patience, practice, and careful work, with modern sewing machine technology you can now master techniques that were formerly done by hand. Projects can include small items, such as a bonnet; parts of a garment, such as a blouse yoke; or a total garment.

Basic heirloom techniques consist of joining strips of fabrics and trims. Strips may be placed either horizontally or vertically on the garment piece. The fabric strips are cut or torn on the straight grain to the length needed; it is easiest to use the crosswise grain. The width of the strips may vary as long as the proportions are pleasing. Fabric strips may be machine-embroidered, using a wing needle and machine embroidery thread; gathered on both sides to form a puffing strip; or pin-tucked, using a twin-needle and pin-tuck presser foot.

Use fine woven cotton or cotton blends in sheer fabrics, such as batiste and broadcloth. Select from three weights of 100 percent cotton Swiss batiste. All will wrinkle, which is part of the effect of these fabrics. Lightweight Swiss batiste is sheer enough to allow the color of a slip to show through. The batistes that are easiest to work with are the mediumweight and heavyweight fabrics. Imperial® batiste is an economical polyester/cotton blend that is wrinkle-resistant and is available in several colors.

Laces and trims of 100 percent cotton, or of 90 percent cotton and 10 percent nylon, feel soft and are easiest to handle. You may use insertion laces, which have two straight edges; edgings, which have one scalloped edge; or beadings, which have woven holes to accommodate ribbon trims. Use double-faced satin ribbon in beading and for ties. In heirloom sewing, entredeux is always used between fabrics and laces to reinforce seams decoratively. Entredeux resembles hemstitching with seam allowances on both sides.

How to Design an Heirloom Project

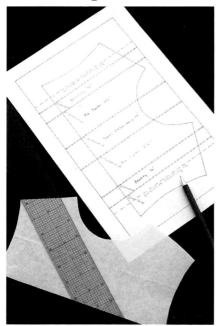

1) **Make** a full-size pattern piece from tissue. Trace onto firm paper. Plan design, using fabrics, trims, and entredeux; widest trim should be at the center, fabric strips at the curved edges, and the entredeux between fabric and trims.

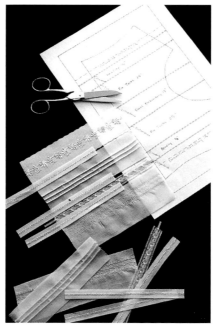

2) **Measure** pattern at its widest and longest points. Cut all strips 1" (2.5 cm) longer than width or length, depending on direction of the strips. Sew pin-tucks, decorative stitching, or puffing strips, if used (pages 160 and 161).

3) **Join** fabrics, laces, and trims (pages 162 and 163) to form a rectangle or square. Block fabric to original shape by pinning in place and steaming to set. Let cool. Cut garment piece.

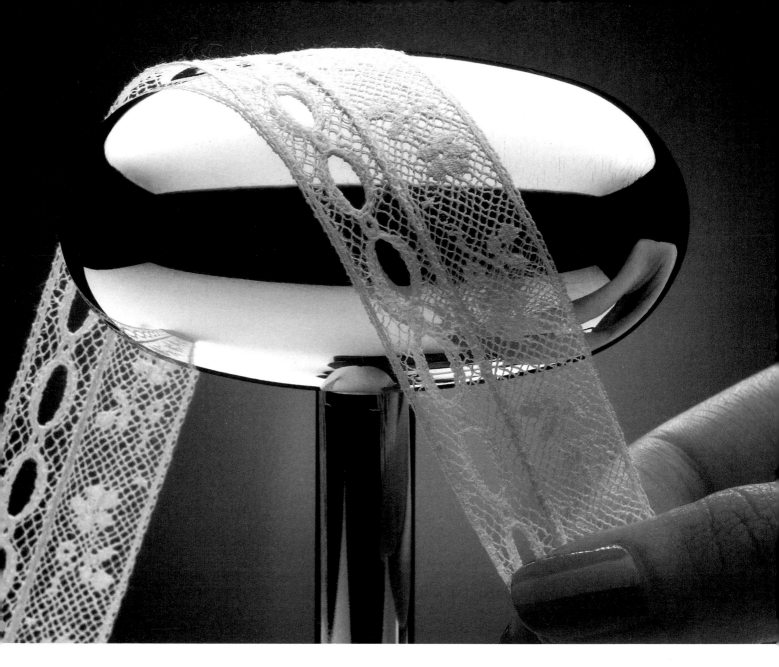

Heirloom Techniques

You may want to practice heirloom techniques before making your project. To produce different looks and designs, creatively combine the methods that follow. For pressing convenience, set up a puff iron near your sewing machine. Use spray starch on both sides of the fabric and trim, except for puffing strips, and press over the puff iron to make fabric easier to handle. Some pieces, such as the puffing strips, cannot be ironed once they are sewn.

When sewing fine, soft fabric, laces, and trims, use an extra-fine thread that will not add bulk to the seams. Use cotton machine embroidery thread on the conventional sewing machine; use extra-fine cone

thread on the serger. White thread is appropriate for white, ecru, and pastels. The fine thread blends into the fabric.

A size 8 (60) or 9 (65) needle is recommended because it is compatible with the fabric and thread. Stitch length is determined by the distance between the holes of the entredeux. Stitch width will vary depending on the technique.

A new needle is an essential for machine heirloom sewing. Check frequently for burrs on the needle point. Change the needle after every five hours of use, even if the needle point feels smooth.

How to Prepare Straight-grain Fabric Strips

Swiss cotton. Clip into selvage. Pull a thread across to other selvage; cut fabric on pulled thread line. Clip selvage and pull another thread across fabric at desired width or length of fabric strip; allow for two ¼" (6 mm) seams in the width.

Polyester/cotton batiste. Clip selvage and tear fabric. Clip again and tear at desired width or length of fabric strip; allow for two ¼" (6 mm) seams in the width. Press edges of strip flat. Edges may be trimmed, using ruler and rotary cutter; serger knives will trim fibers.

How to Set Machine Stitch Length

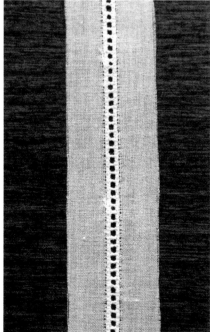

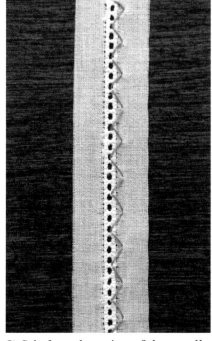

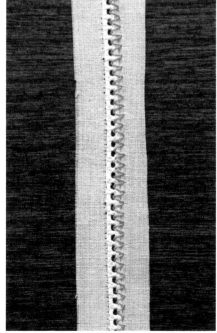

1) Cut entredeux strip about 4" (10 cm) long to use for determining stitch length. Set machine for a zigzag stitch 3 mm wide and for a length of 12 to 16 stitches per inch (2.5 cm).

2) Stitch so the swing of the needle zigs into the middle of a hole of the entredeux and zags into the batiste seam allowance.

3) Adjust stitch length so needle zigs into each hole of the entredeux. Once the stitch length is established, it will remain the same for the entire project.

Heirloom Strips

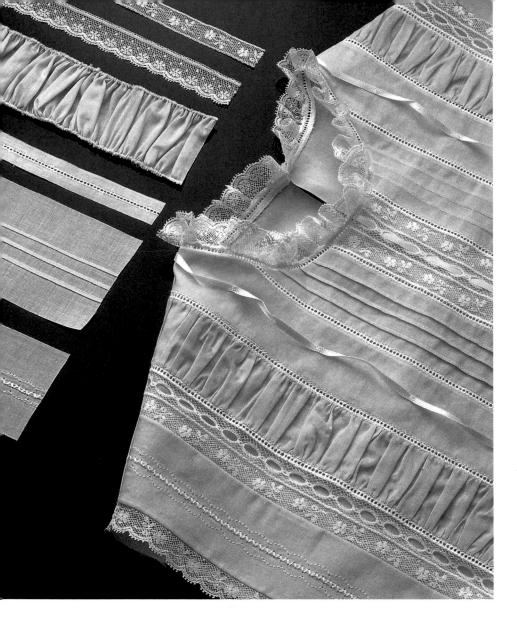

Fabric strips for machine heirloom sewing may be embellished with machine embroidery and pin tucks, or gathered for puffing strips.

Machine embroidery is the easiest technique to use. Experiment with wing needles, decorative stitches, and machine embroidery thread.

Make pin tucks, using a pin-tuck presser foot and a twin needle. Twin needles are sized according to the distance between needles and the thickness of the needles. Use a 1.8 (70) or 2 (80) needle for fine fabrics. The fabric strip should be wider than the finished width to allow for the fabric that forms the tucks. Make an uneven number of tucks, with the middle tuck at the center.

Create puffing strips by gathering both sides of a fabric strip before joining it to entredeux. Cut fabric to the desired width plus ½" (1.3 cm) for two seam allowances, and one and a half times the finished length. Set the zigzag stitch length (page 159); set the stitch width to zigzag over ⅛" (3 mm) of the edge of the fabric. Press, but do not starch, the fabric strip before gathering; do not press after gathering.

How to Machine-embroider Using a Wing Needle

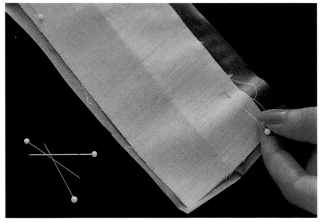

1) Cut fabric to desired width plus ½" (1.3 cm) for two seam allowances. Apply spray starch to fabric strip; press. Fold strip lengthwise; lightly finger press fold to mark stitching line. Pin a strip of water-soluble stabilizer to back of fabric.

2) Stitch one or more rows, using a decorative stitch and a wing needle. Remove stabilizer according to manufacturer's directions; press fabric strip.

How to Roll, Whip, and Gather a Puffing Strip

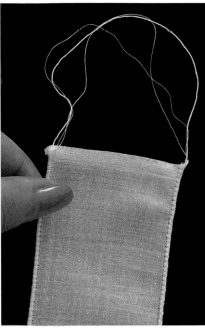

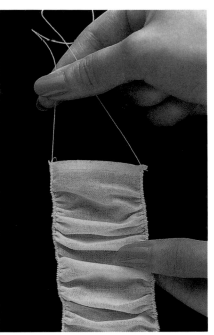

1) Cut fabric and set stitch length and width, opposite. Place a thread along edge on right side of fabric, leaving a 3" (7.5 cm) thread tail. Zigzag stitch over thread; fabric will roll over thread.

2) Zigzag stitch one edge of fabric. Turn fabric, and leave a 4" (10 cm) loop of thread before stitching down other side. Leave 3" (7.5 cm) thread tail at end.

3) Pull encased threads from each end to evenly gather both sides of puffing strip. Gather to desired length; distribute gathers. Knot gathering threads at each end.

How to Sew Pin Tucks

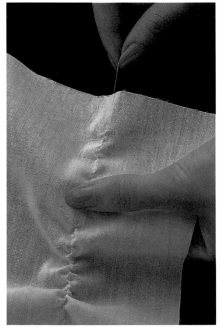

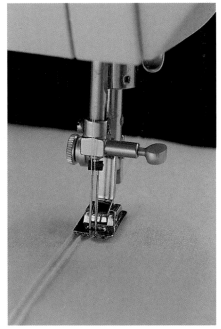

1) Cut fabric strip about 2" (5 cm) wider than finished width. Pull thread lengthwise on strip to mark position for center tuck. Tighten upper thread tension slightly; set stitch length to 12 to 14 stitches per inch (2.5 cm).

2) Apply spray starch to fabric strip; press. Using pin-tuck presser foot and twin needle, stitch over pulled-thread mark; hold the fabric taut. Bobbin thread draws two needle threads together, creating pin tuck.

3) Place first tuck under channel of pin-tuck presser foot; determine distance from first tuck by channel selection. Stitch additional tucks. Trim equal amounts on each side of strip, allowing for ¼" (6 mm) seam allowance on each side.

Joining Heirloom Strips

Join fabric strips, laces, and trims for heirloom sewing with a narrow seam that is neat and durable. Machine methods closely duplicate traditional hand stitches but are much faster to do and easier to master. For additional strength, use entredeux between fabrics and laces or trims. Use spray starch on all strips except puffing strips. Press all strips before stitching.

Several techniques are used for joining strips. One of the joining techniques used in heirloom sewing is rolling and whipping. This technique rolls a tiny amount of fabric around the adjoining lace or trim, adding strength to the seam. When applying flat lace to a hem edge, press the seam allowance toward the fabric. You may also want to edgestitch through all layers. A rolled seam sewn on the serger produces the same result as rolling and whipping.

The narrow zigzag stitch on a conventional sewing machine or the flatlock stitch on a serger may be used to join two laces with finished edges. Use a narrow zigzag stitch to join trimmed entredeux to lace with finished edges.

Gather laces before joining them to trimmed entredeux. Pull a heavy thread in the lace heading to create gathers or, if the lace lacks a heavy thread, machine-stitch a gathering line. Trim the remaining seam allowance on the entredeux and use entredeux with gathered lace to highlight a yoke seam or neck edge (page 165).

Selecting Joining Techniques

Edges to Be Joined	Conventional Machine	Serger
Entredeux to puffing strip	Rolled and whipped seam	—
Fabric to entredeux	Rolled and whipped seam	Rolled seam
Fabric to flat lace	Rolled and whipped seam	Rolled seam
Lace to entredeux	Zigzag seam	—
Lace to lace	Zigzag seam	Flatlock seam

How to Gather Lace and Join to Entredeux

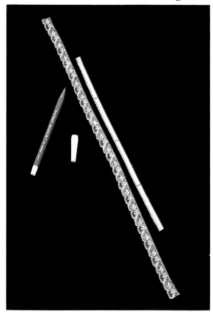 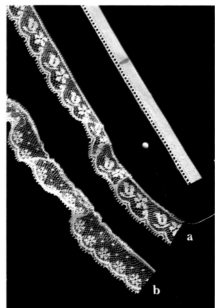 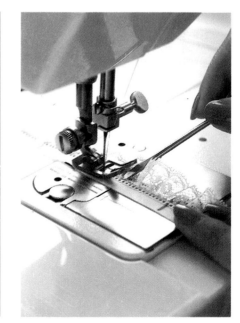

1) **Cut** entredeux 1" (2.5 cm) longer than needed; trim away one seam allowance. Cut flat lace 1½ times longer than entredeux. Divide lace and entredeux into fourths; mark.

2) **Pull** heavy thread in lace heading from both ends to gather lace (a). For laces without a heavy thread, stitch next to lace edge, using 14 to 16 stitches per inch (2.5 cm); pull bobbin thread to gather (b). Match marks on lace and entredeux.

3) **Set** zigzag stitch length (page 159). Butt trimmed entredeux edge to lace; zigzag 1" (2.5 cm) at a time, using a narrow stitch. Use a small screwdriver to hold gathers under presser foot. Continue to end; remove gathering thread.

How to Use the Zigzag and Flatlock Joining Methods

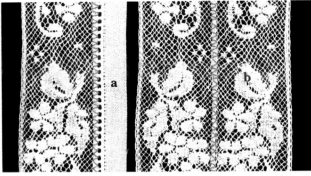

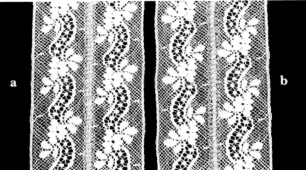

Zigzag seam. Set zigzag stitch length (page 159); set width for narrow stitch. For entredeux **(a)**, trim one seam allowance and butt trimmed edge to lace; stitch. For laces **(b)**, place right side up and butt edges; stitch.

Flatlock seam. Adjust server for flatlock stitch following manufacturer's directions. Stitch; pull laces flat. Ladder of stitches **(a)** shows on right side when laces are stitched with right sides together. Trellis of stitches **(b)** shows on right side when laces are stitched with wrong sides together.

How to Use the Rolled and Whipped and the Rolled Seam Joining Methods

Roll and whip fabric to flat lace. 1) Set zigzag stitch length (page 159). Lay starched and pressed strips, right sides together, with bottom strip extending ⅛" to ³⁄₁₆" (3 to 4.5 mm) beyond top strip.

2) Set zigzag stitch width so left swing of stitch is ⅛" (3 mm) from edge of top strip and right swing of stitch extends over edge of bottom strip. As needle moves to the left, edge of bottom strip rolls over seam; upper thread tension may need to be loosened.

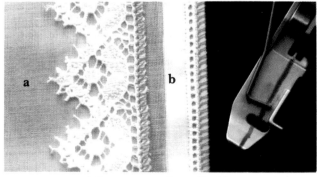

Roll and whip fabric to entredeux. Set zigzag stitch length (page 159). To join entredeux and flat fabric **(a)**, place starched and pressed strips right sides together and raw edges even; stitch in the ditch next to the entredeux holes. Trim seam allowances to scant ⅛" (3 mm). To join entredeux to a puffing strip **(b)**, trim entredeux seam allowance to scant ⅛" (3 mm); position strips, and stitch in the ditch. Remove the gathering thread. Finish both seams as in step 2, above.

Rolled seam. Adjust serger for rolled hem setting, following manufacturer's directions; set stitch length at 2 to 3 mm. Stitch lace to fabric **(a)**, with right sides of strips together and raw edges even. To stitch entredeux to fabric **(b)**, mark line from needle position to end of presser foot (arrow). Use line as a guide to stitch in the ditch next to holes of entredeux.

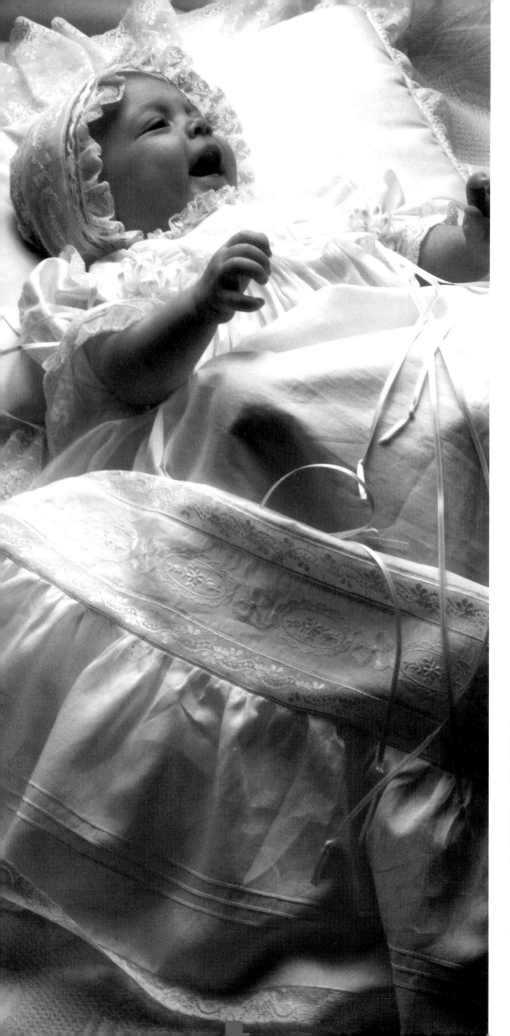

Sewing an Heirloom Dress

Any dress or blouse pattern yoke may be adapted to machine heirloom sewing. Read about machine heirloom techniques (pages 157 to 163) before sewing an heirloom garment.

Plan an heirloom design to fit the yoke. When using Swiss cotton, line the yoke to support the fabric. Interfacing, which shows through sheer fabric, may be eliminated.

A variation of the yoke design may be used for a bonnet or as an heirloom band on the skirt. The band may be used as an insert, placed above a ruffle, or used at the lower edge of the skirt.

The yoke seam and neck edge will be trimmed with entredeux and gathered lace (page 162). Make a strip of entredeux with gathered lace the length of all edges plus 6" (15 cm).

A slip of opaque batiste will prevent the undergarments from showing through. A ribbon rosette may be used as an accessory.

Beauty pins can be used to close an heirloom garment. The pins replace the buttons and buttonholes in fine, sheer fabrics that are not interfaced. Beauty pins may be gold-plated or hand-painted.

How to Make an Heirloom Dress

1) **Cut** front yoke from heirloom fabric; cut lining from dress fabric, if desired. Layer front yokes, wrong sides together. Place foldline of back yoke pattern on fold of dress fabric; cut two yokes. Join front and back yokes at shoulders, using French seams (page 168).

2) **Construct** band for skirt. Join entredeux to upper and lower edges of band. Cut ruffle according to pattern. Finish lower edge of ruffle with edging lace; gather upper edge as for puffing strip. Stitch ruffle to lower edge of band.

3) **Shorten** skirt pattern by width of band. Join skirt front and back at one seam. Complete placket. Join skirt and band. Stitch other side seam, matching seams of band and ruffle. Gather upper edge of skirt; join to yoke, step 3, page 171.

4) **Slash** sleeve pattern at line for elastic. Cut sleeve in two pieces; gather both edges of sleeve as for puffing strips. Cut beading 2" (5 cm) longer than circumference of arm; join to gathered edges of sleeve. Finish lower edge with flat lace. Set in sleeve. Apply French binding (page 169). Insert ribbon in beading; tie bow.

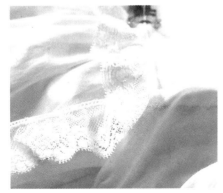

5) **Join** entredeux to gathered lace; trim seam allowance of entredeux. Position entredeux on yoke next to seam, with end folded at placket edge as in step 7, right; zigzag to within 2" (5 cm) of corner. Fold trim under diagonally at corner.

6) **Fold** trim to miter corner at outer edge of lace so right side is up; place entredeux just above yoke seamline. The outer edge of the lace forms a right angle, and entredeux overlaps at inner corner. Miter other corners, and continue zigzagging trim to within 2" (5 cm) of placket.

7) **Cut** trim to extend ½" (1.3 cm) beyond placket edge. Turn under ¼" (6 mm) twice so trim ends at placket edge; stitch. Attach entredeux with gathered lace to neck edge; finish ends as for yoke, above.

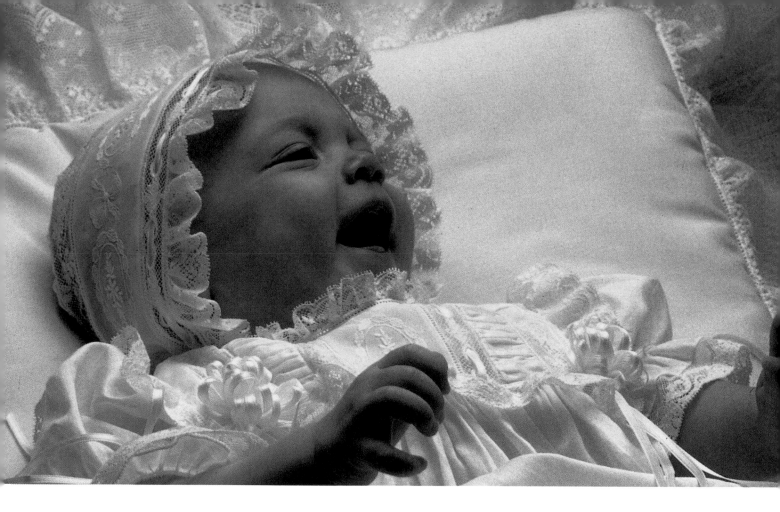

How to Make Heirloom Accessories

Rosettes. Cut 5 yards (4.6 m) of 1/16" (1.5 mm) or 1/8" (3 mm) double-faced satin ribbon. Mark every 2" (5 cm) or more; stop marks 12" to 15" (30.5 to 38 cm) from ends. Stitch through each mark, using double thread; draw up tightly, and arrange loops. Knot thread. Hand-stitch rosette to garment.

Slip. Trim neck and armhole seam allowances to 1/4" (6 mm). Make placket at center back. Stitch both shoulder seams. Finish neck and armhole edges with entredeux joined to gathered lace (page 162); finish ends at placket as in step 7, page 165. Stitch side seams. Finish hem with flat lace (page 163).

How to Sew an Heirloom Bonnet

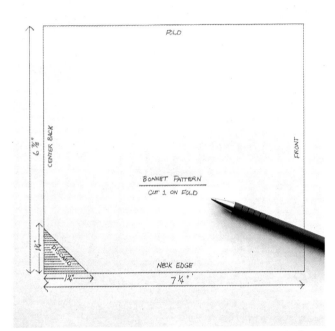

1) **Draw** rectangle 7¼" × 6⅞" (18.6 × 17.2 cm). Label long ends as neck edge and fold; label short sides as front and center back. Mark 1¼" (3.2 cm) on each side of center back and neck edge corner; connect dots with diagonal line for cutting line.

2) **Join** 15" (38 cm) lengths of fabric strips and trims (page 163) to 7¼" (18.6 cm) width. End with beading strip at back edge and gathered lace at front edge. Fold in half; position pattern on fabric. Cut bonnet. Stitch diagonal seam, using French seam (page 168).

3) **Gather** neck edge to 9" (23 cm). Finish with French binding (page 169). Cut 2 strips of ½" (1.3 cm) double-faced satin ribbon, each 24" (61 cm) long. Fold under ½" (1.3 cm) on one short end of each ribbon. Fold ribbon in half lengthwise; make running stitches, ¼" (6 mm) apart, on finished edges for 2" to 3" (5 to 7.5 cm).

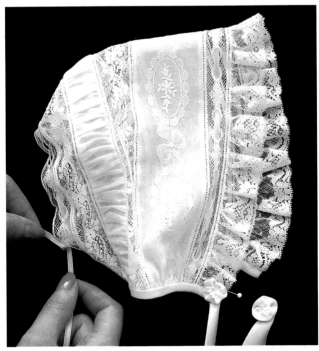

4) **Pull** thread to gather ribbon into circle. Secure end to ribbon, closing rosebud circle; hand-tack to bonnet at front edge of neck binding. Trim free ends of ribbons diagonally. Thread narrow ribbon through beading at center back; tighten and tie to finish.

Other Finishing Techniques for Heirloom Garments

French seams and French bindings are used for seam finishes in delicate heirloom garments. French seams are used only for straight seams. French bindings are used for curved seams, such as armhole seams of set-in sleeves, opposite. They are also used for seams with gathers, such as gathered waistlines.

Eliminate facings whenever possible, and bind the edges of the neckline and sleeveless armholes with French binding. Or use lace and entredeux at the neckline as a pretty finish; gather the lace and join it to the entredeux as on page 162. Then sew the entredeux to the garment edge as for rolling and whipping flat fabric to entredeux on page 163.

Rolling and whipping may be used for a narrow hem finish on a ruffle or at the lower edge of a garment.

How to Sew Narrow French Seams

1) Place garment pieces with *wrong* sides together. Stitch seam, within the seam allowance, ³⁄₁₆" (4.5 mm) from the seamline, using 16 to 18 stitches per inch (2.5 cm).

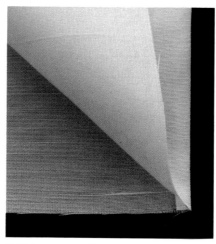

2) Trim seam allowances to scant ⅛" (3 mm); press seam allowances to one side. Fold on stitching line, right sides together; press.

3) Stitch seam ⅛" (3 mm) from fold, encasing raw edges. Press seam allowance to one side.

How to Finish Seams and Edges with French Binding

Seams. 1) Cut 1¾" (4.5 cm) bias strip of lightweight fabric 1" (2.5 cm) longer than edge. Press the strip in half lengthwise, wrong sides together. Trim seam allowances on garment to scant ¼" (6 mm).

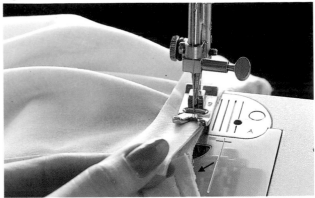

2) Pin binding to garment, raw edges even. Stitch, using ¼" (6 mm) seam; stretch binding slightly on inside curves. For continuous edge, tuck ½" (1.3 cm) to inside of binding at beginning of strip (arrow). For edge at garment opening, wrap ½" (1.3 cm) of binding around ends.

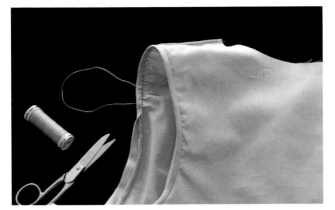

3) Press binding toward seam allowances. Fold the binding in half over raw edges; pin. Slipstitch folded edge of binding to previous stitching line. Press.

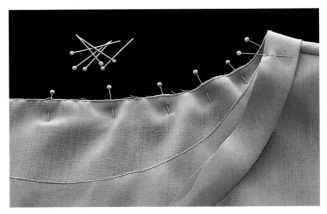

Edges. Staystitch just beyond the seamline to prevent stretching; trim at seamline. Cut and press bias strip, as in step 1. Pin binding to right side of garment, raw edged even; attach as in steps 2 and 3.

How to Sew a Narrow Hem Using Rolling and Whipping

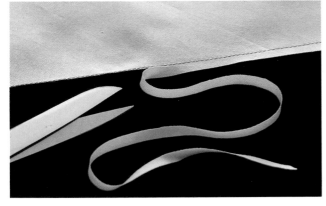

1) Staystitch bias edges ¼" (6 mm) from edge; then trim fabric close to stitching. It is not necessary to staystitch edges that are on the straight of grain.

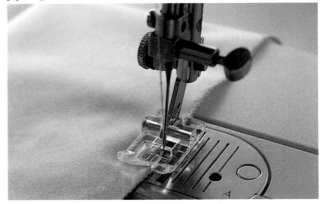

2) Set stitch width to 12 to 16 stitches per inch (2.5 cm); set stitch width so left swing of needle stitches ⅛" (3 mm) from raw edge and right swing of needle extends over raw edge. As needle moves to the left, edge of fabric will roll.

Dresses

Choose construction methods that add a professional finish to the dresses you sew for girls. Line the yokes of dresses and blouses to eliminate facings that show through fabric and to add stability to the yoke. Select a fabric for the lining that is appropriate for the garment fabric you are sewing. For example, line lightweight or mediumweight fabrics with self-fabric, line bulky fabrics with a lightweight fabric, and line transparent print fabrics with solid-colored fabrics.

Use narrow French seams (page 168) for sewing straight seams in sheer or lightweight fabric. For curved seams or seams with gathers, bind the edges, using the French binding technique on page 169; French seams are unsuitable for curved and gathered seams. Special techniques for gathers, ruffles, and collars, as well as tips for sewing dresses from velvet, are included on the following pages.

How to Line a Yoke or Bodice

1) **Cut** yoke and yoke lining. Stitch shoulder seams, using French seams for sheer and lightweight fabrics. Attach collar to right side of yoke.

2) **Stitch** yoke to lining at neckline with right sides together, using short stitch length. Trim the seam allowances to a scant ¼" (6 mm); clip curves, and understitch seam allowances to lining. Turn; press.

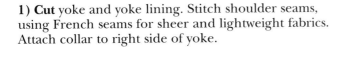

3) **Pin** yoke to lining at lower edge; pin to skirt, right sides together, and stitch. Finish raw edges; press seam allowances toward yoke.

Alternative method. Stitch yoke to skirt, right sides together. Press seam allowances toward yoke. Turn under seam allowance of lining; slipstitch to seam.

Gathers & Ruffles

Dress patterns often require the techniques of applying elastic, gathering fabric, and making ruffles. The methods that follow can simplify these techniques.

Transparent elastic may be substituted for elasticized casings to gather sleeves and waistlines. Stitch the elastic directly to the garment. The stitches are hidden in the folds of the fabric.

To create soft, fine gathers in lightweight fabrics, stitch gathering lines, using short stitches. To gather a long piece of fabric, you can zigzag stitch over a heavy thread or pearl cotton, which will not break when pulled.

Ruffles may be made from a double or single layer of fabric. Make double-layer ruffles from soft, lightweight fabrics. To cut, fold the fabric, and place the outer edge of the ruffle pattern on the fold to eliminate a hem. The doubled fabric adds body to the ruffle.

Make single-layer ruffles from firm fabrics or fabrics that show through when doubled, such as eyelets and sheer prints. When adding lace to a single-layer ruffle, you may want to reduce the pattern at the outer edge by the width of the lace.

How to Gather Sleeves with Elastic

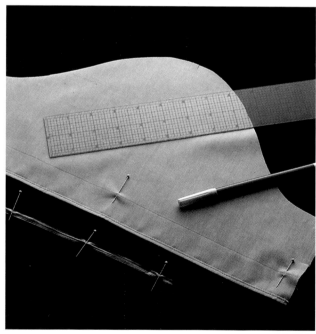

1) Cut ¼" (6 mm) elastic to fit the body comfortably plus seam allowances. Sleeve elastic does not need to fit snugly. Mark stitching line for elastic on wrong side of garment, using washable marking pen. For sleeves, pin-mark elastic and sleeve at seamlines and midpoint; for waistlines, divide elastic and garment into fourths, and pin-mark.

2) Pin elastic to wrong side of garment at pin-marks. Zigzag elastic to garment over marked line; stretch to fit between pins, but do not stretch elastic in seam allowances. Finish garment according to pattern directions, catching elastic in seam.

How to Gather Lightweight Fabrics

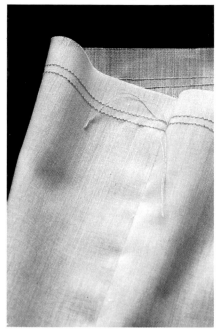

1) Loosen upper tension; set stitch length at 14 to 18 stitches per inch (2.5 cm). Stitch two gathering rows on right side of fabric, ⅛" (3 mm) apart, on each side of seamline.

2) Pull both bobbin threads, and distribute gathers evenly. Stitches automatically pull to wrong side of garment for gathering ease. Wrap threads around a pin to anchor at each end.

3) Stitch on seamline between rows of gathering when joining to garment. Do not remove gathering stitches; outer row of stitches is hidden in fabric fullness.

How to Make Ruffles

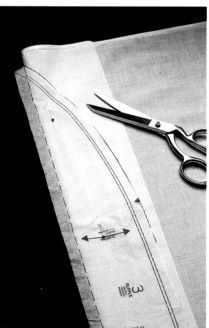

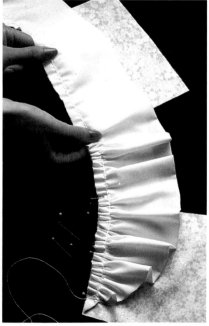

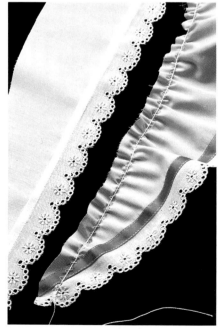

Double-layer ruffle. 1) Fold fabric, wrong sides together; place outer seamline or hemline of the ruffle pattern on fold. Cut ruffle. Using a wide zigzag setting, stitch ½" (1.3 cm) from raw edges over a heavy thread.

2) Pull heavy thread, and distribute gathers evenly. Wrap thread around a pin to anchor at each end. Stitch ruffle to right side of garment; remove heavy thread.

Single-layer ruffle. Stitch flat lace to outer edge of ruffle, wrong sides together. Trim seam allowance to ¼" (6 mm); press toward ruffle. Edgestitch ⅜" (1 cm) ribbon over seam allowances through all layers. Gather ruffle.

Velvet

The handling of velvet depends primarily on its fabric content. Cotton velvet, shown on the left, is made from all-cotton or a cotton/rayon blend. It has a fairly firm hand. Cotton velvet is resilient and can be stitched and pressed similar to velveteen. It can be machine washed, using mild detergent and a gentle cycle, and then tumble dried.

Lustrous velvets. Velvets made of rayon, acetate, or silk blends have a softer texture and hand than cotton velvet. Most of these velvets have a high luster (**1**). Handle the rich, lustrous pile carefully because it mars easily. Panne, the shiniest of the lustrous velvets, has a nap that is permanently pressed down during manufacturing (**2**). The flat nap adds to the sheen of the fabric. Drycleaning is necessary for all lustrous velvets.

Pattern Selection

The best patterns to use with velvet are softly draped silhouettes with a minimum of seams and darts and without buttonholes or topstitching. Velvet can be gathered or formed into unpressed pleats, and is often used for girls' party dresses.

Layout, Cutting & Marking

Many apparel velvets are 39"/40" (100 cm) wide, a width rarely given in the fabric requirements on the back of a pattern envelope. To estimate how much velvet to buy, test the pattern layout at home or at the store, using a "with nap" layout.

In general, the less velvet is handled during the entire sewing project, the better. Make fitting changes on pattern pieces before layout; ripped-out seams leave marks.

Spread velvet, unfolded, right side up on the cutting surface. Lay out and cut the pattern pieces one layer of fabric at a time because velvet slips when folded. Cut facings from a lightweight lining fabric to keep bulk to a minimum. Cut the undercollar on a tailored garment from finely woven wool flannel to reduce bulk and to ensure a smoothly rolled collar.

Transfer only the essential pattern markings, using a marking pen or pins and chalk for symbols such as dots that show sleeve placement. As you sew, use the pattern tissue as an overlay to locate foldlines, pocket placement, and similar markings.

How to Lay Out Velvet

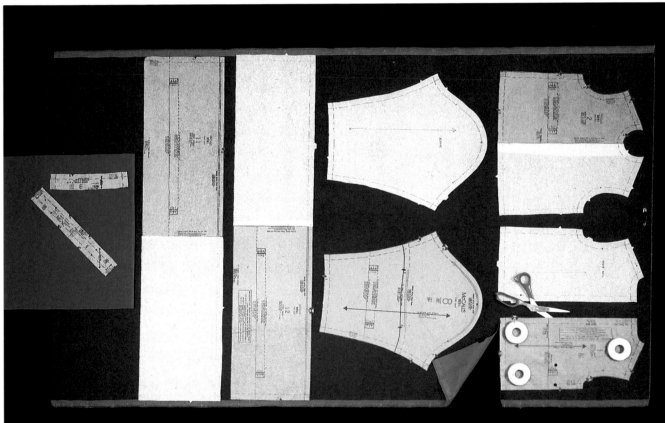

Mark direction of pile with safety pin at one crosswise edge, and place all pattern pieces in this direction. Lay out pattern on a single layer of fabric, positioning pattern pieces without pins until ready to cut. Working with one pattern piece at a time, pin in seam allowances only or use weights; cut in direction of the pile, toward safety pin marker. Cut around pattern notches; snipping seams to mark notches could cause a tear. Remove pins immediately after cutting out pattern section to prevent imprints on pile texture. Use lightweight woven fabrics for facings and undercollars.

Interfacings & Underlinings

Fusible interfacings can be used on cotton velvets if a test sample shows the pile is undamaged. To fuse, cover pressing surface with a velvet scrap, right side up, or a thick terry towel. Place test scrap plush side down for fusing. If pile looks crushed, use a sew-in interfacing. If a ridge shows at the edge of the interfacing, pink the edges of another sample of interfacing and test-fuse again. Pinking sometimes helps the interfacing edges to blend better with the pile. Use sew-in interfacings on lustrous velvets.

Underline cotton velvet with an easy-care fabric such as polyester/cotton batiste to prevent wrinkles. All velvets benefit from underlinings and gain support and strength from this extra fabric backing. Zigzag or overlock the raw edges of velvet and underlining together to finish the raw edges at the same time as you apply the two fabrics back to back. When overlocking an edge, mark notches with marking pen or chalk because they will be trimmed by the overlock stitch.

Pressing

All velvets require careful steam pressing to prevent flattening the pile, but extra caution is necessary with delicate lustrous velvets. Try finger pressing, wearing a thimble on your finger and lightly creasing the seam on the wrong side. Never rest the iron directly on velvet. Before handling, allow to dry completely.

Stitching Techniques

Two main problems in sewing velvet are puckered seams and uneven feeding of the fabric layers. Before you can achieve an acceptable seam, you may need to make some sewing machine adjustments.

Loosen the upper thread tension if puckers are a problem. Decrease the pressure on the presser foot if uneven feeding occurs, or try using an Even Feed™ or roller foot on your machine. Generous basting with pins, fine needles, or thread may be necessary as well. Stitching in the direction of the nap is always a good practice, and especially important with velvet, but cleaning the machine and inserting a new needle can make a difference, too.

Because velvet ravels, raw edges require finishing. In lined garments, pink the edges. In unlined garments, bind the edges with sheer tricot bias binding, or overlock them. Grade enclosed seam allowances to reduce bulk, but do not trim raw edges to less than ¼" (6 mm).

How to Stitch Velvet

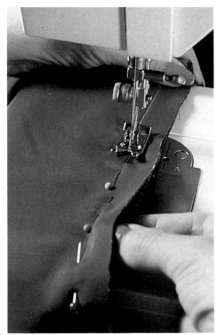

Pin-baste by placing pins parallel to seamline, with heads toward you. Do not stitch over pins, but remove them as you come to them. Use long stitches, 10 to 12 per inch (2.5 cm). As you sew, hold bottom fabric layer taut to encourage even feeding of seams.

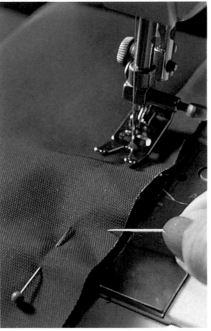

Stop stitching every 2" to 3" (5 to 7.5 cm). Raise presser foot with needle in fabric. Allow both fabric layers to relax. Lower presser foot and resume stitching. Use a pin to help ease the top layer along.

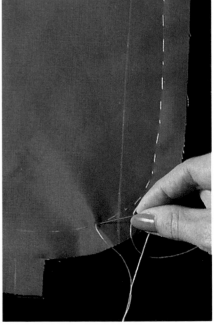

Hand-baste on curved seams that may be more difficult to handle. Use a fine thread, and backstitch every couple of inches (2.5 cm). Machine-stitch seam as directed at left, holding bottom layer taut.

How to Hem Velvet

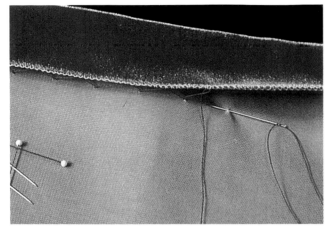

1) Finish the raw hem edge by overlocking or binding; then sew blind catchstitch hem between hem edge and garment, keeping the stitches loose.

2) Place hem on needle board or scrap of self-fabric. Steam hem from inside. To set hemline, pat along the foldline with a stiff-bristled brush.

Four Ways to Press Velvet

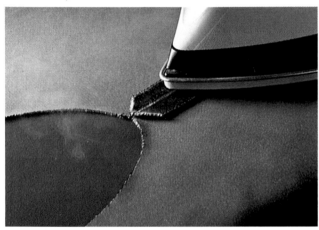

Cover pressing surface with velvet scrap, plush side up. Place garment with plush side down. Steam lightly, using hands to pat seam allowances. Never rest iron directly on velvet pile.

Use a needle board. Place velvet, pile side down, on needle board and press with steam iron or hand steamer from wrong side of garment.

Revive overpressed pile by steaming right side gently. Brush pile lightly with brush or scrap of fabric. Some piles may be permanently damaged.

Hang garment on a plastic or padded hanger in a steaming bathroom for about half an hour. Allow garment to dry thoroughly before handling.

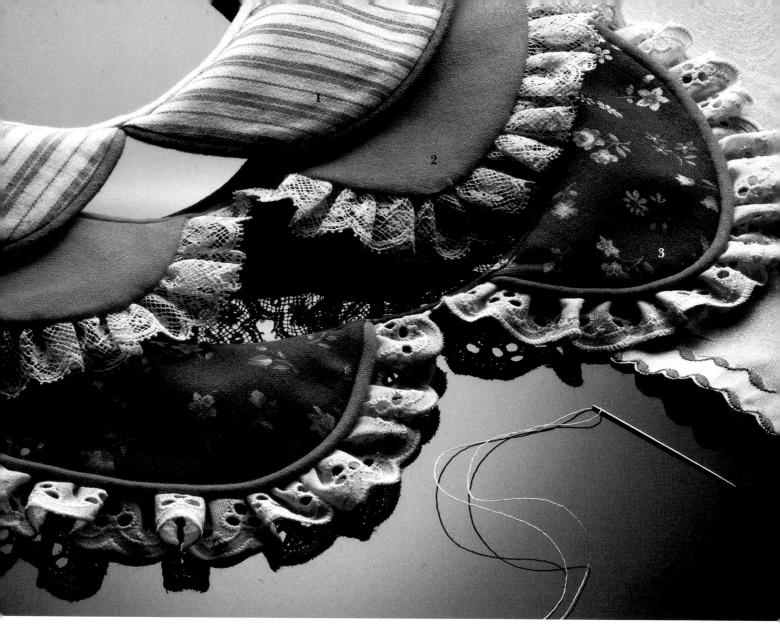

Collars

Collars with trim are an easy and inexpensive way to dress up children's clothes, and are a practical and popular choice for adding special touches to classic styles. Collars may be edged with piping (1), lace (2), or both (3); they may be joined by fagoting to a bias strip (4) or to lace (5); or they may be machine-embroidered (6). See pages 180 to 183.

Fabrics such as lightweight batiste, broadcloth, calico, organdy, and voile are suitable for collars. Opaque fabrics minimize seam show-through. Crisp fabrics prevent curling of collar edges. Pipings and trims stabilize outer collar edges and eliminate the need for bulky, hard-to-handle interfacing in a small, curved collar.

Detachable Collars

Detachable collars permit a sewer to concentrate detail work on a small project. The collars can be worn with many garments or handed down to other children. Since the size of a child's neck changes slowly, a detachable collar may continue to be used as the child grows. Detachable collars may be finished with ties or hand-stitched to the inside of the neckline. Any of the collars on the following pages may be made as detachable collars, or stitched to the garment according to the pattern directions.

How to Make a Detachable Collar

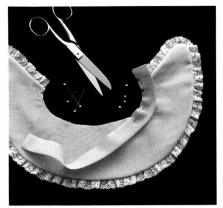

1) Prepare collar. Staystitch neck edge of collar ⅛" (3 mm) from seamline; trim seam allowance on seamline. Apply French binding (page 169).

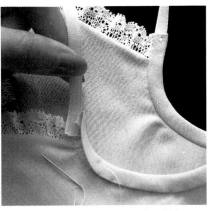

2) Insert ½" (1.3 cm) of a 10" (25.5 cm) length of ¼" (6 mm) satin ribbon in each end of binding. Bar tack by zigzagging in place.

Alternative method. Prepare collar. Staystitch on collar seamline; trim seam allowance to ¼" (6 mm). Apply French binding (page 169). Hand-stitch binding to inside of garment at neck edge.

Collars with Piping

Piping adds a tailored look to a collar, and may be used for a boy's or girl's collar. String or fine cord is an appropriate filler for piping in children's collars; preshrink the filler. Cut fabric strips for piping, page 101. Collars may also be trimmed with a combination of piping and lace, opposite.

How to Apply Piping to a Collar

1) Cut bias fabric strip 2" (5 cm) wide and length of outer edge of collar. Lay string or fine cord in center, and fold strip in half, wrong sides together. Stitch close to string, using zipper foot. Trim outer edge of collar and bias strip seam allowances to ¼" (6 mm).

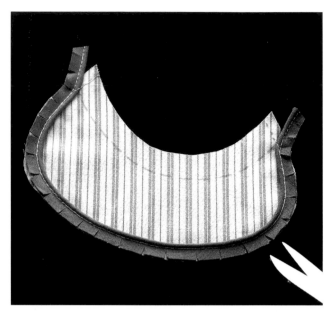

2) Baste piping to right side of upper collar, raw edges even. Clip seam allowance of piping at curves and neckline. Taper piping into seam allowance.

3) Stitch upper collar to undercollar on outer edge, with right sides together; stitch over basting line to join collars and piping.

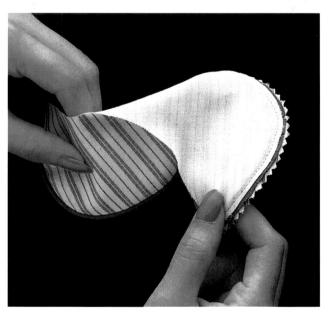

4) Trim undercollar and piping seam allowances to a scant ⅛" (3 mm). Trim upper collar seam allowance slightly with pinking shears; the upper collar seam allowance prevents piping seam allowance from showing through. Turn right side out. Press gently.

Collars with Lace Edging

Lace edging adds a feminine touch to a collar; it may be used alone or with piping (below). To keep the original size of a collar, reduce the width of the pattern by the width of the lace that is to be added at the edge. To make adding trims easier, adjust all seam allowances at the outer edge of the collar to ¼" (6 mm).

How to Apply Lace Edging to a Collar

1) Trace collar pattern onto paper. Gather lace as in step 2, page 162; pin to pattern, with finished edge of lace at pattern seamline. Draw new seamline (arrow) at gathering line of lace. Draw new cutting line ¼" (6 mm) from new seamline. Cut collar, using adjusted pattern.

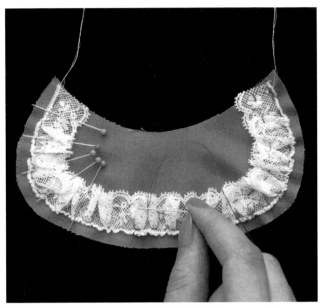

2) Baste lace to upper collar, right sides together, placing gathering line at new seamline. Adjust gathers so extra fullness is at curves. Baste ruffled portion of lace down to prevent catching in seam while stitching.

3) Stitch upper collar to undercollar on outer edge, right sides together, stitching over basting line to join collars and lace. Trim seam allowances as in step 4, opposite. Turn right side out. Remove basting. Press gently.

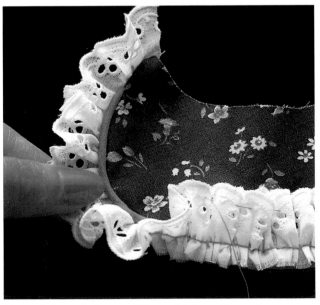

Combining piping and lace. Make adjusted pattern and cut collar as in step 1, above. Baste piping in place, step 2, opposite. Complete collar as in steps 2 and 3, above.

Collars with Fagoting

Fagoting is a method of joining two finished edges with an open, decorative stitch. The edges to be joined are basted to water-soluble stabilizer. Set the sewing machine for the fagoting stitch, or use a three-step zigzag stitch. Experiment with the stitches and make a test sample to determine the desired stitch width and length.

For a boy's collar, join a bias strip to the outer edge of the collar. For a girl's collar, join lace to the outer edge of the collar.

How to Make a Boy's or Girl's Collar with Fagoting

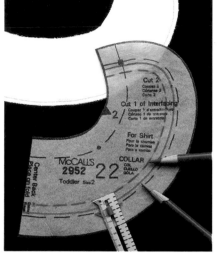

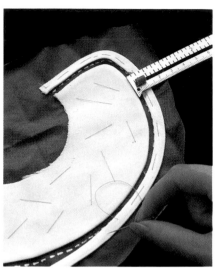

Boy's collar. 1) Cut 2" (5 cm) bias strip the length of the seamline at outer edge of collar. Fold right sides together. Stitch ¼" (6 mm) from fold, stretching fabric; trim to scant ⅛" (3 mm). Use loop turner to turn right side out.

2) Decrease size of pattern at outer seamline by ⅜" (1 cm). Add ¼" (6 mm) seam allowance. Cut collar from adjusted pattern, and stitch upper collar to undercollar, using short stitch length; trim, turn, and press collar.

3) Baste collar to water-soluble stabilizer. Draw line ⅛" (3 mm) beyond outer edge. Press bias strip to follow curve of line, with seam on inner edge of curve. Baste bias strip to stabilizer at line.

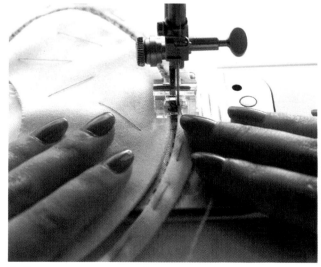

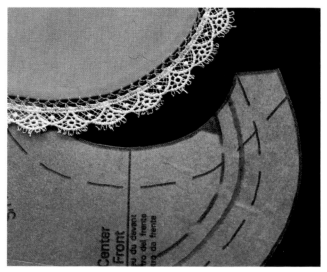

4) Center open area under presser foot. Stitch bias strip to collar, using fagoting stitch or 3-step zigzag stitch, *barely catching* the collar edge and bias strip alternately as you stitch. Remove stabilizer. Steam or spray with water, and blot with a towel; allow to dry.

Girl's collar. Decrease size of collar pattern at outer seamline by width of lace plus ⅛" (3 mm). Add ¼" (6 mm) seam allowance. Cut and stitch collar as in step 2, above. Baste to water-soluble stabilizer. Draw line ⅛" (3 mm) from collar edge. Baste lace to stabilizer at line. Join lace to collar, using fagoting or 3-step zigzag stitch. Remove stabilizer as in step 4, left.

Collars with Machine Embroidery

Simplify the planning of stitch placement for machine-embroidered collars by choosing a collar pattern with rounded, rather than square, corners. Experiment with decorative stitches, and vary the stitch combinations. You may want to create different looks, using machine embroidery threads. Rayon thread produces a shinier finish than cotton thread.

For a sheer machine-embroidered collar, use silk organza or cotton organdy. When two layers of these fabrics are used, a shadow effect can be created by trimming away portions of one layer. Use appliqué scissors; the large, duckbill-shaped edge and angled handles allow you to trim close to the fabric without cutting into adjacent fabric.

How to Machine-embroider a Sheer Collar

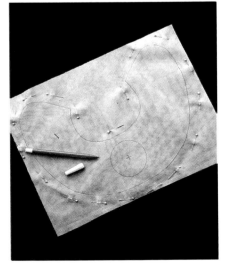

1) Cut two layers of fabric 2" (5 cm) larger than the pattern; pin wrong sides together. Trace pattern, without seam allowances, onto fabric. Mark center of collar for placement of embroidery.

2) Embroider center design, using machine or hand stitches; outline with twin-needle stitching. Stitch decorative border pattern on outer edge; stitch additional row of stitching, if desired.

Shadow effect. Trim one layer of fabric from underside of collar; use appliqué scissors, with duckbill flat on fabric not being cut. Cut close to stitching. Trim outer edge close to stitching.

Especially for Boys

Boys' clothing usually ranges from traditional classic to well-worn sports clothes. However, some occasions call for special attire. Accessorize a boy's suit with suspenders, a bow tie, or a reversible vest.

Suspenders are quick and easy to make, using belting, or decorative elastic. Suspenders should be ⅛" (3 mm) narrower than the hardware.

There are two styles of suspenders: crisscross and cross-brace. Both styles require clips to fasten to the pants

waistband and adjusters for easy length alterations as the child grows.

To prevent suspenders from slipping off the shoulders, you may use a slide for crisscross suspenders or make a cross-brace to hold suspenders together in front.

To determine the finished length of crisscross suspenders, measure the child diagonally across the shoulder. For cross-brace suspenders, measure straight over the shoulder.

How to Make Crisscross Suspenders

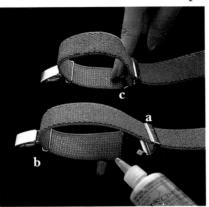

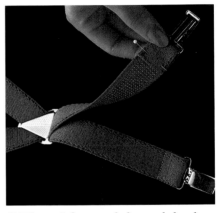

1) Cut two straps 10" (25.5 cm) longer than finished suspender length. Apply liquid fray preventer to cut ends. Insert one end through adjuster **(a)**, then through clip **(b)**, then back to adjuster; insert, and close tab **(c)**.

2) Insert free ends through slide by bringing both ends of straps through side openings and out lower end of slide. Straps cross on back of slide.

3) Thread free end through back clips; turn 1" (2.5 cm) to wrong side. Double-stitch through both thicknesses of strap. Position back slide and front adjusters for comfortable fit.

How to Make Cross-brace Suspenders

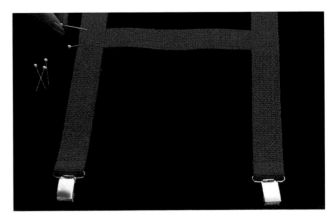

1) Cut two straps 10" (25.5 cm) longer than finished suspender length. Apply liquid fray preventer to cut ends. Attach adjusters and clips, as in steps 1 and 3, above.

2) Try on suspenders with adjusters in back; position adjusters for comfortable fit. Cut cross-brace to fit at mid-chest between outer edges of straps. Apply liquid fray preventer to cut ends. Place cross-brace under straps; stitch as shown.

Reversible Vest with Bow Tie

A reversible vest may be coordinated with a bow tie and suspenders. For the vest, select two fabrics that are similar in weight and have the same care requirements. Interface the entire vest front for a crisp look and for support in the closure area. Gripper snaps, attached with a decorative prong for both the ball and socket, allow the vest to lap correctly when reversed.

For an easy-to-sew bow tie, cut fabric either on the bias or straight grain. Cut fabric for the bow 3½" × 9" (9 × 23 cm), for the knot 3" × 2" (7.5 × 5 cm), and for the neck band 2½" (6.5 cm) wide by the length of the neck measurement plus 1½" (3.8 cm). (Take neck measurement over the shirt.) For interfacing, cut a piece of polyester fleece, 1½" × 9" (3.8 × 23 cm). Attach hook and loop tape to the ends of the neck band for easier dressing. This size will be appropriate up to a Boys' size 10.

How to Make a Bow Tie

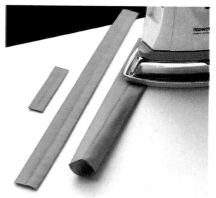

1) Fold all fabric strips lengthwise, with right sides together, and stitch with ¼" (6 mm) seam; press open. Turn the strips right side out; press flat, centering seam.

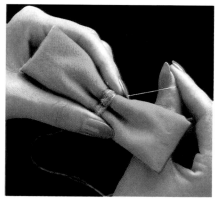

2) Insert fleece in strip for bow. Fold ends of strip to center back, overlapping ends ¼" (6 mm); stitch. Wrap center of bow tightly with double thread. Tack center back of bow to center of neck band.

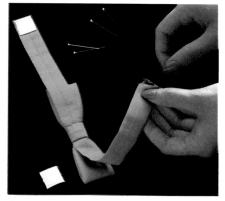

3) Wrap strip for knot around bow and neck band, lapping ends; hand-stitch in place. On ends of neck band, turn in raw edges ¼" (6 mm). Stitch hook and loop tape to ends of neck band (page 126).

How to Make a Reversible Vest

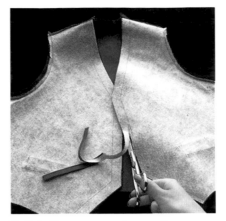

1) Cut two fronts and one back from fabric; repeat, using coordinating fabric. Follow pattern directions to attach pockets to interfaced vest front. Stitch all shoulder seams; press open.

2) Stitch vests together at front, neck, and armhole edges, right sides together, matching shoulder seams. Trim seam allowances to ¼" (6 mm); clip curves to stitching. Press seams open.

3) Turn vest right side out by pulling front through shoulder to back, one side at a time. Press, positioning seamline exactly on the edge.

4) Stitch side seams of both layers in one continuous step, matching armhole seams. Press seams open. Trim seam allowances to ⅜" (1 cm).

5) Stitch lower raw edges, with right sides together and side seams matching; leave 3" (7.5 cm) opening for turning. Trim seam allowances to ¼" (6 mm); trim corners.

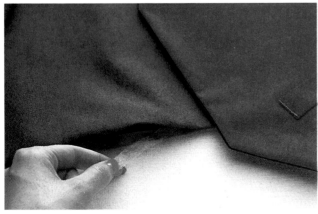

6) Turn vest right side out through opening at lower edge. Press lower edge, positioning seamline exactly on the edge. At opening, turn in raw edges, and fuse. Topstitch vest ¼" (6 mm) from edges, if desired.

7) Mark snap positions on both sides of each vest front. Apply snaps according to package directions, using decorative caps on both parts of snaps.

Personalizing

Adding a Personal Touch

Use your imagination to create personal touches that will make a garment special to the child. The techniques for personalizing clothing can be adapted to a single garment or repeated on several garments in a coordinated wardrobe.

Consider color blocking, especially when you are sewing more than one garment; use the remnants from one garment for blocks of color in another. Or highlight and coordinate garments with piping. You may want to add appliqués; purchase them ready-made, or design your own. Trapunto, an appliqué variation, can be used to add dimension to a garment.

Patchwork trims can add greatly to the cost of ready-to-wear garments, but some techniques permit you to make designs with small amounts of fabric in a short time. Fabric paints may be used to personalize a garment. They can also be used to decorate fabric shoes.

When personalizing children's garments, remember that special touches can be added to fronts, backs, and sides of garments, and all trims must be attached securely and safely.

Tips for Placement of Design

Balance design shapes. For example, you can offset a small design at the upper left of a shirt with a larger design at the lower right.

Place a placket at a shoulder or raglan seam so a design can be centered on a shirt front.

Add a design to the back of a shirt that has a plain front, or repeat a design used on the front.

Machine-stitch trim to sleeves while the piece is still flat to eliminate the need for handwork in areas too small for your sewing machine to reach.

Decorate sleeves using elbow patches or by placing designs down the center of the sleeve.

Highlight shoulder seams with piping, twill or bias tape, or ribbing.

Repeat a design to make a border at the neckline, yoke, or hemline.

Create interest with fabric strips or trims placed diagonally, vertically, or horizontally; an uneven number of strips or trims may be more pleasing than an even number.

Fabric Painting

Fabric paints can be used to decorate garments. Wash and dry fabric to remove sizing before applying the paint. Help children to plan and practice their own designs before they begin painting on fabric. Or trace an existing picture onto fabric, and then paint it. Fabric paints may be combined with iron-on transfers or appliqués. Decorate the fabric before cutting out the pattern, or decorate the completed garment.

Select acrylic fabric paints for projects painted by children. The cleanup of these water-soluble paints is easy while the paint is wet. Most paints require four hours or longer to dry.

Create different looks with four types of fabric paint: stencil, slick, puff, and glitter. Stencil paint dries with a matte, washed look; set this paint permanently with heat. Use slick paint for a wet-looking, plastic surface; it does not require heat setting. Puff paint lacks luster and is flat when first applied; however, it rises and

assumes a soft, marshmallow texture when heated with an iron. If garments will be washed by machine, apply puff paint in thin layers; thick layers of paint require hand washing. Glitter paint sparkles when dry and does not require heat to set.

For paints in tubes or accordion bottles, shake the paint into the applicator tip before using, to eliminate air bubbles. Apply it with steady, even pressure to prevent puddles.

Follow the manufacturer's directions for application of paint. Allow one color to dry before overlapping it with a second color or stencil. After the paint is completely dry, press to heat-set, if recommended by the manufacturer, using a press cloth. Lay garments flat when painting, and place wax paper between layers to prevent liquids from bleeding through the fabric layers. Launder painted garments inside out and use fabric softener to keep paints soft and flexible.

How to Stencil on Fabric

1) Place the garment flat on clean paper, with wax paper between fabric layers. Use purchased stencil design or cut an original design from thin cardboard. Tape stencil in position on garment.

2) Dilute stencil paint, using one drop of water to ten drops of paint. Dampen sponge; squeeze until almost dry. Dip sponge in paint, and use to paint inside stencil. Lift stencil gently. Heat-set according to manufacturer's directions.

Alternative method. Cut sponge into desired shape. Dampen the sponge; squeeze until almost dry. Dip sponge in paint, and apply to garment. Allow garment to dry flat. Heat-set according to the manufacturer's directions.

Techniques with Fabric Paint

Hold paint tubes 2" (5 cm) above the fabric to paint dots, squiggles, and zigzags. For dots, hold tube still, and squeeze. For squiggles and zigzags, move tube steadily, and squeeze continuously. Heat-set paint if recommended by manufacturer.

Dilute paint with water for colored splashes. A solution of one part water and ten parts paint produces a good consistency. Wet brush with paint, and gently shake over fabric to decorate large areas of fabric quickly. Heat-set paint if recommended by manufacturer.

Use puff paint or slick paint to outline shapes or write words. Outline fused appliqué to seal raw edges; paint replaces all stitching. For puff paint, heat with an iron, following manufacturer's directions, to cause puffing.

Use a child's hand for printing on fabric. In shallow pan, mix paint solution of one drop water and ten drops paint. Dip hand in paint; place on fabric. Press down on fingers and palm; lift hand straight up. Heat-set paint if recommended by manufacturer.

Color & Design Blocking

Create a distinctive look with color and design blocking. Choose two or more fabrics to use in one garment; plan the fabric arrangement, and cut individual pattern pieces from each fabric. Or trace a pattern piece, cut the traced pattern apart, and cut each piece from a different fabric. Choose a simple pattern design. For variety, you can mix woven and knit fabrics, or solids and prints. Combine colorfast fabrics that are compatible in weight and have similar care requirements.

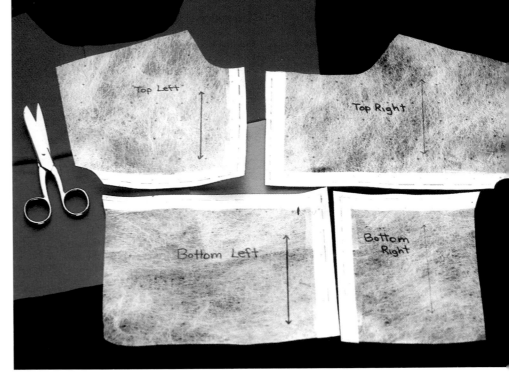

Adapt a pattern. Divide the pattern piece into sections by drawing new seamlines; cut pattern apart, and add ¼" (6 mm) seam allowance at new seams. Join sections before completing the garment.

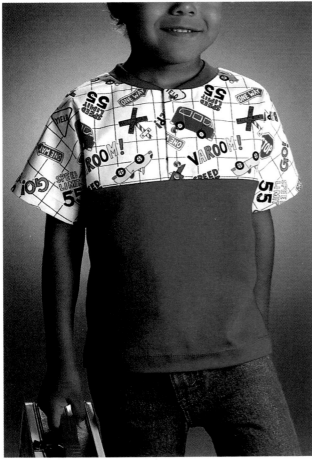

Combine woven and knit fabrics. When using a pattern designed for knit fabric, use woven fabric in areas that will not affect wearing ease, such as collars, cuffs, yokes, and pockets.

Combine striped fabrics. Cut pattern pieces from two or more striped fabrics, each with stripes of a different size. Combine stripes horizontally, vertically, or diagonally.

Patchwork Trims

Versatile patchwork trims can be made from small amounts of woven fabrics. Use coordinating colors and the garment fabric, if desired, for diagonal or Seminole patchwork trims. Stitch the fabric strips together on the straight grain for either type of trim. Diagonal patchwork trims can be constructed faster, and from less fabric, than Seminole patchwork trims.

Constructing Seminole patchwork trims is not difficult, but this method of piecing does require precise measuring, cutting, and stitching. A rotary cutter and ruler help you to cut strips accurately.

To vary the size of Seminole patchwork trims, vary the size of the squares. For a border, sew wide strips at the edges, or cut a border strip on the straight grain, and sew it to the Seminole patchwork trim.

Diagonal or Seminole patchwork trims may be applied to garments in several ways. Insert them as stripes or garment borders, or use color blocking techniques (page 195). An entire yoke, bib, or other pattern piece may be cut from a patchwork trim.

How to Make a Diagonal Patchwork Trim

1) Cut fabric strips on straight grain the finished width plus two ¼" (6 mm) seam allowances. Cut two strips each of three or more fabrics; widths of strips may vary. Stitch strips together lengthwise, with right sides together and in desired sequence, repeating the pattern once.

2) Press seams in one direction. Cut pieced fabric into bias strips, and stitch strips together as necessary, step 2, page 101. Attach to garment, being careful not to stretch strip.

How to Make a Seminole Patchwork Trim

1) Measure, and cut fabric strips on straight grain the finished width plus two ¼" (6 mm) seam allowances. Join strips in sequence, right sides together; stitch accurate seams. Press seams in one direction.

2) Cut pieced fabric into strips. The width of each strip should be equal to the width of center strip as cut in step 1, left.

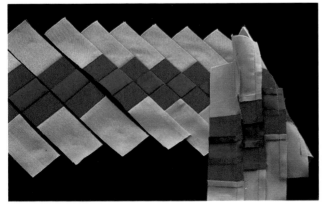

3) Join strips, right sides together; use ¼" (6 mm) seams and stagger color blocks to form diagonal pattern. Alternate direction of seam allowances on strips to help match seams. Edges along sides are staggered. Press seams in one direction.

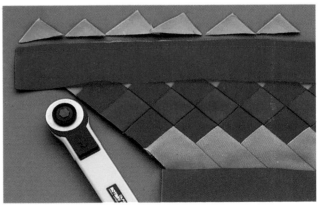

4) Trim long sides even. To add a border, cut two edging bands of straight-grain self-fabric or coordinating fabric; stitch to long sides of patchwork trim, right sides together.

Applied Stripes

Applied stripes are made by topstitching one or more strips of fabric onto garment sections. They offer an easy way to achieve the look of fine detailing on fashion sportswear. Creative variations of applied stripes all use similar, basic sewing techniques.

The simplest form of applied stripe is a single strip of contrasting fabric. The strip may be as wide or narrow as desired. Use a single strip on the front of a garment, or position it on all garment sections so the stripe encircles the garment. For a custom touch, use the same fabric for small sections, such as undercollar and front facings.

You can also combine strips of various fabric prints and textures. Knits can be mixed with wovens, and mesh can be layered over smooth fabric textures. For an effective contrast in texture on knit garments use the wrong side of the fabric for applied stripes. Give applied stripes a soft, raised dimension by padding them with polyester batting.

Another way to add fashion interest is to use lightweight trims, such as ribbons, knitted braids, or flat piping, along the edges of fabric stripes. Braids and ribbons can also be used instead of fabric strips to make stripes.

An important guideline for applied stripes is to combine compatible fabric weights. The applied stripe should match the weight of the garment fabric or be lighter in weight. Also, use fabrics that have the same care requirements. If combining dark or bright fabric colors with white or light fabric colors, be sure the dyes are colorfast so the dark or bright colors will not bleed or stain the lighter colors. Preshrink all fabrics before you cut.

How to Add an Applied Stripe

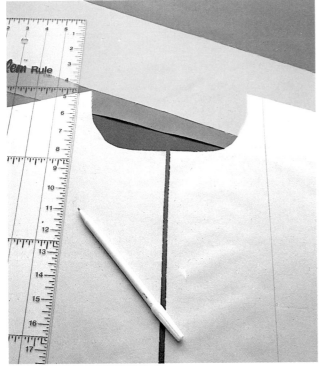

1) Mark placement guide for stripe ¼" (6 mm) inside the finished edge of stripe. Use liquid marking pen, or press a crease across garment section to indicate placement of stripe.

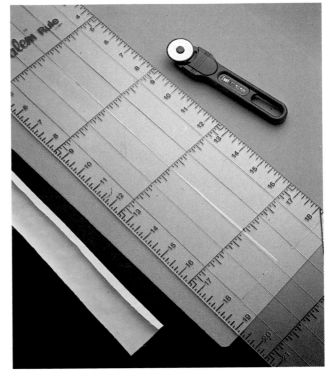

2) Cut out strip of desired width on straight fabric grain, allowing ¼" (6 mm) seam allowance on each long raw edge. Use transparent ruler and rotary cutter for quick, accurate cutting. Fold under one long raw edge ¼" (6 mm), and press.

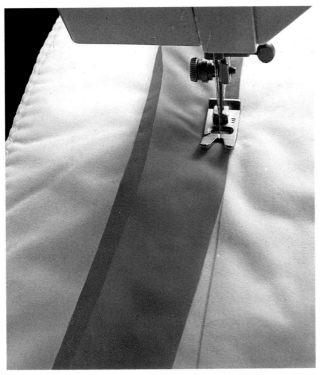

3) Place strip so unfolded raw edge lines up with marked placement guide. Right side of strip and garment section are facing. Stitch strip to garment ¼" (6 mm) from raw edge of strip.

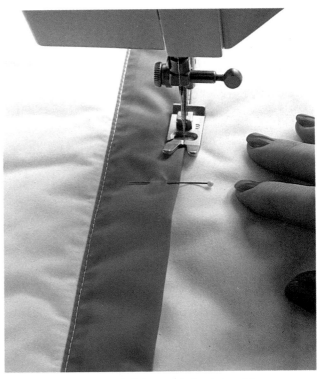

4) Fold strip over stitching so it is right side up. Press; pin. Edgestitch fold. Edgestitch opposite side of strip in same direction to prevent shifting.

How to Apply a Narrow Stripe

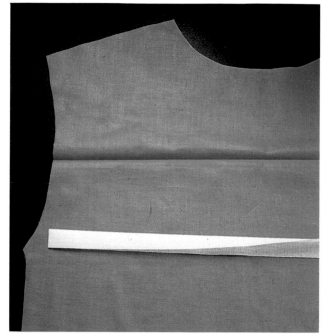

1) Cut strip as in step 2, page 199, but cut it double width. Fold strip along its length, wrong sides together, and press. Mark placement guide as in step 1, page 199.

2) Stitch on side of strip to garment as in step 3, page 199. Fold strip over raw edges, press, and edgestitch. Edgestitch opposite side of strip in same direction. Since this side is prefinished, it is not necessary to turn under the edge.

How to Apply a Braid Stripe

1) Preshrink braid; steam it thoroughly because knitted trims can shrink considerably. Hold steam iron slightly above surface of braid.

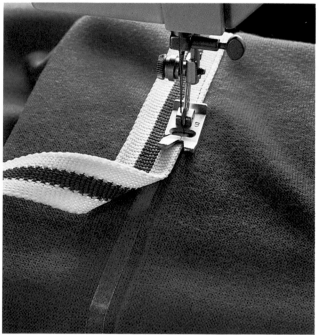

2) Mark placement guide for braid on garment section; pressing a crease is fastest marking method. Align one edge of braid with marking. Position braid with dissolvable basting tape. Stitch with conventional foot; or pin and edgestitch, using Even Feed™ foot. Edgestitch both sides of braid in same direction.

Applying Multiple Stripes

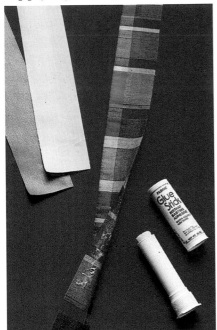

Lapped method. 1) Apply first fabric strip using basic method, page 199, but omit pressing under raw edge and final edgestitching. Use glue stick to baste raw edge of strip to garment.

2) Stitch second strip over first, using raw edge as placement guide. Stitch succeeding strips same way, turning under raw edge of final strip for edgestitching. Lapped method makes lightweight fabrics and narrow stripes easier to handle.

Pieced method. Join all fabric strips, using ¼" (6 mm) seam allowances. Press seams toward one side, pressing all seams in same direction. Apply strip using basic method, page 199, treating the pieced strip as one strip of fabric.

Padded stripes. Use basic method, page 199, but insert strip of polyester batting under fabric strip before edgestitching second side. Batting is cut to match finished size of applied stripe. Baste batting in place with glue stick or basting tape if necessary.

Multiple padded stripes. Stitch fabric strips together using pieced method, above. Cut polyester batting to match finished size of multiple stripe. Apply multiple stripe to garment, using basic method on page 199 and inserting batting before final edgestitching. Topstitch through all layers, stitching on top of seams that join individual strips.

Using Decorative Stitch Patterns

Accent a collar or cuffs with rows of decorative stitching. Mark placement lines and sew decorative stitches before assembling the collar or cuffs.

Decorative stitches can add just the right accent to a child's playsuit or a pretty blouse.

Deciding which of the many decorative stitches to use is the first step in planning a project. Whether you have a basic sewing machine with utility stitches or a top-of-the-line machine that also has automatic decorative stitches, there are several designs you can stitch (pages 204 and 205). On some machines, you can change the look of the stitches by varying the stitch length and stitch width.

Experiment with the stitches by sewing on fabric scraps, turning both left and right corners; some stitches may be attractive at both left and right corners, while others may look good only in one direction.

Also experiment with different types of thread. Changing from an all-purpose thread to a specialty thread, such as a shiny rayon, can change the effect of the stitching from sporty to dressy.

Sew the decorative stitches on the garment section before the seams are sewn, whenever possible, so the bulk of the seam allowances does not interfere with the stitching. It may be easier to sew the decorative stitches on the fabric before cutting out the garment piece.

Topstitch ribbed openings or hems of a T-shirt, using a utility stretch stitch instead of the straight stitch.

Make your own trim by sewing decorative stitches on a strip of contrasting fabric; then apply the trim with topstitching. You can also use rows of decorative stitching to add body to the brim of a hat.

Center a monogram on a turtleneck collar. Place tear-away stabilizer under the area to be monogrammed, to prevent the fabric from stretching.

Utility Stitch Patterns

The utility stitch patterns on a sewing machine were designed primarily to serve specific functions, such as blindstitching a hem or overcasting a seam; however, they can also be used as decorative stitching.

A twin needle can be used with utility stitches for a decorative look, following the guidelines in your manual for twin-needle stitching. You can also vary utility stitches by changing the stitch width or stitch length. Or change the look of the stitches by aligning or staggering the stitch patterns in two or more rows of stitching.

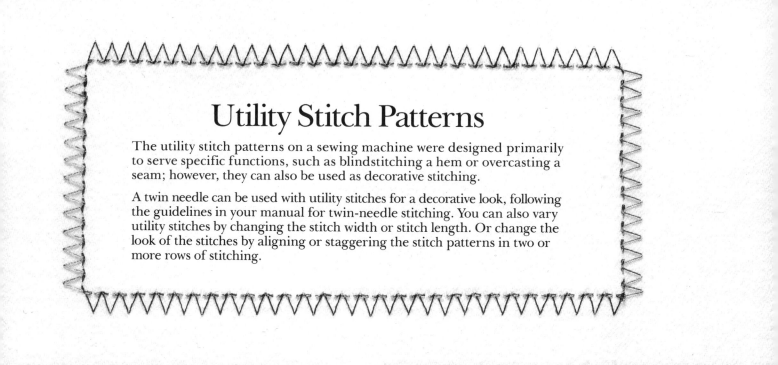

Straight stitch pattern can be stitched using a twin needle for two parallel rows of stitching in one step.

Zigzag stitch pattern or other utility stitch patterns can also be stitched using twin needle for an echo effect.

Fagoting stitch pattern can be varied by changing the stitch width and stitch length.

Multistitch-zigzag stitch pattern can be varied by changing the stitch length.

Blindstitch stitch pattern forms a new design when two rows of stitching are aligned opposite each other.

Overedge stitch pattern forms a new design when two rows of stitching are staggered.

Decorative Stitch Patterns

Decorative stitch patterns are available on both computerized and mechanical sewing machines. Computerized machines usually offer a wider selection of stitches; some offer large stitch patterns.

Features for sewing decorative stitches vary, depending on the machine. Computerized machines have many features that are helpful for decorative stitching, such as reverse-image and mirror-image patterns. Computerized machines can sew detailed stitch patterns in a single motif. The motifs can be repeated a specific number of times or combined with other stitches.

Continuous stitch patterns can be used as border designs.

Single-motif stitch patterns can be stitched one motif at a time.

Large stitch patterns of 25 mm width are available on some computerized machines.

Reverse-image stitch patterns are alternated so motifs face outward in opposite directions.

Mirror-image stitch patterns are alternated so motifs face each other.

Alphabet stitch pattern can be programmed to write words. Monograms, shown at right, are available on some computerized machines in various sizes and styles of lettering.

Appliqués

Appliqués can be the focal point of a garment; they can also be used for other projects, such as framed artwork, wall hangings, and tablecloths. Appliqués can be made from one fabric or from a combination of fabrics in various colors and textures. They can be bright and bold, or soft and subtle. Satin appliqués can add the perfect touch to a child's party dress; velour appliqués can embellish a toddler's playsuit. The direction of the grainline can be varied on appliqué pieces for an interesting effect.

Select a background fabric that has enough body to support the weight of the appliqué and that will not stretch out of shape. Then check that the background fabric does not show through any light-colored fabrics in the appliqué. Appliqué fabrics can be interfaced with fusible knit interfacing, if necessary, to prevent show-through or to add body to the appliqué. The fusible knit interfacing will not cause the appliqué to become stiff.

Appliqués are stitched to the garment using satin stitching (pages 210 and 211). The width of the

stitches depends on the size of the appliqué; use wider stitches for larger appliqués. Machine embroidery thread is recommended for satin stitching, but all-purpose thread, which is available in a wider color selection, may be used. After threading the machine, adjust the tension so the bobbin threads do not show on the right side of the fabric. The color of the thread may be changed as desired, to blend or contrast with different areas of the appliqué.

Choose either the fused technique (page 212) or the padded technique (page 214), depending on the fabrics used and the effect you want to create. With either method, tear-away stabilizer is used on the wrong side of the background fabric to prevent the stitches from puckering.

Appliquéd garments may be washed and dried by machine if the fabrics are washable. To prevent excessive abrasion of the appliqué, turn the garment wrong side out before washing.

Fused appliqués (page 212) can be sewn in an endless variety of designs, such as the school bus above. For a horn, a squeaker is inserted in the front of the bus. Colorful buttons are used for the wheels.

Padded appliqués (page 214) have a soft, dimensional effect, created with the addition of polyester fleece or low-loft quilt batting.

Dragon appliqué makes this child's jacket one of a kind.

Jester is created from fabrics in a variety of textures, including broadcloth, polyester satin, and corduroy.

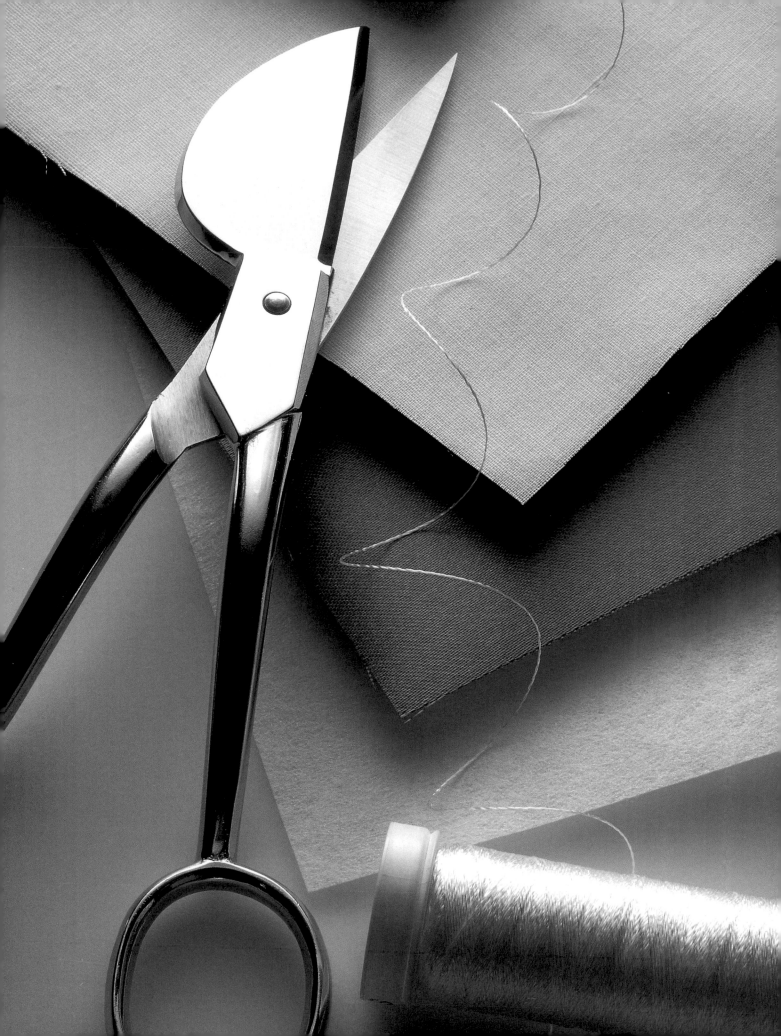

Selecting an Appliqué Technique

Appliqués may be applied using either a fused technique (page 212) or a padded technique (page 214). Keeping in mind the considerations below, choose the method that works best for the fabrics you are sewing and the look you want to achieve.

Whichever method you select, the outer edges of the appliqué are covered with satin stitching. To neatly follow the edges, use the techniques for satin stitching corners, curves, and points on pages 210 and 211.

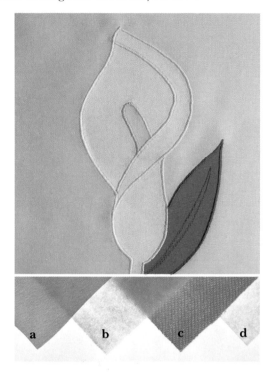

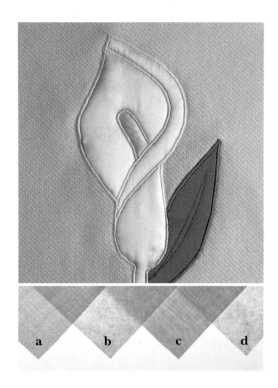

Fused Appliqués

The appliqué fabric (**a**) is cut to shape and secured with fusible web (**b**) to the background fabric (**c**). Tear-away stabilizer (**d**) is placed under the background fabric; then satin stitching is done from the right side to cover the raw edges.

Considerations

Fusible web causes appliqué to become somewhat stiff.

Appliqué cannot shift or ripple during stitching, because it is fused to the background fabric.

Use basic fabrics, such as cotton broadcloth, poplin, or other lightweight to mediumweight fabrics that fuse securely.

Avoid using fabrics that will become too stiff when fusible web is applied, such as chintz, or those that will bubble when fused, such as some silky fabrics.

Padded Appliqués

The appliqué fabric (**a**) is placed over layers of polyester fleece or quilt batting (**b**) and background fabric (**c**); the appliqué shape is not cut out. The design is marked on tear-away stabilizer (**d**) and the stabilizer is placed on the wrong side of the background fabric.

The design lines are stitched from the wrong side, using straight stitching. Then the appliqué fabric and fleece are trimmed close to the stitching, and satin stitching is done from the right side to cover the raw edges.

Considerations

Appliqué fabric and polyester fleece or quilt batting are secured to the background fabric by straight stitching from the wrong side of the project before cutting them to the shape of the design.

Use lightweight to mediumweight appliqué fabrics. Because the polyester fleece or quilt batting adds bulk to the appliqué, avoid using bulky or stiff appliqué fabrics. Heavier background fabrics may be used with padded appliqués.

How to Satin Stitch Corners and Curves of Appliqués

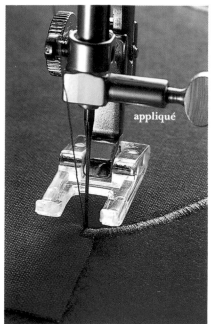

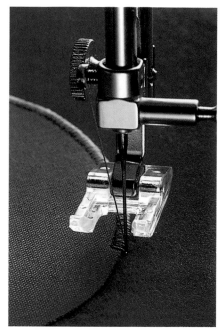

Inside corners. Stitch past corner a distance equal to width of satin stitch, stopping with needle down at the inner edge of satin stitching; raise presser foot. Pivot and satin stitch next side of appliqué, covering previous stitches at corner.

Outside corners. Stitch one stitch past corner, stopping with needle down at outer edge of satin stitching; raise presser foot. Pivot and satin stitch the next side of appliqué, covering previous stitches at corner.

Curves. Pivot fabric frequently, pivoting with needle down at longest edge of satin stitching.

How to Satin Stitch Outside Points of Appliqués

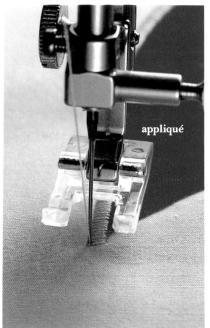

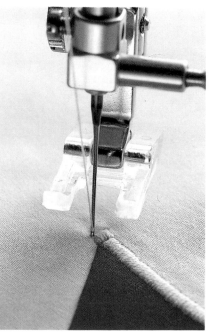

1) Stitch one stitch past the point, stopping with needle down at outer edge of satin stitching; raise the presser foot.

2) Pivot fabric to a 90° angle. Stitch two to four stitches, stopping when stitches just cover previous stitches; stop with needle down on outer edge of satin stitching. Raise the presser foot.

3) Pivot fabric; satin stitch next side of appliqué.

How to Satin Stitch Outside Points of Appliqués

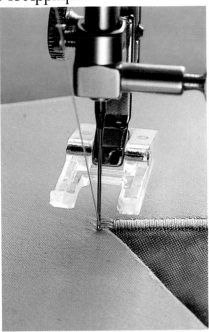

1) Stitch one stitch past the point, stopping with needle down at outer edge of satin stitching; raise the presser foot.

2) Pivot fabric to a 90° angle. Stitch two to four stitches, stopping when stitches just cover previous stitches; stop with needle down on outer edge of satin stitching. Raise the presser foot.

3) Pivot fabric; satin stitch next side of appliqué.

How to Satin Stitch Tapered Outside Points of Appliqués

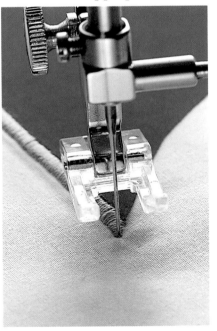

1) Stitch, stopping when inner edge of satin stitching meets other side of appliqué. Raise presser foot.

2) Pivot fabric slightly. Continue stitching, gradually narrowing stitch width to 0 and stopping at point. Raise presser foot.

3) Pivot fabric and stitch back over the previous stitches, gradually widening stitch width to original width. Pivot fabric slightly and stitch next side of appliqué.

Fused Appliqués

Appliqués are a traditional method for decorating children's garments. Select from three basic types of appliqués; purchase iron-on or sew-on appliqués, or design your own. For a fast and easy decorative touch, fuse purchased iron-on appliqués to a garment, following the manufacturer's directions. Purchased sew-on appliqués may be fused to the garment using fusible web. You may wish to topstitch to secure the appliqué through many launderings.

You may want to design your own custom-made appliqués. Look at magazines, ready-to-wear garments, or coloring books for ideas. Fruit, animals, numbers, toys, hearts, and rainbows are all popular shapes for children's appliqués. Consider cutting motifs from printed fabrics.

Before assembling the appliqué, plan the work sequence. Smaller pieces may need to be positioned on and stitched to larger pieces before applying appliqué to the garment, and some pieces may overlap other pieces.

Embellish the appliqués with bows, buttons, ribbons, pom-poms, fabric paint, or cord. Cut ends of cord may be placed under appliqué pieces before fusing. Trims may be stitched or glued in place, using permanent fabric glue.

Tips for Appliqués

Practice stitching an appliqué on a test piece before working with the garment piece.

Select a colorfast fabric for an appliqué that is compatible with garment fabric in weight and care requirements; preshrink all fabrics.

Remember that it is easiest to stitch around large, simple shapes with few corners.

Leave a fabric margin in a geometric shape around intricate motifs cut from printed fabrics.

Apply paper-backed fusible web to the wrong side of the appliqué fabric before cutting out the shape.

Add durability to a garment by applying an appliqué with fusible web at knees or elbows.

Add ½" (1.3 cm) to sides of appliqué pieces that will go under another piece; trim to reduce bulk when final placement is determined.

Remember that shapes drawn on paper backing of fusible web will be reversed on the garment; draw mirror images of letters or numbers.

Apply tear-away stabilizer to the wrong side of a garment for smooth satin stitching at the edge of an appliqué.

Use a special-purpose presser foot with a wide channel to prevent buildup of satin stitches.

Apply an appliqué to garment before joining seams. It is easier to apply an appliqué while fabric is flat.

How to Make and Apply an Appliqué

1) **Apply** paper-backed fusible web to wrong side of appliqué fabric, following manufacturer's directions. Allow fabric to cool.

2) **Draw** mirror image of design on paper backing; add ¼" (6 mm) to sides of appliqué pieces that go under another piece. Cut out design, and remove paper backing.

3) **Position** appliqué pieces on the garment fabric. Fuse appliqué pieces to garment.

4) **Cut** tear-away stabilizer 1" (2.5 cm) larger than appliqué. Glue-baste to the wrong side of garment, under appliqué. Zigzag stitch around appliqué, using short, narrow stitches.

5) **Decrease** the upper tension, and adjust stitches for short, wide zigzag; satin stitch around appliqué edges to cover all raw edges. Remove tear-away stabilizer.

Appliqué with squeaker. Apply fusible interfacing to wrong side of appliqué. Place squeaker under appliqué; glue appliqué in place at edges. Complete appliqué as in steps 4 and 5, left.

Padded Appliqués

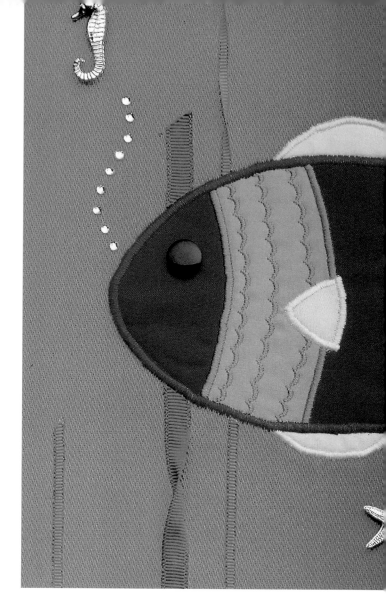

A softly padded effect can be achieved by placing polyester fleece or low-loft quilt batting under the appliqué fabric. A padded appliqué is stitched from the wrong side before cutting the appliqué fabric and batting to the shape of the design. This eliminates any concern about keeping the layers even at the edges of the appliqué during stitching and is especially helpful if you are sewing an appliqué from lightweight or silky fabrics. If necessary, fabrics can be secured in an embroidery hoop to prevent rippling while the design outline is stitched.

How to Sew a Padded Appliqué

1) Cut tear-away stabilizer at least 2" (5 cm) larger than entire appliqué area. Trace design onto stabilizer; if using an asymmetrical design, trace mirror image.

2) Mark placement of the appliqué on fabric, using pins. Position the stabilizer on the wrong side of the garment, matching the placement points of design to pins. Baste or pin stabilizer to garment.

3) Cut polyester fleece or quilt batting larger than motif; place on right side over design area. Cut fabric for appliqué piece larger than design area; do not cut out appliqué shape. Place appliqué fabric, right side up, over fleece; baste.

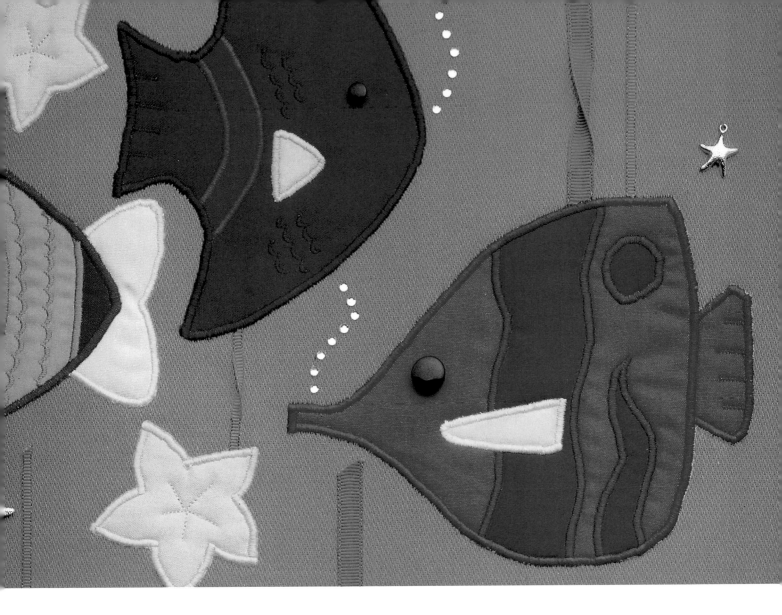

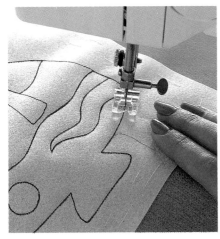

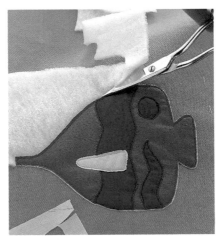

4) Stitch design lines on stabilizer, using short, straight stitches. Remove basting. From right side, trim excess appliqué fabric close to stitching.

5) Cut fabric for next appliqué piece and place over fleece as in step 3; stitch and trim as in step 4. Repeat for all remaining appliqué pieces. Trim fleece close to stitching.

6) Satin stitch from right side, as on pages 210 and 211. Remove the stabilizer. Embellish appliqués as desired.

Embellishing Appliqués

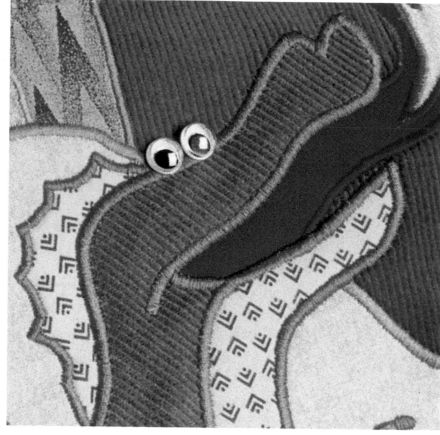

Moveable eyes (above) and embellishments (below) can be stitched or glued into place.

Ribbons or cords can be tacked in place or inserted under edge of appliqué before satin stitching to secure them.

Notions, such as charms, buttons, rhinestones, and ribbons, can be stitched on appliqués or glued in place with permanent fabric glue.

Decorative stitching can embellish some of the appliqué pieces and add detail to the appliqué.

Repair

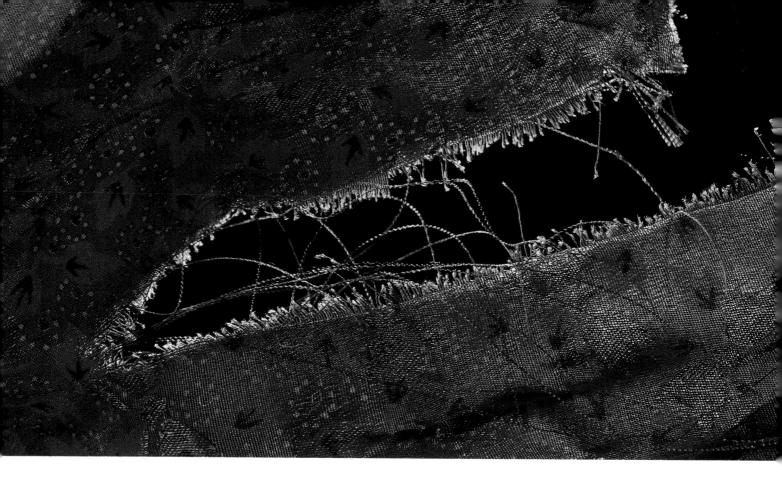

Tears, Cuts & Holes

Rips, tears and cuts are usually the result of an accidental snag on a sharp object. The threads or yarns of a rip or cut are usually not missing as they are in a hole, but they may have been pulled off-grain. Holes leave a gap in fabric with threads missing. What starts as a worn spot or small tear may become a hole, and the longer it is ignored the larger it becomes. Repair it as soon as possible.

Repair without sewing. Use fusible interfacing, iron-on mending tape or fabric, or fusible web with a patch of matching fabric. If a tear has not raveled excessively, the fusible prevents further tearing or raveling. On most fabrics it will barely be noticeable; however, fusibles add stiffness and bulk that may not be desirable on lightweight or sheer fabrics. Before making a repair, test the fusible on a hidden area of the garment, such as in a seam allowance, a shirttail or the inside of a pocket.

Hand darning. Use thread that is suitable to the weight of the fabric. Thread that is too heavy strains the darned area and makes the mend more obvious; thread that is too fine may not cover the hole adequately. To match woven fabrics perfectly, ravel some threads from a seam or cut edge to use for hand darning. Steam press to remove the crimp.

Machine darning. Some machines have a special darning foot to use with a free-hand straight stitch.

For straight-stitch darning, drop or cover the feed. To manipulate the area to be darned more easily, place it in an embroidery hoop.

Machine darning may be done with or without an underlay of lightweight or matching fabric. If the tear is so large that the trimmed edges of the fabric do not meet smoothly, an underlay gives strength and support to it without excessive stitching. This is a sturdy mend, ideal for fabrics that receive a lot of stress or require frequent laundering. To make this mend less obvious, use thread one shade darker than the fabric. Use extra-fine thread for light to mediumweight fabrics.

When darning denim jeans, use matching navy thread on top and gray thread in the bobbin. Loosen upper tension. The bobbin thread will pull slightly to the top of the work, giving an almost invisible mend.

Use multi-stitch zigzag, serpentine or honeycomb stitch for darning and reinforcement with zigzag machines. These stitches keep the fabric flat and allow the mended area to stretch slightly after it has been repaired.

Sometimes a tear is hidden, such as in a gathered area. If a tiny tuck will not affect the fit of the garment, the tear can be mended on the inside with a narrow seam.

How to Repair a Tear or Cut without Sewing

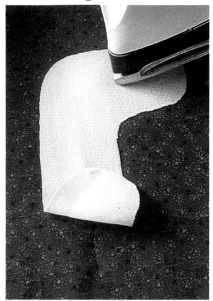

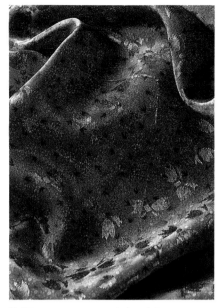

1) Press torn area to realign threads which may have been pulled off-grain. Trim loose threads from edges of tear with sharp scissors. Clip into each end about ½" (1.3 cm), or enough to taper to a point.

2) Place tear, face down, on pressing surface and gently bring edges together. Cut patch of fusible interfacing or mending fabric 1" (2.5 cm) larger than tear. Round corners. Place patch, adhesive side down, over tear. Touch tip of iron to patch to tack in place.

3) Turn garment right side up. Check that cut edges meet, covering patch. Press to fuse, following directions on package. Let cool before handling.

How to Hand-darn a Tear or Cut

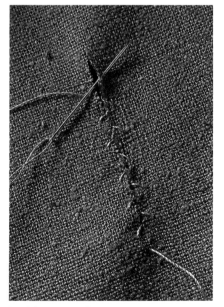

1) Prepare tear as in step 1, above. Use fishbone stitch to hold torn edges together. Use matching thread because it may be impossible to remove. Do not secure thread. Insert needle ¼" (6 mm) from end of tear, then on one side of tear at end.

2) Alternate slanted stitches on each side of tear with needle in position as at left; alternate direction of needle with each stitch. Place stitches ⅛" to ¼" (3 to 6 mm) apart. Insert needle as close to torn edge as possible.

3) Stitch back and forth across tear with closely spaced rows of tiny running stitches. Work parallel to fabric grain, duplicating weave of fabric. Keep stitches loose so darned area does not have tight, pulled appearance. (Contrasting thread is used for detail.)

How to Machine-darn a Tear or Cut

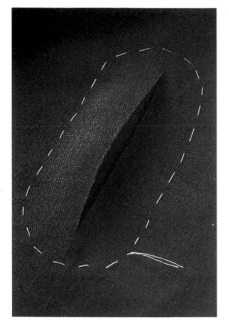

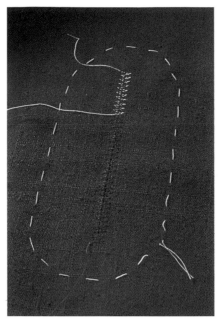

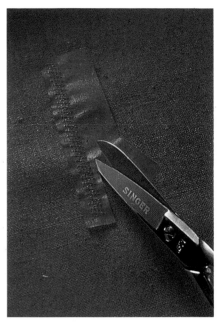

1) Follow step 1 for repairing a tear (page 67). Cut a patch of lightweight fabric in matching color, 3" (7.5 cm) larger than tear. Baste it in position on back of tear.

2) Multi-stitch zigzag, serpentine or honeycomb stitch on right side of garment, catching both edges of tear in stitching. (Contrasting thread is used for detail.)

3) Turn garment to wrong side; trim underlay patch close to stitching. If fabric ravels or frays easily, stitch again on each side of first row before trimming, overlapping stitches slightly.

How to Machine-darn a Hole or Reinforce a Worn Area

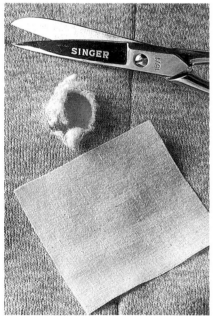

1) Trim ragged thread ends from hole. If using an underlay for reinforcement, cut a patch of lightweight woven fabric at least 1" (2.5 cm) larger than hole or worn area. Baste underlay on wrong side, covering area to be darned.

2) Place area to be darned in embroidery hoop, right side up over outer ring. Place smaller ring inside outer ring so area to be darned will lie flat on machine. Pull fabric taut in hoop.

3) Attach darning/embroidery foot and feed cover (or lower feed). Raise needle to highest position; carefully position hoop under needle. Lower presser foot lever. Insert needle into fabric. Bring bobbin thread up through fabric and pull threads behind needle.

4) Stitch a circle around hole, holding hoop with both hands. Stitch slowly; do not rotate hoop. Clip thread ends. Move hoop slowly back and forth under needle to fill in with vertical stitches. Control stitch length by hand movements.

5) Move work from side to side under needle after vertical threads have been stitched. Continue stitching until hole is filled in with vertical and horizontal stitches.

Reinforce a worn area or darn a hole with multi-stitch zigzag, serpentine or honeycomb stitch. Place underlay under worn area. Stitch back and forth over worn area, overlapping stitches.

Patches

Whether a repair is invisible or decorative, patching is a sturdy way to repair holes in garments. A favorite skirt with a tear that is inconspicuously patched may remain in your child's wardrobe instead of being discarded. A worn snowsuit mended with decorative knee patches can start the season with a new look.

Methods of patching include fusing, gluing, and hand or machine stitching. The patching technique you choose depends on how much time you have, the use of the garment and the type of fabric.

Time. Fusing a patch usually takes the least amount of time, especially if you buy a precut, iron-on patch. Other timesaving notions include mending fabric or tape and fusible web. Use a hole-and-tear mending appliance to repair small holes and tears. For successful application, follow package or wrapper directions when using any fusible or iron-on product.

Applying fabric glue or adhesive is another simple way to patch when stitching is too obvious and fusing is not possible. Special adhesive products are available for vinyl, leather, and nylon outerwear.

Machine-stitch a patch for a fast, secure repair that will withstand frequent laundering. With this method you can use decorative stitch patterns around the edge of the patch. Use a free-arm sewing machine to machine-stitch patches on sleeves or pants legs.

Hand stitching is the most time-consuming method of patching, but may need to be used in an area that is hard to reach with a machine. The patch can be applied so that it is nearly invisible on carefully matched plaids.

Use. Another consideration, besides the amount of time a patching technique takes, is the use of the garment. Expensive dressy clothes require less obvious patching than rugged work clothes or children's play clothes. A fused patch of matching fabric is the best technique to use for a good pair of gabardine pants, but a sturdy machine-stitched patch would be appropriate for jeans. Machine or hand stitching may be best for children's clothes whenever fusing or gluing would cause the fabric to become uncomfortably stiff.

Fabric. Consider, too, the type of fabric. Tweeds, plaids and overall prints are easier to repair invisibly than fabrics of solid colors. Textured fabrics are easier to patch than smooth ones. Solid colors, smooth surfaces and lightweight fabrics may require lace or appliqué trims to cover the repaired area.

To cover a hole least conspicuously, use a patch that matches the fabric of the garment. Save any scrap material from clothing you have sewn. If the garment was purchased, cut a small patch from the hem, the back of a pocket or another concealed area of the garment. Apply the patch *under* the hole for a hidden application. Apply it *over* the hole and stitch around the edge for a decorative application.

Apply purchased iron-on patch that is compatible with fiber, color and texture of garment. Wash or dryclean garment before applying patch. Preheat worn area with dry iron before applying patch.

Cut mending fabric or tape 1" (2.5 cm) larger than hole or tear; round off corners. Place shiny side of mending patch on right side of garment, covering hole. Use press cloth to prevent scorching.

Use fusible web to make an iron-on patch from any fabric. Cut fabric patch and web 1" (2.5 cm) larger than hole. Place web between fabric patch and hole. Adhere, using steam iron.

Fuse and reinforce with stitching to keep edge smooth and secure on garments that need frequent laundering. Use straight, zigzag or decorative stitch.

Use preventive fusing to reinforce areas that receive hard wear, such as elbows. Back with fusible interfacing, cut wide enough to stitch into seams.

How to Hand-stitch a Patch

1) Press fabric around hole. Trim hole to square or rectangle. Reinforce corners with short machine stitches, or small running stitches ¼" (6 mm) from edge. Clip corners up to stitching. Reinforce corners with liquid fray preventer.

2) Turn edges under ¼" (6 mm) and press. Cut patch on matching grain 1½" (3.8 cm) larger than hole. With right sides up, center patch under hole. Baste in place along folded edge.

How to Machine-stitch a Patch on the Inside

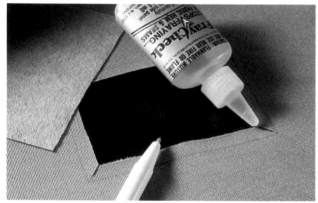

1) Press fabric around hole. Trim hole to square or rectangle. On wrong side, mark ¼" (6 mm) seam along edge of hole or reinforce as in step 1, above. Clip to marks at corners. Reinforce corners with liquid fray preventer. Cut matching fabric patch 1" (2.5 cm) larger than hole.

2) Press edges of hole under ¼" (6 mm). With right sides together, line up one edge of patch with edge of hole, opening out pressed seam allowance. Work from wrong side of garment. Using short stitches, stitch ¼" (6 mm) from edge, starting at middle of one side. Stitch to corner.

How to Patch with Fabric Glue or Adhesive

1) Trim hole or tear to a simple shape with smooth edges. Cut a patch of matching fabric the exact same size and shape as hole. Cut underlay of lightweight matching fabric at least 1" (2.5 cm) larger than patch.

2) Apply a narrow bead of permanent fabric glue to edge on wrong side of patch; use toothpick or pin to spread. Press patch onto underlay fabric and allow to dry thoroughly.

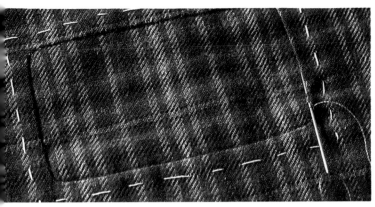

3) Slipstitch folded edges of fabric to patch, using tiny, closely spaced stitches, ⅛" to ¼" (3 to 6 mm) long. Use a short, fine needle.

4) Catchstitch edge of patch to garment on inside, picking up only one or two threads of garment so stitches are not visible on outside. On lightweight fabrics, turn under edge of patch and slipstitch.

3) Pivot at corner. To pivot, leave needle in fabric; raise presser foot. Turn patch a quarter turn. Rearrange garment in front of needle, lining up raw edge of hole with patch. Lower presser foot.

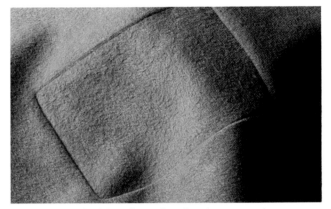

4) Stitch each side of patch, pivoting at each corner. Overlap stitching at starting point. Press patch and seams to one side.

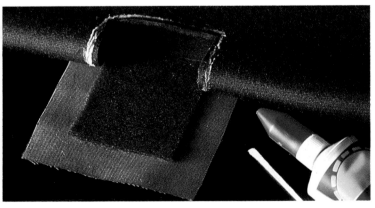

3) Apply glue sparingly to edge of hole. From underneath, place patch right side up into hole. Remove any excess glue with damp cloth.

4) Place tape at right angles to edges until glue is dry. Let dry for a few minutes. Trim underlay close to glue line.

Elbow & Knee Patches

Worn elbow and knee areas do not always need to be invisibly repaired. Instead, apply decorative patches. Appliquéd knee patches are ideal for jeans. Synthetic or genuine suedes make handsome elbow patches for sweaters, jackets and wool shirts. You can cut your own, or buy precut suede and leather patches with perforations around the edges to aid in sewing through the heavy patch.

To cut patches, first make a paper or cardboard pattern. For nonwoven fabrics that do not ravel, such as synthetic suede, cut the patch the same size as the pattern. For woven fabrics that ravel, such as corduroy, cut patch ½" (1.3 cm) larger, press edges under ¼" (6 mm).

Baste or fuse patches in place for stitching. To fuse, cut fusible web from pattern. Place fusible web between patch and right side of garment. Place heavy brown paper or aluminum foil under worn area to prevent fusible web from sticking to inside of garment.

How to Apply Elbow and Knee Patches

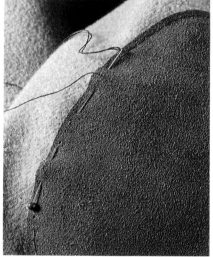

1) Make a paper or cardboard pattern 4" by 5" (10 by 12.5 cm) for sleeve patch and 5" by 6" (12.5 by 15 cm) for knee patch, depending on size of garment. Trim corners into rounded curves. Cut and fuse patch as above.

2) Machine-stitch edge of patch in place (or hand-stitch). Use medium stitch length with thread and needle appropriate to fabric. Free-arm machine makes it easier to sew patches on sleeves and pants legs.

Hand-stitch edge of patch in place, using backstitch (above), or blanket stitch (page 230). Use single strand of buttonhole twist for perforated suede or leather patches and for lined jackets.

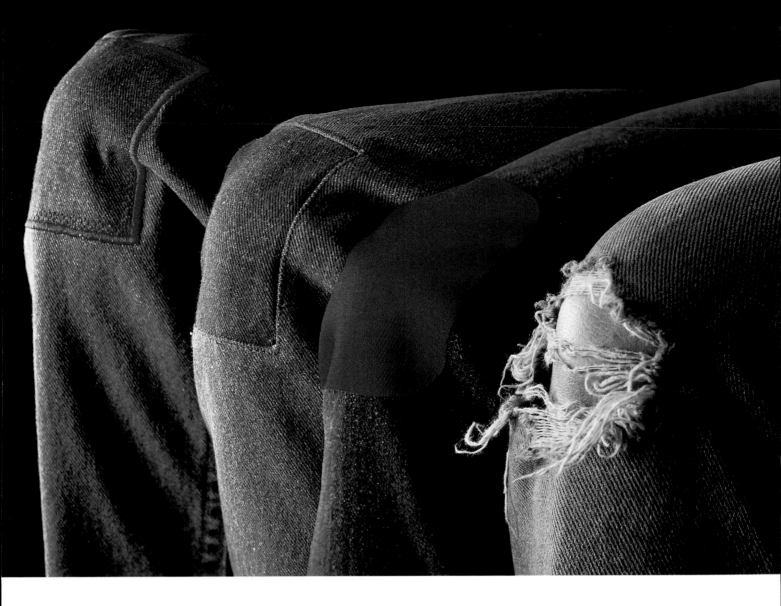

How to Appliqué a Patch on the Outside

1) Press garment area to be patched, but do not trim worn area. Cut matching patch 1" (2.5 cm) larger than area to be patched. With right sides up, center patch over hole or worn area and baste in place.

2) Open part of seam, if necessary, for access to narrow areas. Zigzag around patch, using closely spaced stitches to cover raw edges of patch. Use widest zigzag setting and matching thread.

3) Stitch again using multi-stitch zigzag or decorative stitch to reinforce patch. Use short stitch length and full width. Overlap stitching at corners. Trim worn fabric area from under patch.

Decorative Patches

Patches can enhance the appearance and durability of children's clothes. Bright colors and fanciful appliqués provide contrast; quilted patches add extra strength and padding for the knees. If only one knee or elbow area wears out, reinforce and patch both pants legs or sleeves for a decorative effect. You will be satisfied knowing the garment will last longer, and children will be delighted with the new look that a patch or appliqué gives to their clothes.

To coordinate a child's outfit, repeat the fabric or design of the patch on another area of the garment. Trim the pockets, for example, with fabric or a stitch pattern used on the patch. Or coordinate piped patches with piped collar and cuffs on a shirt.

Consider comfort when selecting the patching method you will use. Fusing the patch (page 225) may add too much stiffness to be comfortable. Machine-stitching takes a little longer but is generally softer than fusing.

A free-arm machine aids machine stitching of tubular areas, such as sleeves and pants legs, because you can stitch around the patch all at once. Even with some free-arm machines, you may have to reposition the garment after sewing halfway around the patch and sew from the other end of the tube.

On narrow legs or sleeves, open the inside seam before stitching to provide a flat area. Stitch the patch in place, then restitch the seam. An alternative for hard-to-reach areas is to hand-stitch the patch with backstitch or blanket stitch.

How to Blanket-stitch a Decorative Patch

Use three strands of embroidery floss or a single strand of buttonhole twist. Secure thread under patch. Bring needle to right side. Holding thread loop down with thumb, bring needle through patch and garment and over thread. Pull up stitch. Continue around patch with stitches ⅛" to ⅜" (3 to 10 mm) apart. Secure thread on inside.

How to Apply Padded Knee Patches

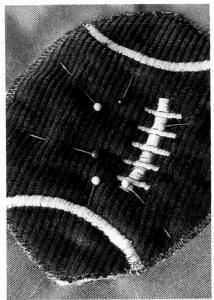

1) Cut patch, backing and batting at least 1" (2.5 cm) larger than worn area. Apply any decorative or quilting stitches before sewing patch onto garment. If necessary, edgestitch layers together to prevent shifting.

2) Baste patch onto worn area of garment. Replace presser foot with special-purpose foot for appliqué work. Set machine for narrow zigzag and medium stitch length. Zigzag around edge of patch.

3) Satin-stitch around edge, completely covering narrow zigzag and edge of patch. To satin-stitch, set machine for wide zigzag and short stitch length; loosen tension. A test sample is advisable.

How to Apply a Quilted Patch with Piped Edges

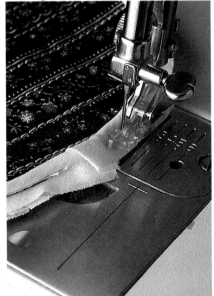

1) Cut patch with rounded corners. Using zipper foot, stitch piping to right side of patch, beginning 1" (2.5 cm) from end of cord so other end can be lapped around it. Allow 1" (2.5 cm) overlap at ends. Snip a few stitches at overlapped end to open piping. Clip encased cord so ends meet.

2) Fold under ½" (1.3 cm) of overlapped end of piping. Lap it around the other end and stitch in place. Turn seam allowance to wrong side of patch and press raw edges toward center.

3) Baste patch in position and topstitch close to piping, using zipper foot. Stitch a second row approximately ¼" (6 mm) from topstitching.

Creative Repairs with Trimmings

Sometimes the best repair solution is to disguise a tear or hole with lace, ribbon, a pocket, an applique or an insert. If conventional mending techniques would be obvious because of the fabric, or the tear is in a prominent location, turn the repair into a design feature.

Consider the style and fabric of the garment when selecting which trimming to use. Laces, ribbons and ruffles are good choices for little girls' dresses, lingerie and blouses. An applique adds whimsical decoration to children's clothing, even when in an unusual location such as on a sleeve cuff, a dress hem or the seat of pants. A fabric insert is ideal for replacing an area of fabric that would be difficult to trim with another technique or an area that has a large tear in it. Use an insert to replace a yoke, or add a decorative band near the hem of a skirt or inverted pleats in the sleeves of a dress.

Designers use pockets as decorative features in surprising positions. The same idea works as a strategy for repair. Add two or three contrasting pockets, one to hide the tear and the others to call attention to the pocket as a design feature. Not only will the tear be covered, but the garment will have a new look as well.

When selecting trimmings, also consider the garment care and use. Purchased items, such as lace collars or silk flower pins, are also possibilities. For denim or corduroy, sporty appliques or grosgrain ribbons can hide repairs without adding frills.

How to Use Ribbon to Hide Repairs

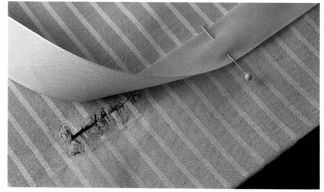

Tears on skirts can be easily hidden with trimmings. Choose a coordinating trimming wide enough to cover the tear. Baste ribbon or lace over the tear and stitch in place. Use liquid fray preventer or fusible interfacing on inside to prevent further raveling. Attach additional trimming at waistband or sleeve to extend the design feature to the whole garment.

How to Use Pockets to Hide Repairs

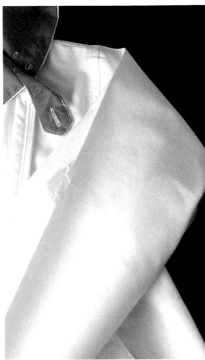

1) Consider the position of the tear when deciding what technique to use. A pocket is a creative way to conceal a tear on a sleeve.

2) Make pockets from contrasting fabrics; add several for emphasis. On a windbreaker, zippered pockets are ideal for a casual look.

3) Coordinate with other pockets on garment.

How to Use Fabric Inserts to Hide Repairs

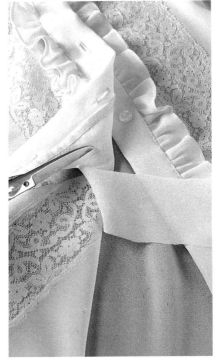

1) Replace torn area with lace or fabric insert if hole or tear is in a position that is not appropriate for trimming.

2) Position lace over hole or tear. Attach with narrow zigzag on finished edge of lace. Trim torn area from behind insert. Use liquid fray preventer on inside cut edges.

3) Use handkerchiefs, embroidered linens or contrasting fabrics for decorative inserts.

233

Repairing Hems

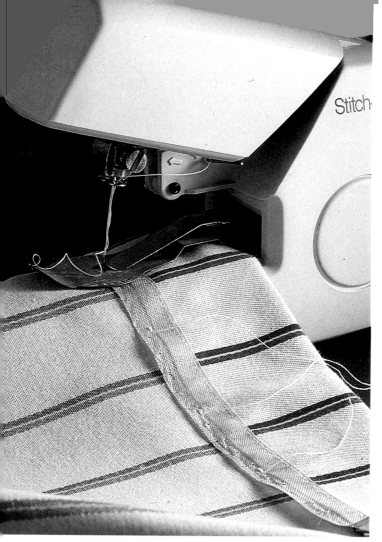

It takes only minutes to repair a hem that has pulled out. Make emergency repairs with double-faced mending tape, fabric glue or a portable hem-and-seam tacker.

Non-sewing repairs can be made with strips of fusible web. This permanent hem withstands washing and drycleaning.

Hand-stitching the repair gives a custom finish. Use blindstitch for woven, ravelly fabrics finished with seam binding or an overcast edge; catchstitch is durable for flat hems in pants, knits and heavy fabrics. Use slipstitch for woven fabrics with a turned-under edge.

Machine-stitched repair takes less time and is sturdier than hand stitching, and it achieves the same professional finish. Machine blindstitch provides an invisible hem. A straight-stitched hem shows on the right side.

When in doubt about which hemming or stitching technique to use, duplicate the technique used by the manufacturer in the original hem. Many commercial hems use a blind chainstitch that pulls out when one end of the thread is pulled. Replace this hem with a stitch appropriate to the fabric and the garment use. You may also need to replace poor quality seam binding that has worn from abrasion.

Hem-and-seam tacker makes individual thread tacks, useful for tacking permanent or temporary hems. Place hem under clamp. Squeeze and release hand lever five or six times to stitch. Use built-in thread cutter to automatically cut thread. Make as many tacks as necessary to secure hem in place.

Emergency Repairs

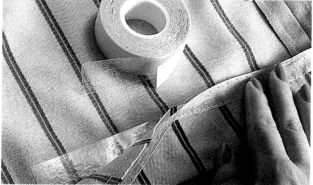

Double-faced mending tape needs no iron to apply. Place tape on garment with edge along hemming line; leave backing on tape. Press firmly with fingers. Remove paper backing. Fold hem up at ends of tape and pinch in place. Smooth hem, applying pressure from center outward. Remove tape before washing or drycleaning.

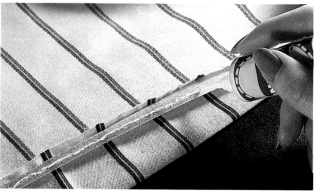

Fabric glue is washable but not drycleanable. Test for staining in a hidden area. Spread foil under fabric to protect work surface. Apply thin line of glue to hem edge. Spread lightly with finger or tube tip. Fold hem in place. Blot excess with damp cloth. Apply light pressure with fingers or use straight pins to hold. Glue dries in five minutes.

Six Ways to Repair a Hem

Fusible web is available by the yard or in precut strips. By the yard it is more economical, but you'll need to cut it into strips ½" to ¾" (1.3 to 2 cm) wide for hemming. Apply web strips between two layers of fabric. Steam press with damp press cloth as directed on package.

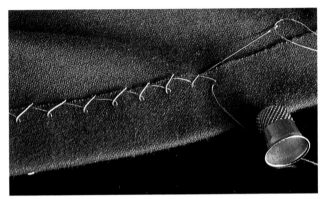

Blindstitch a pinked, overedged or seam-taped hem. Work from right to left. Roll hem edge back about ¼" (6 mm). Take a tiny stitch in the garment. Take next stitch in hem ¼" to ½" (6 mm to 1.3 cm) to left of first stitch. Continue alternating stitches. Keep stitches in garment small and do not pull too tightly.

Replace worn and frayed seam binding on fabrics that ravel. Lap seam binding ¼" (6 mm) over hem edge on right side of fabric. Straight-stitch binding in place, overlapping ends at a seamline. Hem by hand, using blindstitch.

Catchstitch hems on knits and heavy fabrics to provide give, and to hold hem edge flat to garment. Work from left to right. Take a small horizontal stitch in hem edge. Take next stitch in garment, about ¼" (6 mm) to right, crossing the stitches.

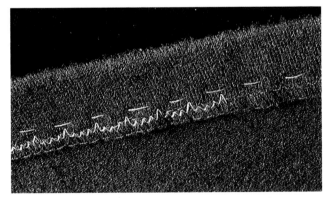

Machine blindstitch for sturdy hems. Baste hem to garment ¼" (6 mm) from raw edge. Adjust machine to blindstitch setting, and attach blindstitch foot or zigzag foot with hemming guide. Place hem face down and fold garment back to basting line. Stitch close to the fold, catching garment only in wide zigzag stitch. Press flat.

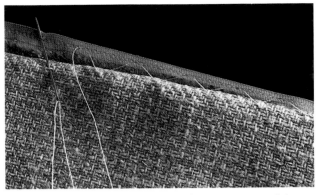

Straight-stitch to hem and finish raw edge in one step, or to add decorative detail. Turn up hem 1½" (3.8 cm) and pin in place. For ravelly fabrics, pink or turn under raw edge. On right side, topstitch 1" (2.5 cm) from folded edge. As a design detail, add a second or third row of stitching.

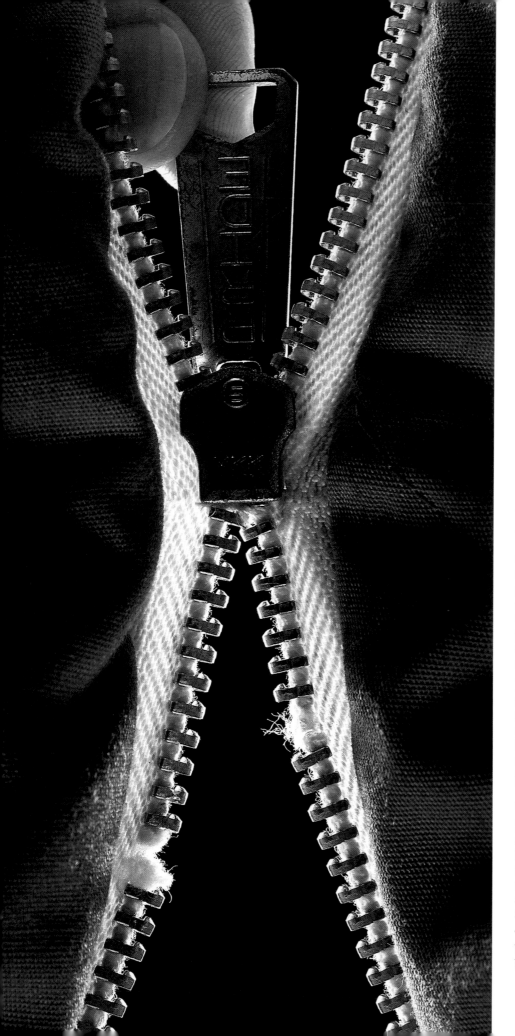

Zipper Repairs

Knowing how to replace a broken zipper can extend the life of many favorite garments. It is easy to replace a zipper because the original folds and stitching lines are already in position to guide every step.

The most common zipper ailments are teeth or coils that break in the middle of the zipper chain and sliders and pull tabs that separate from the zipper. These mishaps usually need a complete zipper replacement.

A zipper may break because it is not strong enough for its use or the fabric. Although coil zippers are lightweight and flexible, a metal or brass zipper may stand up better for heavy-duty wear.

Often the bottom of a separating zipper pulls loose from the garment. This can be repaired by replacing the stitching. Use thread that matches the color of the garment. As a reinforcement, stitch a bar tack at the bottom of the zipper (page 241).

Lengthening the zipper opening may be to your advantage. Most skirts and pants use 7" (18 cm) zippers, but an 8" or 9" (20.5 or 23 cm) zipper may provide just enough extra length to make the garment easier to get on and off. This will prevent putting too much strain on the bottom stop.

If metal zippers stick, rub beeswax or wax candle stub on the teeth to lubricate them. If metal teeth have rusted, place a drop of rust-eroding fluid on the rusted spot. Use paper towels under the zipper to absorb excess fluid.

To save wear and tear on the bottom stop, always close zippers before laundering and drycleaning.

Three Basic Steps to Replacing a Zipper

1) Remove zipper stitching with a seam ripper or point of sharp scissors, one or two stitches at a time. To avoid cutting fabric, do not slide seam ripper along seam. Also remove any stitching and fasteners that will interfere with zipper stitching.

2) Use a replacement zipper as similar as possible to original in color, weight and length. Preshrink zipper tape by soaking zipper in hot water for 30 minutes. Allow to air dry. Press tape with cool iron. Do not press over teeth.

3) Baste zipper in place with hand basting, pins, glue stick or basting tape. To machine-stitch close to zipper teeth, use zipper foot, which adjusts to either side of needle. Follow original stitching lines. Press lightly from right side, using a press cloth.

Two Ways to Shorten a Zipper

Shorten a zipper from top or bottom. Measure and mark correct length on longer zipper. Most zippers can be shortened from bottom. Fly-front and separating zippers are shortened from top to maintain bottom stop.

From the bottom. Line up tab of new zipper with tab of original. Zigzag or whipstitch several times over coil or teeth to form new bottom stop. Trim off excess zipper ½" (1.3 cm) below stitching.

From the top. Insert zipper before shortening, leaving excess zipper tape above opening. With zipper open, stitch across both ends of tape on original stitching line. Trim off excess zipper tape ½" (1.3 cm) above stitching line.

Replacing Lapped & Centered Zippers

Lightweight zippers are usually inserted with a lapped or centered application. The lapped zipper has a wide overlap on one side which covers the zipper teeth, and an underlap stitched close to the zipper teeth on the other side. A centered zipper is sewn in a seam with equal folds of fabric on each side of the zipper.

Zippers may be inserted by hand or machine. Although machine stitching is more durable, hand stitching may be preferred for velvets and other specialty fabrics that are more difficult to work with. The tiny stitches on the outside of the garment may look fragile, but the long stitches on the underside of the garment are strong and secure enough to hold a zipper in place, provided the closure is not subject to a lot of stress or heavy use.

How to Insert a Zipper by Hand

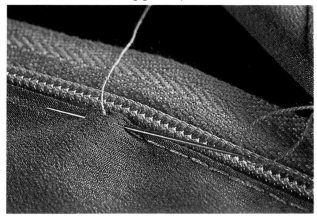

1) **Follow** basic directions for replacing a lapped or centered zipper, opposite. After basting zipper in place, thread a fine needle with double all-purpose thread, silk thread or single strand of buttonhole twist; knot. Run thread over beeswax or white candle stub to strengthen and prevent tangling. Replace machine stitching with backstitch on underlap.

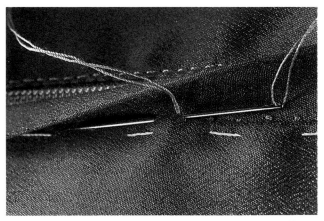

2) **Prickstitch** overlap. To prickstitch, bring needle through fabric to right side just below bottom stop. Insert needle two to three threads behind this point; bring it up ⅛" to ¼" (3 to 6 mm) in front of first stitch. Continue to top of zipper. Stitches on surface show as very small pricks.

How to Replace a Lapped Zipper

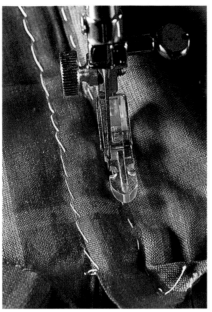

1) Baste zipper to underlap with teeth close to folded edge and bottom stop of zipper at seam opening. Attach zipper foot and adjust to left side of needle. Starting at bottom of zipper, stitch through underlap and zipper tape.

2) Baste overlap edge to stitching on underlap. Then baste other side of zipper in place just outside original stitching. Adjust zipper foot to right side of needle. Starting at bottom, stitch across and up on original stitching line.

3) Tuck zipper tape into the waistband or facing. Replace any stitching that was removed from waistband or facing using all-purpose presser foot.

How to Replace a Centered Zipper

1) Open zipper. Position bottom stop at bottom of seam opening. Baste one side of zipper to one side of opening, positioning zipper teeth under folded edge so they are just covered. Close zipper.

2) Whipstitch edges together at center of zipper. Baste other side of zipper in place. Adjust zipper foot to right side of needle. Starting at top of zipper, stitch down one side, across bottom and up other side on original stitching lines.

3) Remove whipstitches. Tuck zipper tape into waistband or under facing. Align waistband or facing evenly on both sides. Restitch in place.

Replacing Separating & Fly-front Zippers

Several methods are used for inserting separating and fly-front zippers, so it is important to examine the original method of insertion closely before ripping out a zipper. Try to replace the zipper when you have uninterrupted sewing time available. It is easy to forget the order of the steps when there is a time lapse between work periods.

When replacing a separating zipper, remove the stitching from one side at a time. Then you will still have part of the original insertion in place to use as a guide for replacing linings and facings.

Note that in the fly-front zipper application the overlap side of the zipper is stitched to a facing, not to the garment. Topstitching holds the facing and zipper in place. On the right front of boys' pants, an extension may be a separate piece or cut in one piece with the garment and folded back. When a separate extension is used, the zipper is inserted between the extension and the outside of the pants, so only the zipper teeth are visible. When the extension is folded back, the zipper tape is stitched on top of it.

These instructions show the left fly front lapping over the right front as in boys' pants. On girl's pants, the fly may lap the other direction.

How to Replace a Separating Zipper

 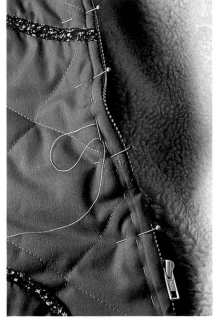 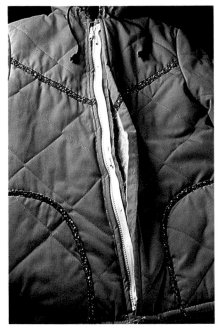

1) Separate zipper. Place one side of zipper between jacket and facing with zipper tab toward outside of garment. Baste tape to facing only. Using zipper foot, stitch zipper to facing on basting line.

2) Pin jacket front over zipper. To hold securely for stitching, baste through all thicknesses. Using zipper foot, stitch on original zipper stitching line.

3) Zip both sides of zipper together to align jacket edges. Pin second side of zipper tape to facing; stitch, following steps 1 and 2, left. For added reinforcement, place a short bar tack across bottom of each zipper tape.

How to Replace a Fly-front Zipper

1) Mark overlap topstitching line with transparent tape or washable marking pen before removing zipper stitching. Remove top-stitching. On inside, mark along edge of zipper tape for placement of new zipper. Remove zipper.

2) Open out facing on overlap. Baste zipper tape to facing along marked line on inside. Using zipper foot, stitch next to zipper teeth. Stitch again, ¼" (6 mm) from first row for reinforcement.

3) Open zipper. Pin folded edge of underlap over other side of zipper with fold along zipper teeth. Close zipper to check that it lies flat. Baste extension back in original position. Stitch through all thicknesses.

4) Shorten zipper from top, if necessary. Open zipper tab. Cut off top of zipper tapes ½" (1.3 cm) above original waistband stitching line. Tuck top ends into waistband. Replace waistband stitching.

5) Fold underlap extension back so it is out of the way. Using an all-purpose presser foot, replace topstitching on overlap side. Be careful not to catch extension in stitching line.

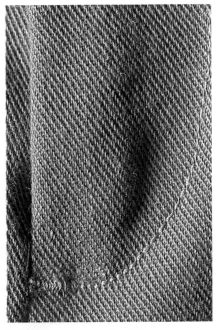

6) Replace bar tacks. Use narrow, closely spaced zigzag stitch ¼" to ½" (6 mm to 1.3 cm) long, directly below zipper stop. Be careful not to hit stop with needle. Bar tack may also be placed inside to hold facing and extension together.

Special Projects

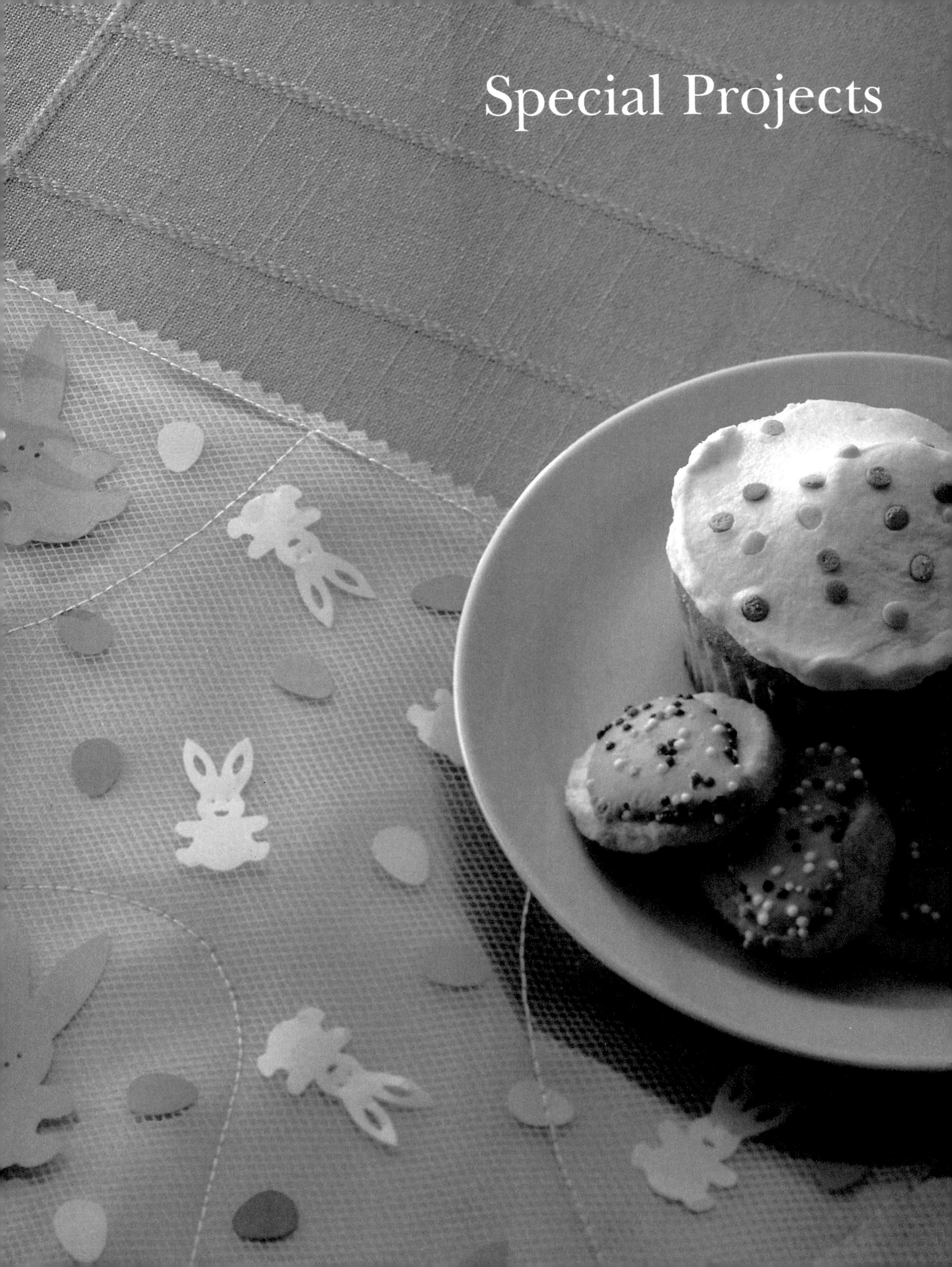

Cookie-cutter Ornaments

Cookie cutters provide a variety of shapes to be used as patterns for tree ornaments. To make the patterns, simply trace around the cookie cutters and add ¼" (6 mm) seam allowances. Stitch the ornaments wrong sides together and leave the seams exposed for a homespun look.

Make the ornaments from cotton or cotton-blend fabrics. Add decorative details to the ornaments with fabric paints in fine-tip tubes. Hand-paint your own designs or follow the imprints of plastic or metal cookie cutters as a guide for painting the details.

For best results in painting, prewash the fabrics to remove sizing. Practice painting on a scrap of fabric before painting on the ornaments to perfect the painting techniques. To keep the paint flow even, tap the tip of the bottle gently on the table to eliminate air bubbles. Wipe the tip of the bottle often while painting, to prevent paint buildup. If the tip becomes clogged, squeeze the tube to force paint through the tip onto a sheet of paper or a paper towel. If necessary, remove the cap and unclog the tip with a toothpick or needle.

✂ Cutting Directions

Make the patterns as on page 246, step 1. For each ornament, cut two pieces of fabric, wrong sides together.

YOU WILL NEED

Scraps of cotton fabric in desired colors.
Polyester fiberfill.
9" (23 cm) length of ribbon or cording, for hanger.
Fabric paints in fine-tip tubes, for decorating ornaments.

How to Make a Cookie-cutter Ornament

1) Transfer cookie-cutter design to paper by tracing around cookie cutter with a pencil; add ¼" (6 mm) seam allowances.

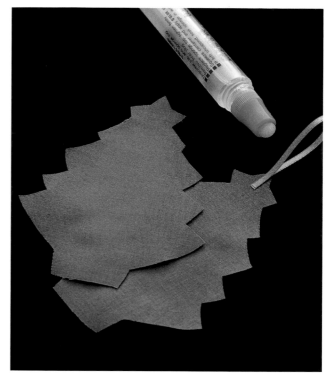

2) Cut fabric pieces for ornaments as on page 245. Fold ribbon in half to make hanger; glue-baste to top of ornament as shown.

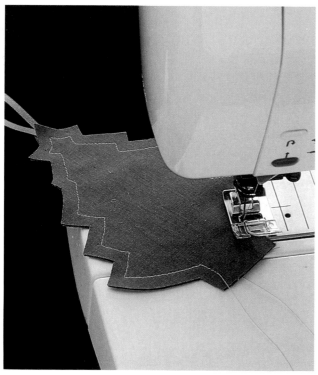

3) Place the fabric pieces *wrong* sides together; pin. Stitch ¼" (6 mm) from raw edges, using short stitch length; leave 1" (2.5 cm) opening for stuffing.

4) Stuff ornament with polyester fiberfill; use eraser end of a pencil to push stuffing into smaller areas.

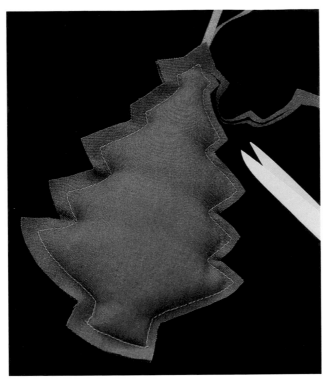

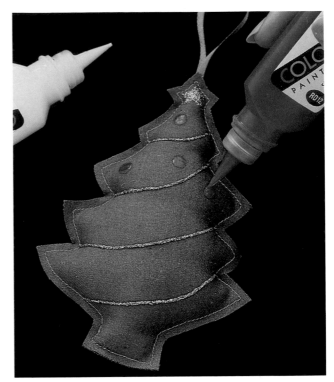

5) Stitch opening closed, using a zipper foot. Trim seam allowance to ⅛" (3 mm), taking care not to trim off hanger.

6) Add painted details to the ornaments as desired, using fabric paints.

Tips for Making Cookie-cutter Ornaments

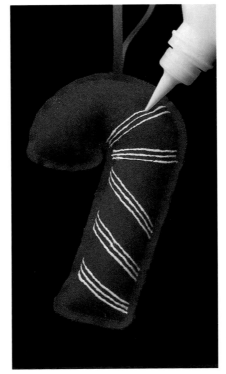

Mark stitching lines lightly with pencil or chalk when the seam allowances overlap.

Paint details on ornaments, using paint tube as a pencil; keep point on fabric while painting to get the finest line.

Trim around the ornament, using pinking shears, if desired, for a decorative edge finish.

Ornaments from Fabric Cutouts

Designs cut from some printed fabrics can be used to make two styles of tree ornaments: a basic cutout ornament and an appliquéd cutout ornament. Both styles are stitched and turned and have cutout designs on one or both sides.

Make basic cutout ornaments using a fabric cutout for the front of the ornament and a solid or coordinating fabric for the back. Or, for symmetrical designs, cut two motifs that are alike and use one for the front of the ornament and one for the back. The shapes of the basic cutout ornaments follow the outline of the cutout designs.

The appliquéd cutout ornaments are cut to simple shapes like rectangles, circles, stars, and Christmas stockings, with the cutout designs used as appliqués. A cup, glass, or cookie cutter may be used as a template for the simple shapes. The cutout designs are fused to the ornaments before the ornaments are stuffed.

How to Sew a Basic Cutout Ornament

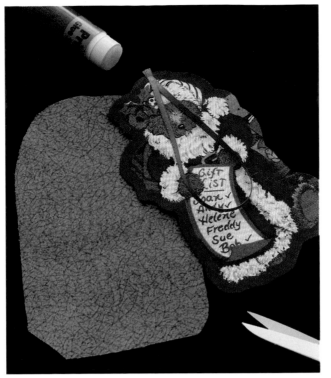

1) Cut design for ornament front from printed fabric, cutting ¼" (6 mm) outside the edge of design. Cut a piece of solid or coordinating fabric slightly larger than design, for ornament back. Baste ends of ribbon to upper edge on right side of design.

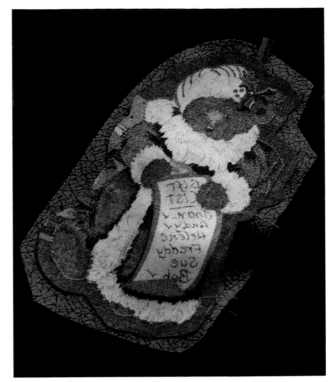

2) Pin front to back, right sides together. Stitch close to outer edge of design, about ¼" (6 mm) from raw edge, using short stitch length. Leave about 2" (5 cm) opening for turning.

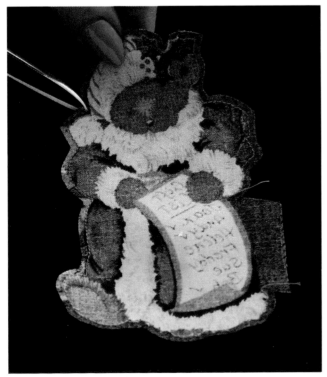

3) Trim close to stitching, clipping as necessary. Turn ornament right side out; press lightly.

4) Stuff ornament with polyester fiberfill. Hand-stitch opening closed.

Christmas Countdown Wall Hangings

Count down the days to Christmas with a Christmas tree wall hanging. Move one miniature ornament from the background to the tree each day beginning December 1 so the tree will be completely decorated by Christmas.

For body, the wall hanging is constructed with a layer of fleece or batting between the front and the back fabric layers. The Christmas tree is appliquéd to the front using a machine satin-stitch. Buttons, stitched to the tree and the background, serve two purposes; they hold the layers together, giving a quilted look, and also hold the ornaments in place.

Hang ornaments in the background area until they are ready to be used on the tree. Display the wall hanging from a rod or dowel, using the tabs across the top.

✂ Cutting Directions

Cut one 26" (66 cm) square each from muslin and fleece or batting.

Cut one 20½" (52.3 cm) square from the fabric for the background.

Cut two 2½" × 20½" (6.5 × 52.3 cm) rectangles from the border fabric, for the upper and lower borders; cut two 2½" × 24½" (6.5 × 62.3 cm) rectangles from the border fabric, for the sides.

Make the pattern for the tree as on page 252, step 1; cut one tree from fabric.

Cut one 2½" × 3" (6.5 × 7.5 cm) rectangle from the fabric for the trunk.

Cut one 24½" (62.3 cm) square from the backing fabric.

Cut four 2½" × 4½" (6.5 × 11.5 cm) rectangles from the border fabric, for the tabs.

YOU WILL NEED

⅔ yd. (0.63 m) fabric, for background.

⅓ yd. (0.32 m) fabric, for border.

½ yd. (0.5 m) fabric, for tree.

¾ yd. (0.7 m) muslin.

¾ yd. (0.7 m) fabric, for backing.

¾ yd. (0.7 m) fleece or batting.

Tear-away stabilizer.

Scrap of fabric for tree trunk.

Forty-eight buttons.

Twenty-four miniature tree ornaments, about 1" (2.5 cm) long.

One star ornament or button, for top of tree.

1" (2.5 cm) grid, such as cutting mat or graph paper.

Rod or dowel, up to ½" (1.3 cm) in diameter.

Diagram for the Tree

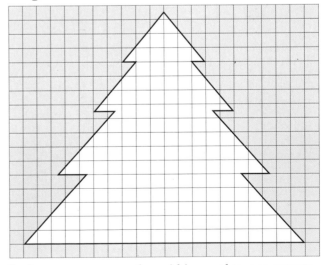

Scale: one square on the grid is equal to one square inch (2.5 sq. cm).

How to Sew a Christmas Countdown Wall Hanging

1) **Place** tracing paper over a 1" (2.5 cm) grid, such as a cutting mat. Make a full-size pattern for the tree, using diagram (page 251); enlarge tree, using grid lines as a guide. Cut the tree from fabric.

2) **Center** the 3" (7.5 cm) width of trunk on background fabric at lower edge; secure with glue stick. Satin stitch sides of trunk to background as on pages 210 and 211.

3) **Center** tree on fabric, over trunk, 2¼" (6 cm) above the lower edge; secure with pins or glue stick. Satin stitch tree to background.

4) **Place** muslin square on the work surface; cover with fleece. Center the background fabric over fleece. Pin-baste layers together.

5) **Pin** around the tree through all layers. Stitch around outer edge of tree along satin stitching, to define outline of tree.

6) **Pin** the upper and lower border strips to background fabric, right sides together; stitch ¼" (6 mm) from edges through all layers. Turn borders right side up; pin to fleece and muslin layers.

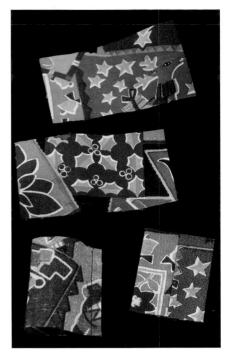

7) Repeat step 6 for the side border strips. Baste close to outer edges of border through all layers. Trim off excess batting and muslin.

8) Secure star ornament or button to top of tree. Stitch 24 buttons to background and 24 buttons to tree, spacing them evenly.

9) Fold one tab in half, right sides together; stitch ¼" (6 mm) seam along edge opposite fold. Turn tab right side out; press, centering the seam on back of tab. Repeat for remaining tabs.

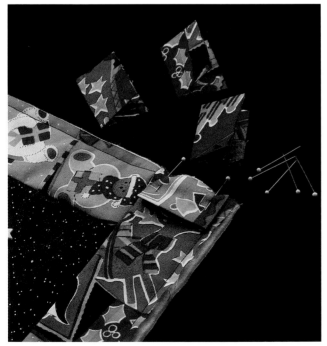

10) Fold tabs in half, with seams to inside, matching raw edges; press. Pin tabs to upper edge on right side of wall hanging front, placing one tab ¼" (6 mm) from each side and spacing remaining tabs evenly across the top; baste.

11) Pin wall hanging front to backing fabric, right sides together. Stitch ¼" (6 mm) from raw edges, leaving 12" (30.5 cm) opening for turning; trim the corners. Turn the wall hanging right side out; press. Slipstitch opening closed.

Pieced Stockings with Appliqués

Brightly colored pieced stockings, with simple appliqué designs, are especially appealing to children. These large stockings made from wool melton or felt are easy to sew. For more body, the felt stocking has an additional layer of felt fused to the front, cuff, and hanger pieces.

Find inspiration for the simple appliqué designs in a children's coloring book, or trace around a cookie cutter. A basic appliqué pattern for a snowflake can be made by folding a 5" (12.5 cm) circle of paper into quarters and making notches along the edges. Straight stitching around the appliqués holds them in place. The cuff and hanger of the stocking are edged with a blanket stitch.

✂ Cutting Directions

For a wool melton stocking, make the full-size pattern below. Cut one stocking back from fabric, with the right side of the fabric facing down. Cut fabric scraps into a variety of shapes for the pieced stocking front. Cut the stocking front from the pieced fabric section, right side up, after completing step 1 on page 256. Cut the desired appliqué designs from scraps of fabric. Cut one 6½" × 20" (16.3 × 51 cm) rectangle

for the stocking cuff and one 1" × 8" (2.5 × 20.5 cm) rectangle for the stocking hanger.

For a felt stocking, make the full-size pattern below. Cut two stocking pieces, right sides together, from felt and one piece from fusible web. Cut felt scraps into a variety of shapes for the pieced stocking front. Cut two 6½" × 20" (16.3 × 51 cm) rectangles from felt and one from fusible web for the stocking cuff, and two 1" × 8" (2.5 × 20.5 cm) rectangles from felt and one from fusible web for the stocking hanger.

YOU WILL NEED

¾ yd. (0.7 m) wool melton, for stocking back; or **¾ yd. (0.7 m) felt,** for stocking back and front underlining.

¼ yd. (0.25 m) wool melton or felt, for contrasting cuff.

1¼ yd. (1.15 m) lightweight fusible web, for felt stocking.

Scraps of wool melton or felt, for stocking front, appliqués, and stocking hanger.

Tear-away stabilizer, for wool melton stocking.

Pearl cotton or rayon thread, for blanket-stitch edging.

How to Make a Full-size Pattern for a Pieced Stocking with Appliqués

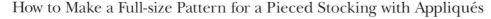

1) Enlarge partial pattern piece (page 258) by about 130 percent on a photocopy machine. Trace enlarged partial pattern onto tissue paper. Draw a line parallel to, and 13½" (34.3 cm) above, dotted line to mark upper edge of stocking. Align quilter's ruler to dotted line at side; mark point on line for upper edge. Repeat for other side.

2) Measure out ½" (1.3 cm) from marked points; mark. Connect outer points at upper edge to sides at ends of dotted line. Add ½" (1.3 cm) seam allowances to make full-size stocking pattern.

How to Make a Pieced Stocking with Appliqués from Wool Melton

1) Butt the edges of fabric scraps for stocking front; place tear-away stabilizer under the scraps. Zigzag scraps together, using wide, closely spaced zigzag stitches. Remove the stabilizer. Cut stocking front as on page 254.

2) Glue-baste or pin appliqués to the stocking front; straight-stitch ⅛" (3 mm) from all edges of appliqués.

3) Pin stocking front to stocking back, right sides together. Stitch ½" (1.3 cm) seam, leaving top open. Stitch again next to first row of stitching, within seam allowances. Trim close to stitches. Turn stocking right side out; press lightly.

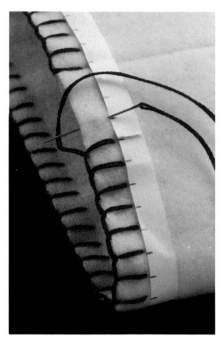

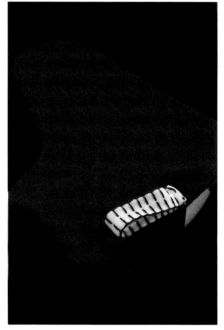

4) Fold cuff in half crosswise, right sides together. Stitch ½" (1.3 cm) seam. Stitch along the lower edge of cuff and long edges of hanger, using blanket stitch, opposite. Tape marked at ⅜" (1 cm) intervals may be used as a guide for stitching.

5) Fold the stocking hanger in half, wrong sides together. At back seam, baste stocking hanger to upper edge of stocking on the wrong side.

6) Place the right side of cuff on wrong side of stocking, matching back seams; pin along upper edge. Stitch ½" (1.3 cm) seam. Turn cuff to right side; press lightly.

How to Make a Pieced Stocking with Appliqués from Felt

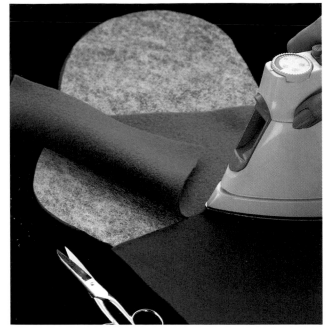

1) Cut stocking pieces as on page 254. Butt edges of felt scraps, and fuse to stocking front, using fusible web; follow manufacturer's directions for fusing. Zigzag over butted edges, using wide, closely spaced zigzag stitches. Trim felt scraps to match outline of stocking.

2) Fuse the cuff pieces and hanger pieces together, using fusible web. Complete stocking as in steps 2 to 6, opposite.

How to Blanket-stitch

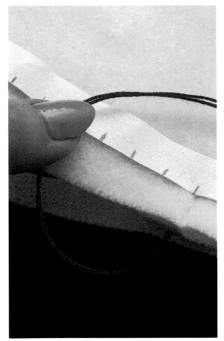

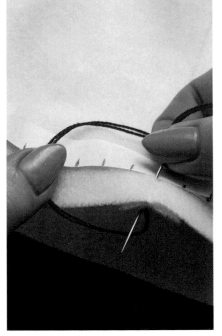

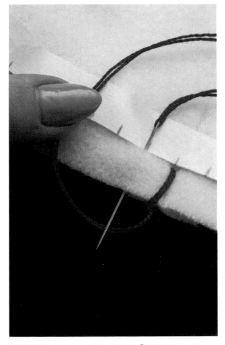

1) Take two short backstitches at lower edge of fabric, within seam allowance, to secure the thread. Form a loop at edge of fabric by bringing thread to left and then right as shown; hold loop with left thumb.

2) Insert needle to underside ½" (1.3 cm) from edge of fabric, then through loop as shown. Pull needle through fabric; release thumb from loop, then pull stitch tight.

3) Make second stitch ⅜" (1 cm) from first stitch as in steps 1 and 2; work stitches from right to left. Tape marked at ⅜" (1 cm) intervals may be used as a guide for stitching.

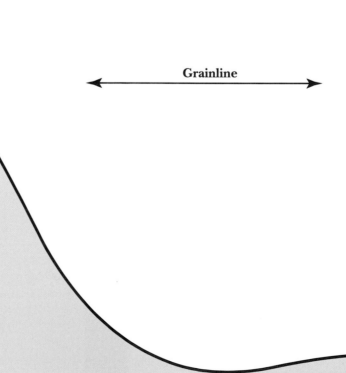

Stocking
Add ¹/₂" (1.3 cm) seam allowance

Grainline

Projects for Easter

Easter offers several opportunities to sew for children. To involve children in decorating for Easter, make several ornaments that they can hang from an Easter tree. And sew confetti placemats for a child's egg-hunting party.

Or follow the instructions on the following pages for Easter baskets trimmed with ribbons and an old-fashioned Easter rabbit.

Cookie-cutter ornaments (page 245) hang from an Easter tree. Embellish the ornaments with fabric paints in fine-tip tubes.

Confetti placemats (page 269) are perfect for a child's party. The placemats are filled with plastic bunnies and eggs.

Easter Baskets

Decorate a wicker basket for Easter by covering it
with bows of various sizes and colors. Or embellish
an open-weave basket by weaving in ribbons and
adding one large bow.

Use satin, organza, or velvet ribbon in various widths.
Wired ribbons work well because they are easily
shaped. Use purchased wired ribbon or make your
own as on pages 261 to 262. Strips of tulle may be
used instead of ribbon. Secure the bows and the
ribbon to the baskets with wire or hot glue.

YOU WILL NEED

Bow-covered basket:

Basket.

Ribbons, such as satin, organza, or velvet.

Hot glue gun and glue sticks or fine-gauge paddle
floral wire and wire cutter.

Woven ribbon basket:

Open-weave basket.

Ribbons, such as satin, organza, or velvet.

Fine-gauge paddle floral wire and wire cutter.

How to Make Wired Ribbon Using the Zigzag Stitch on a Conventional Sewing Machine

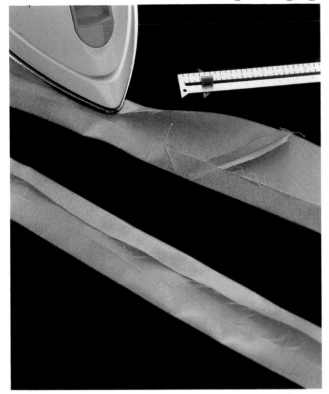

1) **Piece** fabric strips on the bias as necessary, stitching narrow seams. Press under ½" (1.3 cm) on long edges of fabric strip.

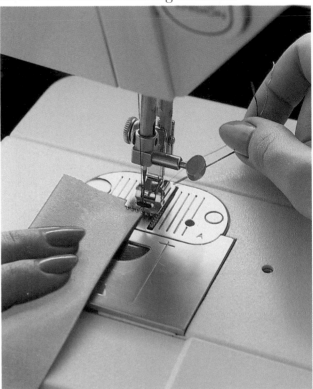

2) **Insert** beading wire into fold on the edge of fabric strip Position folded edge of fabric strip under the presser foot; hold threads and wire firmly.

3) **Encase** wire by stitching over edge of fold, using narrow, closely spaced zigzag stitch. Repeat on the opposite side of the fabric strip.

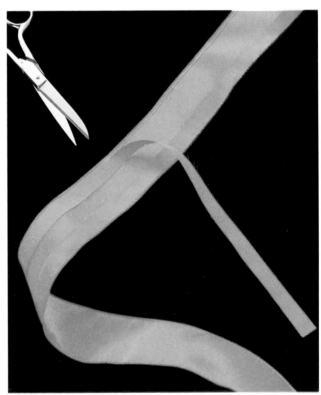

4) **Trim** excess fabric from the underside of ribbon, using small, sharp scissors.

How to Make a Wired Ribbon Using the Rolled Hem Stitch on a Serger

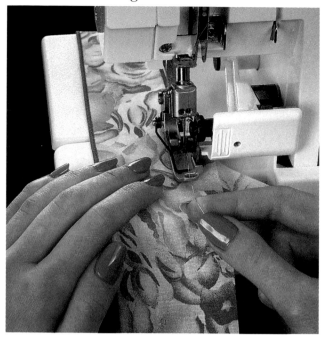

1) Piece fabric strips on the bias as necessary, stitching narrow seams. Adjust serger for rolled hem stitch. Stitch along strip for 2" (5 cm), trimming scant ½" (1.3 cm); stop, and lift presser foot. Place beading wire under back of foot, then over front; lower the presser foot.

2) Hold wire to the right of needle. Stitch over wire, trimming excess fabric; stitches roll to underside.

How to Make a Wired Ribbon Using the 3-thread Overlock Stitch on a Serger

1) Piece fabric strips on the bias as necessary, stitching narrow seams. Adjust serger for balanced 3-thread stitch. Stitch along strip for 2" (5 cm), trimming a scant ½" (1.3 cm); stop, and lift presser foot. Place beading wire under back of foot, then over front; lower presser foot.

2) Hold wire to the right of needle. Stitch over wire, trimming excess fabric; threads lock together at the edge of fabric.

How to Decorate an Easter Basket with Bows Using the Wire Method

1) Tie ribbon into bows; trim ends as desired. Insert wire through loop in center of bow on the back side. Twist ends of wire tightly to secure.

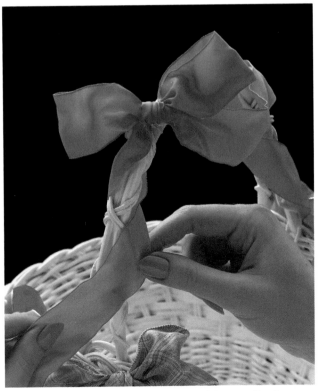

2) Insert ends of wire into basket from the outside, placing wire into different holes of basket.

3) Secure ends of the wire by twisting them together on inside of basket. Trim excess wire; bend twisted ends downward.

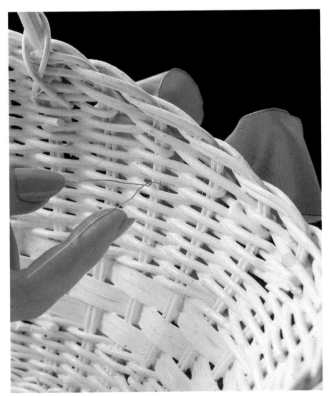

4) Tie bow for handle; leave long ribbon tails. Secure bow to handle with wire; wrap tails around handle.

Old-fashioned Easter Rabbits

Sew a nostalgic Easter rabbit with cut-on arms and legs. The simple pattern can be easily made, using the partial pattern pieces on page 267. The hand-embroidered facial details and covered-button tail add to the old-fashioned quality of the rabbit. For durability, choose a textured wool, wool flannel, decorator cotton, or corduroy. For a dressier look, select fabrics such as velveteen or brocade. Tie a contrasting ribbon bow around the neck of the rabbit for an additional embellishment.

Embroider the nose, mouth, whiskers, and outer two lines marked for the eyes, using an outlining stitch, and fill in the centers of the eyes, using a satin stitch. Three strands of embroidery floss are used for both embroidery stitches.

✄ Cutting Directions

Trace the partial pattern pieces (page 267) and make the full-size rabbit pattern as in step 1, below. Cut the front and back pieces from fabric, placing the center dotted line on the fold.

YOU WILL NEED

⅝ **yd. (0.6 m) fabric,** such as velveteen, brocade, chintz, wool, or corduroy.

Embroidery floss, for embroidered facial details.

Polyester fiberfill.

Button kit, for 1⅛" (2.8 cm) button, to be covered for tail.

Pinking shears, optional.

How to Sew an Old-fashioned Easter Rabbit

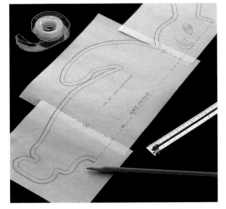

1) Trace the partial pattern pieces (page 267) onto tracing paper. Make full-size pattern by taping pieces A, B, and C together, matching notches and dotted lines. Add ¼" (6 mm) seam allowances.

2) Cut front and back pieces from fabric, above. Transfer the pattern markings for eyes, nose, mouth, and whiskers onto the right side of rabbit front. Transfer placement mark for tail onto rabbit back. Embroider facial details as on page 266.

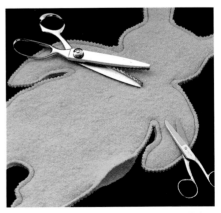

3) Pin rabbit front to rabbit back, right sides together. Stitch around rabbit, leaving 3" (7.5 cm) opening on one side. Clip seam allowances along curves. Or notch outer curves using pinking shears, and clip the inner curves with scissors.

(Continued on next page)

How to Sew an Old-fashioned Easter Rabbit (continued)

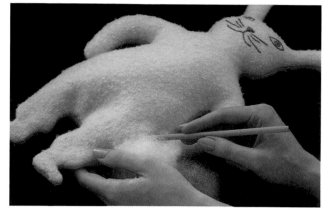

4) Turn rabbit right side out; stuff with polyester fiberfill until plump. Push fiberfill into ears, arms, and feet with the eraser end of a pencil. Hand-stitch opening closed.

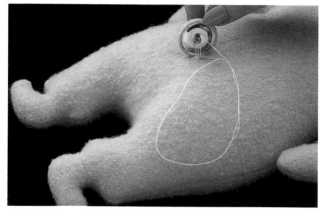

5) Cover the button for tail with fabric, following the manufacturer's directions. Hand-stitch to back of rabbit at tail placement mark.

How to Embroider the Facial Details

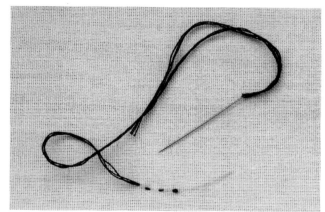

Outline stitch. 1) Secure threads by inserting needle along marked line about ½" (1.3 cm) to right of the starting point. Take short running stitches, as shown, until starting point is reached. Bring threaded needle through fabric from underside, at starting point.

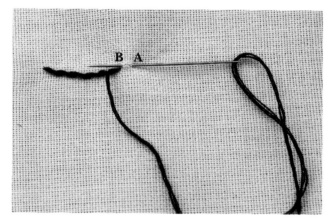

2) Take backstitches by inserting needle to underside at Point A and up a scant ⅛" (3 mm) away at Point B. Continue stitching along marked line to end. Secure threads on underside of fabric.

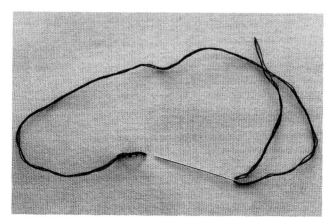

Satin stitch. 1) Secure the threads as in step 1, above. Bring needle through the fabric from underside on marked line. Insert needle on marked line directly opposite to make first stitch.

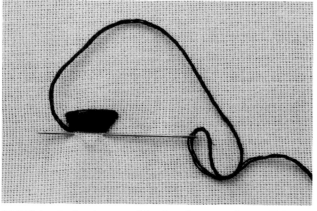

2) Fill in desired area with closely spaced parallel stitches. Secure threads on underside of fabric.

Pattern for an Old-fashioned Easter Rabbit

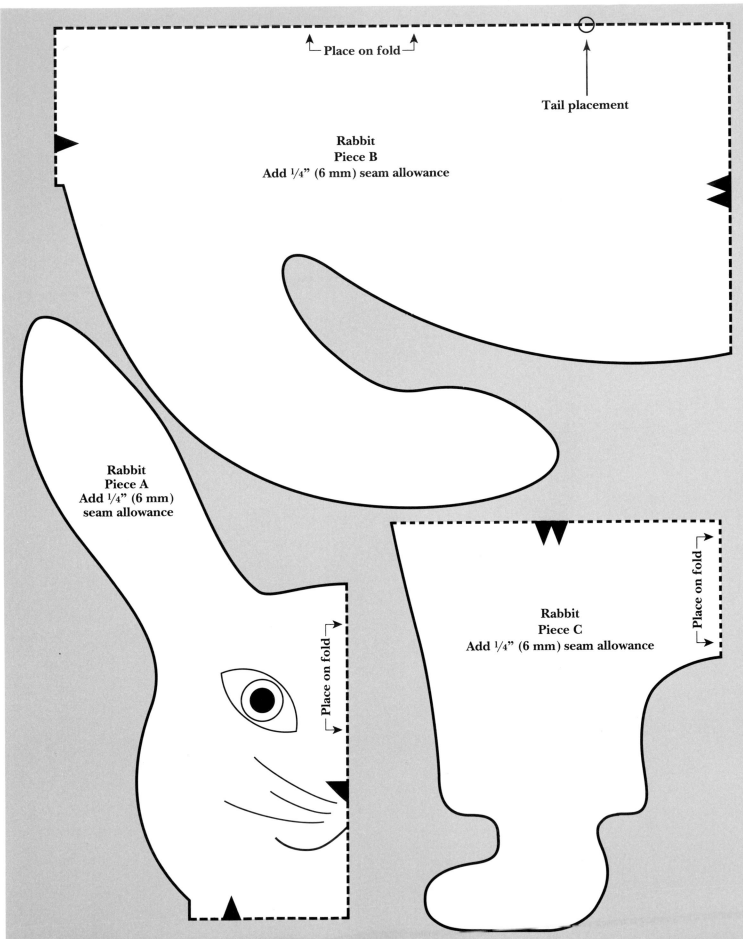

Place on fold

Tail placement

Rabbit
Piece B
Add ¼" (6 mm) seam allowance

Rabbit
Piece A
Add ¼" (6 mm)
seam allowance

Place on fold

Rabbit
Piece C
Add ¼" (6 mm) seam allowance

Place on fold

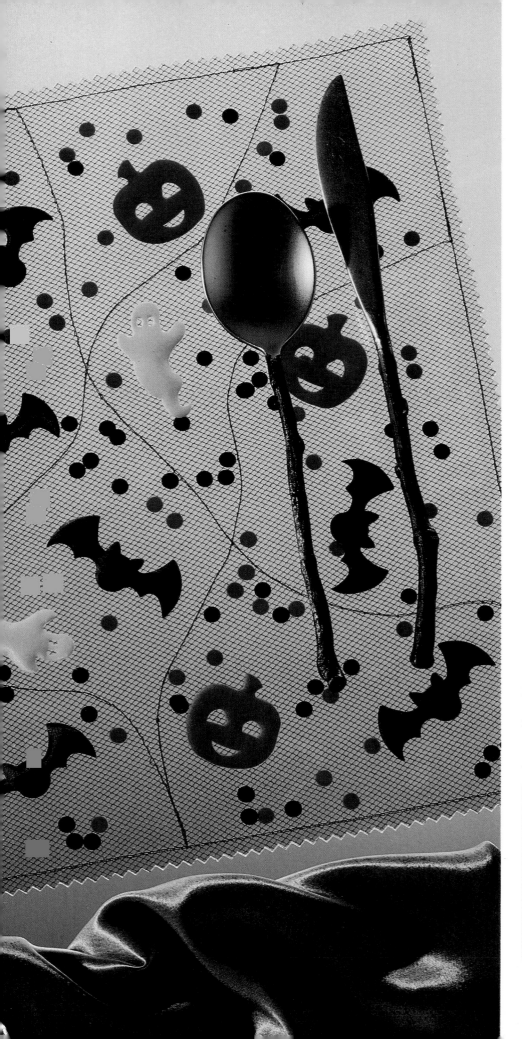

Confetti Placemats

Make durable confetti placemats for Halloween from two layers of clear vinyl, a layer of colored nylon net, and decorative holiday confetti. Small, flat Halloween decorations, like the jack o' lanterns, ghosts, and bats shown here, can be mixed with the confetti. Random rows of machine stitching divide the placemat into compartments.

For ease in stitching on vinyl, use a size 90/14 needle and a long stitch length. Loosen the needle thread tension, and stitch at a slow speed with a sheet of tissue paper under the placemat.

Look for seasonal plastic or metallic confetti in many shapes at craft and fabric stores as well as card and gift shops. The instructions that follow are for finished placemats that measure approximately 12" × 18" (30.5 × 46 cm).

✂ Cutting Directions

For each placemat, cut two 13½" × 19½" (34.3 × 49.8 cm) rectangles from vinyl and cut one 13" × 19" (33 × 48.5 cm) rectangle from net.

YOU WILL NEED

For four placemats:

1⅛ yd. (1.05 m) clear vinyl, 10-gauge or 12-gauge.

1⅛ yd. (1.05 m) of net, 36" (91.5 cm) wide.

Decorative metallic or plastic confetti or other small, flat decorations.

Pinking shears or scalloped scissors.

Spray adhesive.

How to Sew a Confetti Placemat

1) **Mark** a line on one piece of vinyl ¾" (2 cm) from each edge, using a permanent-ink marker.

2) **Place** the nylon net over a protected surface; apply spray adhesive lightly over net. Place confetti on net, at least 1" (2.5 cm) from edges; arrange as desired, pressing in place with finger.

3) **Position** the marked piece of vinyl over the net and confetti; smooth in place. Place vinyl and net over remaining vinyl piece; be sure any large air pockets are removed. Pin layers together outside marked line.

4) **Stitch** around placemat ¼" (6 mm) inside marked line; place tissue paper under placemat while stitching.

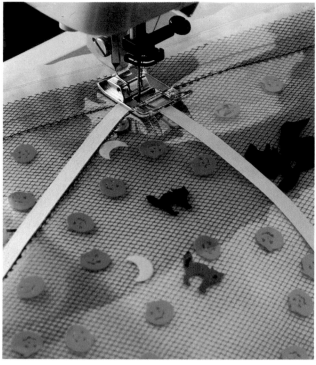

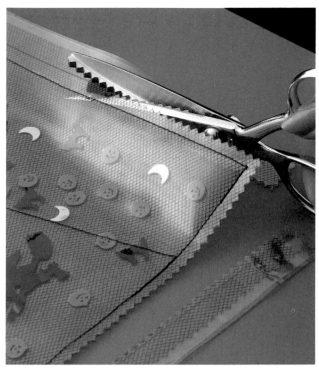

5) Stitch random rows across the placemat, dividing it into compartments; pivot fabric when possible for continuous stitching. Use tape as guide for stitching straight rows.

6) Remove tissue paper. Trim around all sides of the placemat inside marked lines, using pinking shears or scalloped scissors; cut through all layers.

Tips for Sewing Confetti Placemats

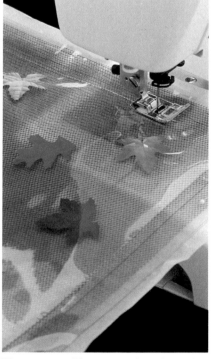

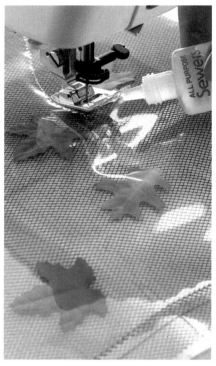

Cut plastic motifs from decorative wired garland, to mix with confetti when larger motifs are desired.

Use a monofilament nylon thread for stitching that is least visible.

Prevent presser foot from sticking to the vinyl by applying silicone lubricant frequently under front of presser foot.

Fabric Ghosts

Remnants of white fabric are used to create stiffened fabric ghosts. Quick and easy to make, these ghosts require little sewing and can be made in different sizes.

Plastic or glass beverage bottles are used to create a frame for supporting the fabric during assembly. A large ghost, about 16" (40.5 cm) tall, can be made using a 64-oz. (2 L) bottle and a balloon or Styrofoam® ball for the head. A smaller ghost can be made using a 16-oz. (0.5 L) bottle and a small Styrofoam ball.

For the best results, use lightweight to mediumweight fabrics of natural fibers, such as bleached cotton muslin, handkerchief linens, and cotton or cotton-blend batistes. The amount of fabric stiffener necessary to saturate the fabric varies with the weight and size of the fabric; ½ cup (125 mL) is enough for sheer fabrics and small pieces. Heavy fabrics and large pieces may require up to 1 cup (250 mL) of stiffener.

✂ Cutting Directions

Cut fabric square as on page 274, step 3. Cut two ½" (1.3 cm) fabric circles for eyes.

YOU WILL NEED

White fabric, such as bleached muslin, handkerchief linen, cotton and cotton-blend batiste.

Scrap of fabric, such as broadcloth, for eyes.

Fabric stiffener.

Aluminum foil, plastic wrap, masking tape, and cording.

Sheet of plastic, to cover work area.

Beverage bottle, 64-oz. (2 L), for large ghost; 16-oz. (0.5 L) bottle, for small ghost.

Balloon or 5" (12.5 cm) Styrofoam ball, for head of large ghost; balloon or 3" (7.5 cm) Styrofoam ball, for head of small ghost.

Embellishments, such as plastic or rubber spider or mouse.

Thick white craft glue, for securing embellishments.

How to Make a Fabric Ghost

1) **Cover** the work area with a sheet of plastic. Press Styrofoam® ball firmly over the top of bottle; cover loosely with plastic wrap (left). Or, blow up balloon to measure about 5" (12.5 cm) in diameter; secure to neck of bottle with masking tape (right).

2) **Form** arms by cutting a length of aluminum foil twice the desired arm length plus about 6" (15 cm); crumple strip lengthwise, and wrap center of strip around neck of bottle. Cover foil with plastic wrap.

3) **Measure** frame for ghost, using a tape measure, from base in front, over the top, to base at back of frame; add to this measurement 2" to 4" (5 to 10 cm), depending on desired amount of fabric puddle. Cut a square from fabric to this measurement.

4) **Narrow-hem** fabric square, if desired. Drape fabric over frame, and mark placement for eyes. Cut eyes from fabric as on page 272. Glue-baste eyes over the markings; satin stitch as on page 210.

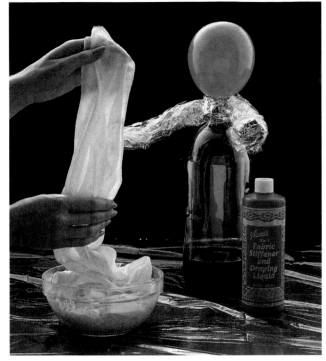

5) Pour fabric stiffener into bowl; dilute with water to a creamy consistency. Immerse fabric in stiffener; work stiffener into the fabric, making sure it is saturated. Remove fabric, squeezing out excess stiffener.

6) Drape the fabric, centering it over top of frame. Arrange the fabric in folds over arms. Using string, loosely tie fabric under head.

7) Press edges of fabric together at sides. Arrange fabric puddle, creating soft folds. Allow fabric and glue to dry completely.

8) Remove the bottle, plastic wrap, and foil, leaving Styrofoam head in place; if using balloon, pop and remove balloon. Attach embellishments as desired, using glue.

Puppy Bath Ponchos

Make this cuddly after-bath poncho for your child from two bath towels. The instructions that follow are for a puppy poncho. By changing the ears and facial features, you can make a poncho that looks like a bunny or a kitty. Prewash the towels and fabrics to preshrink them.

✂ Cutting Directions

From one towel, cut a 10"×22" (25.5×56 cm) rectangle for the hood, with one long edge along the selvage of the towel. From the same towel, cut two ear pieces and two foot pieces, using the patterns on page 283. From contrasting fabric, cut two ear pieces and two foot pieces. From scraps of black broadcloth, cut the pieces for the nose and eyes as on page 278, step 2.

YOU WILL NEED

Two bath towels, about 25"×50" (63.5×127 cm) in size.

¼ yd. (0.25 m) contrasting fabric, such as plaid or animal-print cotton flannel or broadcloth, for ears and feet.

Scraps of black broadcloth, for eyes and nose.

Paper-backed fusible web.

Tear-away stabilizer.

How to Sew a Puppy Bath Poncho

1) **Fold** hood piece in half along selvage. On the side opposite the selvage, use a saucer to round corner from fold to raw edges.

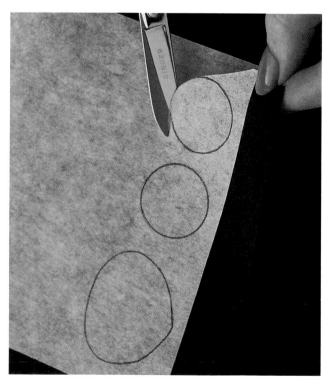

2) **Fuse** paper-backed fusible web to wrong side of black broadcloth; using patterns on page 282, trace eyes and nose onto paper side. Cut out pieces.

3) Remove the paper backing from the eyes and nose. Pin-mark center of hood at selvage. Following placement guide on page 282, fuse pieces to hood.

4) Set machine for satin stitching by adjusting zigzag stitch for closely spaced, wide stitches. Satin-stitch around eyes and nose, placing tear-away stabilizer under hood; satin-stitch the mouth as shown on the placement guide (page 282).

5) Place one ear piece from terry cloth and one from contrasting fabric right sides together. Stitch ⅜" (1 cm) seam around curved edge, leaving the straight end unstitched; clip curves. Turn right side out. Repeat for remaining ear and both feet.

6) Place one ear, contrasting side down, with straight end on placement line and with ear lying above face. Stitch in place along the open end, using wide, short zigzag stitches. Repeat for other ear.

(Continued on next page)

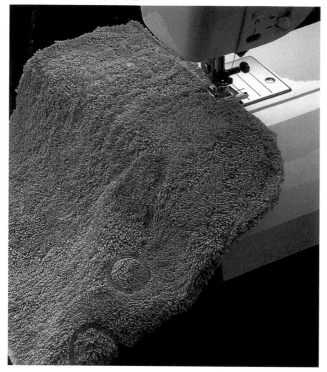

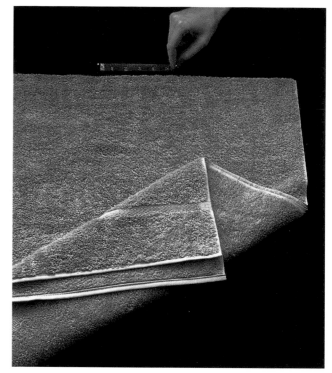

7) Fold the hood in half, with right sides together, matching raw edges. Stitch ⅜" (1 cm) center back seam on the curved side of the hood; finish seam, using zigzag or overlock stitch.

8) Fold remaining bath towel in half, with lower edge of top layer 1" (2.5 cm) above lower edge of bottom layer. Mark the center of the fold; on fold, measure and mark 5¼" (13.2 cm) on each side of center.

9) Unfold the bath towel. Slash the towel between the end markings, for a 10½" (27.8 cm) opening.

10) Pin the hood to the towel at opening, right sides together; match the center back seam of the hood to center marking on longer side of towel. Front edges of hood will not meet.

11) Stitch hood to body in ⅜" (1 cm) seam. Zigzag or overlock seam allowances together, continuing across the slash between edges of hood in front.

12) Fold seam allowances toward the body. Topstitch through all layers, ¼" (6 mm) from the seamline; continue stitching across the front opening.

13) Pin feet, contrasting sides down, to wrong side of towel front, at lower edge and 6" (15 cm) from sides; overlap edges ½" (1.3 cm).

14) Stitch, using short, wide zigzag stitches. Topstitch through all layers, ¼" (6 mm) from the lower edge of the towel.

Placement Guide and Patterns for a Puppy Bath Poncho

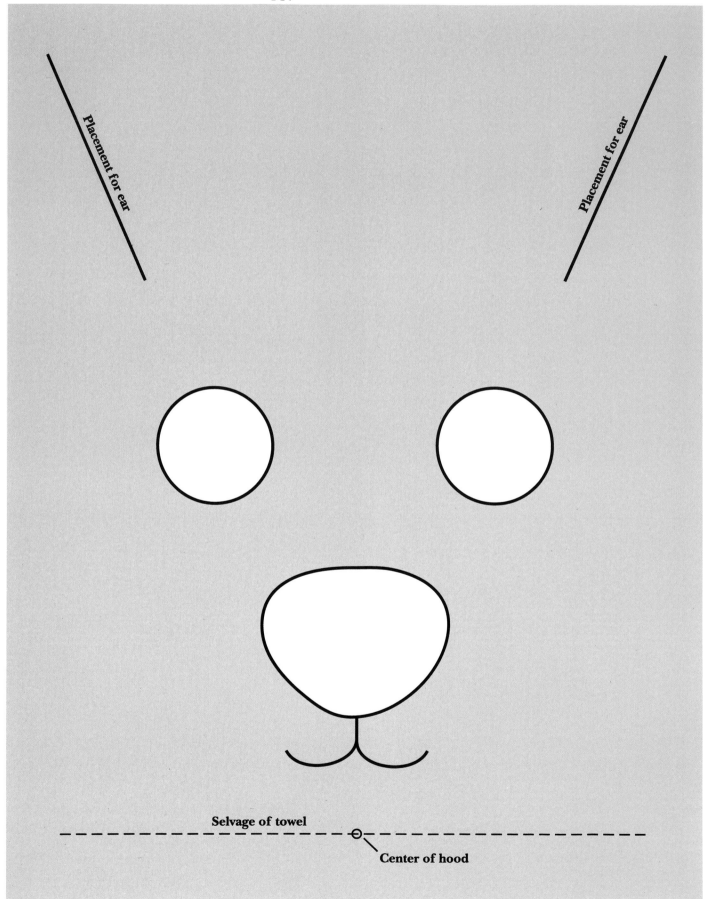

Placement for ear

Placement for ear

Selvage of towel

Center of hood

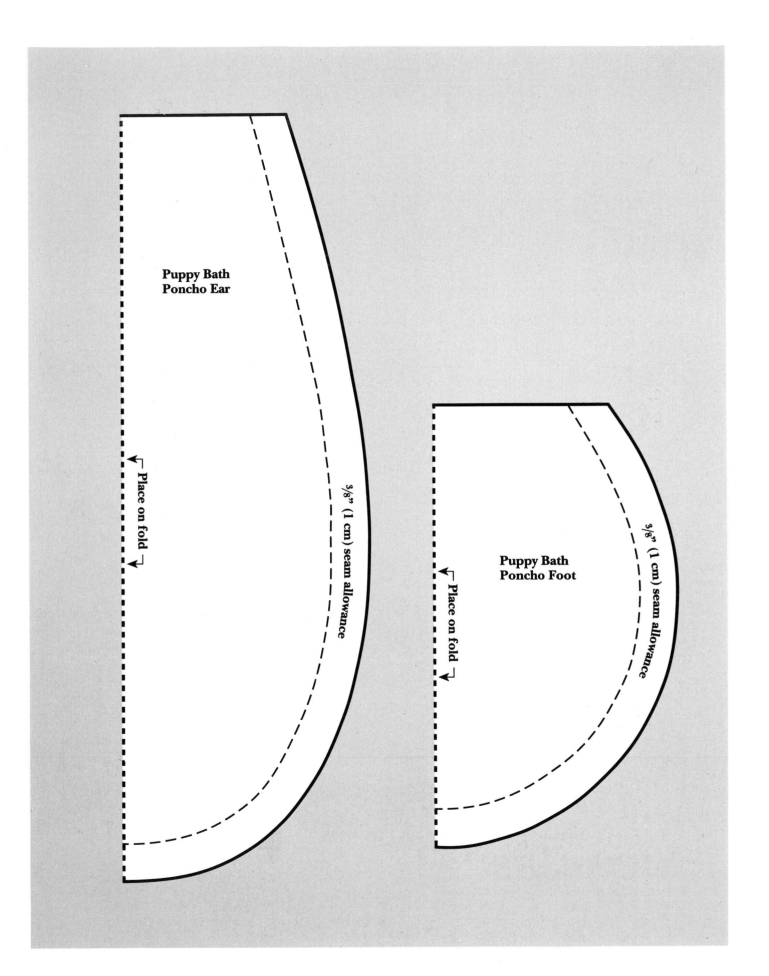

**Puppy Bath
Poncho Ear**

← Place on fold ←

⅜" (1 cm) seam allowance

**Puppy Bath
Poncho Foot**

← Place on fold ←

⅜" (1 cm) seam allowance

283

Birthday Banner

This decorative wall banner features the Ohio Star design (page 288). Decorate a separate fabric square for each family member, and button it over the center of the banner to celebrate each person's birthday.

The lettering on the banner is stenciled onto the fabric before the quilt is assembled. For easy stencil designs, use the precut plastic alphabet stencils available in several sizes and styles at craft stores and office supply stores. Once stenciled, the personalized squares can be customized to each family member's interests with iron-on appliqués, embroidery, or even charms.

The finished banner measures about 31" (78.5 cm) square and hangs easily from a single nail.

✂ Cutting Directions

Cut five 8½" (21.8 cm) squares from background fabric; one of these squares is used for the center square of the quilt. Cut two 9¼" (23.6 cm) squares each from star point fabric and background fabric; layer and cut the large squares as on page 289, step 2.

Cut three 4" (10 cm) strips from border fabric; trim each strip to 24½" (62.3 cm) in length for the side and lower border pieces. Cut two 1¼" (3.2 cm) strips from border fabric; trim each strip to 24½" (62.3 cm) in length for the narrow upper border pieces. The upper border piece with lettering is cut after the letters are stenciled. Cut four 4" (10 cm) squares from star point fabric for the corner squares of the border. For the binding, cut three 2" (5 cm) fabric strips.

For each personalized square, cut two 8½" (21.8 cm) squares from fabric and one 9½" (24.3 cm) square from thin batting or flannel.

Personalized fabric squares highlight interests of family members.

YOU WILL NEED

⅝ yd. (0.6 m) fabric, for background.

⅓ yd. (0.32 m) fabric, for star points and corner squares of border.

⅔ yd. (0.63 m) fabric, for border and binding.

⅛ yd. (0.15 m) light-colored fabric, for upper border with lettering.

1 yd. (0.95 m) fabric, for backing.

Plastic or tear-away paper stencil.

Batting, about 35" (89 cm) square, for banner; thin batting or flannel, 9½" (24.3 cm) square, for each personalized square.

Fabric scraps, and 6" (15 cm) length of ribbon or cording, ⅛" (3 mm) wide, for each personalized square.

Two buttons.

Embellishments, for personalized squares.

Alphabet stencil, 1¼" to 1½" (3.2 to 3.8 cm) in height; fabric paints; disposable plates; stencil brush; medium-grit sandpaper.

Sawtooth picture hanger and 29" (73.5 cm) strip of sealed wooden lattice, for hanging banner.

How to Sew a Birthday Banner

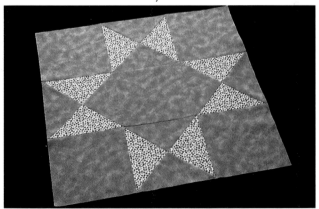

1) Assemble Ohio Star block as on page 289, steps 3 to 7; in step 6, use square from background fabric for center square of block.

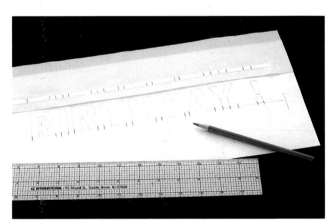

2) Determine spacing of border lettering on paper; finished length of border strip is 24" (61 cm). Mark letter spacing on a strip of tape; then position tape on fabric to use as a placement guide for letters.

(Continued on next page)

3) Place fabric, right side up, on sandpaper to keep fabric from shifting. Wrap tape around the bristles of stencil brush, ¼" (6 mm) from end. Position the first letter; apply tape to the surrounding cutout areas, if necessary to protect fabric.

4) Dip tip of stencil brush into fabric paint; blot onto folded paper towel until bristles are almost dry. Hold brush perpendicular to first letter, and apply paint, using an up-and-down motion. Repeat to stencil the remaining letters, repositioning stencil.

5) Heat-set fabric paint when it is dry, following the manufacturer's directions. Trim fabric to 2½" × 24½" (6.5 × 62.3 cm), taking care to center lettering.

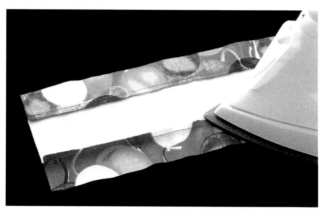

6) Stitch the narrow border strips to upper and lower edges of stenciled border strip; press seam allowances toward the center.

7) Attach borders as on page 66, steps 10 to 12.

8) Cut backing fabric 4" (10 cm) wider and longer than quilt top. Layer and baste the quilt top, batting, and backing (pages 68 and 69). Quilt, using the stitch-in-the-ditch method (pages 70 and 71). Center stencil design on each corner square, and stitch, using template quilting (pages 70 and 72).

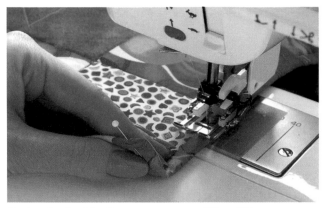

9) Apply the binding as on pages 73 to 75.

10) Embellish right side of personalized fabric square as desired with flat embellishments. Pin 3" (7.5 cm) loop of ribbon or cording to each corner as shown.

11) Place embellished square and lining right sides together; place on batting, and pin layers together. Stitch ¼" (6 mm) from all edges, leaving a 3" (7.5 cm) opening on one side. Trim batting to ⅛" (3 mm); trim corners.

12) Turn square right side out; press lightly. Slipstitch the opening closed. Attach any three-dimensional embellishments as desired. Position the personalized square over center square of banner; mark position for buttons. Stitch buttons in place.

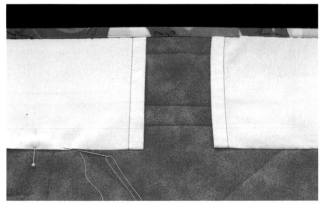

13) Cut fabric sleeve as on page 67, step 1; cut fabric strip in half to make two sleeves. Continue as on page 67, steps 1 to 3; in step 3, allow for 2" (5 cm) space at center of quilt between fabric sleeves.

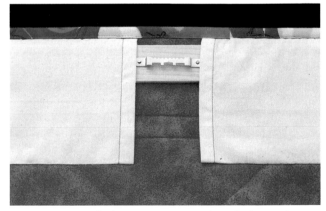

14) Insert a 29" (73.5 cm) strip of sealed wooden lattice through sleeves. Secure a sawtooth hanger to center of lattice. Hang banner from a nail.

Ohio Star Design

The Ohio Star design is created from triangles and squares, and is made from three different fabrics. Select an obvious print for the center square. For the points of the star, use a fabric that is more dominant or darker than the fabric selected for the background. Star points with too little impact will fade into the background, making the center square to be the only design in the quilt block. You can make a 24" (61 cm) or 12" (30.5 cm) finished block with the instructions that follow. The 24" (61 cm) block appears in the Birthday Banner on page 284. The 12" (30.5 cm) block is a popular size, suitable for many other quilt projects.

How to Sew an Ohio Star Block

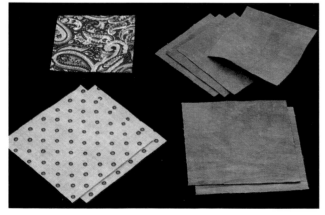

1a) For 24" (61 cm) finished block. Cut one 8½" (21.8 cm) square from the center square fabric and four 8½" (21.8 cm) squares from the background fabric. Cut two 9¼" (23.6 cm) squares each from star point fabric and background fabric.

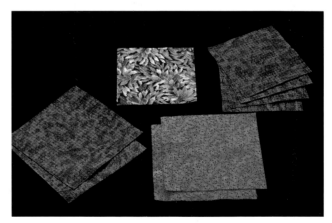

1b) For 12" (30.5 cm) finished block. Cut one 4½" (11.5 cm) square from center square fabric and four 4½" (11.5 cm) squares from background fabric. Cut two 5¼" (13.2 cm) squares each from the star point fabric and background fabric.

288

2) Layer the four large squares, matching raw edges; cut through squares diagonally in both directions.

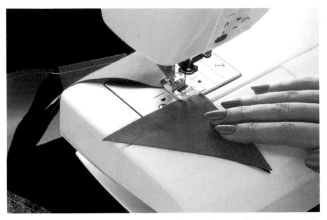

3) Align one star point triangle with one background triangle, right sides together. Stitch along one short side, taking care not to stretch bias edges; repeat for remaining units, using chainstitching as shown.

4) Clip units apart; do not press. Place two units right sides together, alternating fabrics; finger-press seam allowances toward darker fabric. Stitch along long edge, taking care not to stretch bias edges. Repeat for remaining units, using chainstitching.

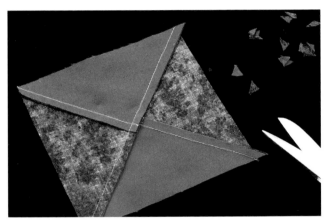

5) Clip the units apart; press the seams. Trim off the points.

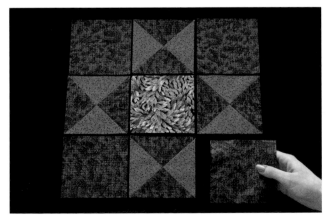

6) Arrange the units into quilt block design as shown.

7) Assemble block. Finger-press seam allowances toward center square. Press block.

Fun Toys to Sew

Nylon Kites

Kites are fun both to make and to fly. The two styles of kites shown here are simple to sew, inexpensive, and fly easily. Because each has its own appeal, you may want to make them both, in brilliant colors.

These kites fit into two different categories: delta and flexible. Delta kites, like the fringed delta kite opposite, are generally triangular in shape and have four spars, or dowels: two along the wing edges, a spine down the middle, and a spreader. By removing the spreader, you can fold the kite for easy storage.

Flexible kites, like the arch-top flexible kite above, are designed to bend, even in light winds, helping them remain stable. This flexible kite has an arched spar and a spine.

YOU WILL NEED

For a fringed delta kite:

1 yd. (0.95 m) nylon fabric, 45" or 60" (115 or 152.5 cm) wide, for sail and keel.

One ¼" (6 mm) dowel, 21½" (54.8 cm) long, for spine.

One ¼" (6 mm) dowel, 19½" (49.8 cm) long, for spreader.

Two ³⁄₁₆" (4.5 mm) dowels, each 26¾" (68 cm) long, for wing spars.

Two caps from ballpoint pens.

Eyelet; kite line.

For an arch-top flexible kite:

¾ yd. (0.7 m) nylon fabric, 45" or 60" (115 or 152.5 cm) wide, for sail.

1¼ yd. (1.15 m) nylon fabric, for tails; this is sufficient yardage for all tails.

⅝ yd. (0.6 m) nylon fabric, optional second color for tails at sides of kite.

One ⅛" (3 mm) dowel, 30" (76 cm) long, for spar.

One ³⁄₁₆" (4.5 mm) dowel, 23½" (59.8 cm) long, for spar.

Kite line.

✂ Cutting Directions

For a fringed delta kite, make the patterns for the sail and keel, opposite. Fold nylon fabric on the bias; cut one sail, using the pattern, placing the foldline of the pattern on a bias fold of the fabric. Cut two fabric triangles for the keel, using the pattern, with the 13" (33 cm) side on the lengthwise grain. For the spreader tabs, cut one 1½" × 6" (3.8 × 15 cm) strip of fabric.

For an arch-top flexible kite, make the pattern for the sail as on page 298. Fold the nylon fabric on the lengthwise grain; cut one sail, using the pattern, placing the foldline of the pattern on the lengthwise fold of the fabric. Cut 2" (5 cm) strips on the bias, for tails. You will need two 5-ft. (1.58 m) tails for the lower point of the kite and two 28" (71 cm) tails for the sides of the kite.

Parts of a Kite

How to Make the Patterns for a Fringed Delta Kite

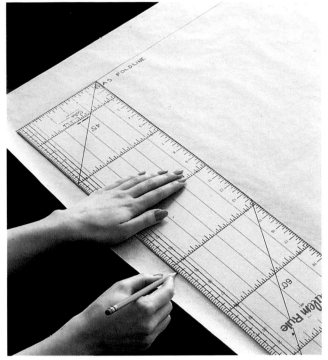

1) Draw 22½" (57.3 cm) line on paper, using pencil; label line as bias foldline. At lower end of line, mark a perpendicular 24" (61 cm) line.

2) Draw 2½" (6.5 cm) line, using pencil, up from and perpendicular to 24" (61 cm) line.

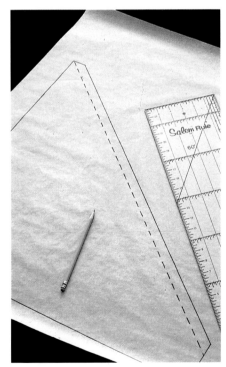

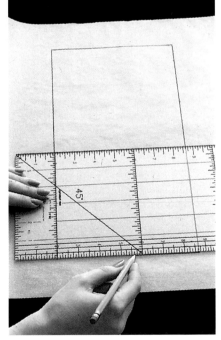

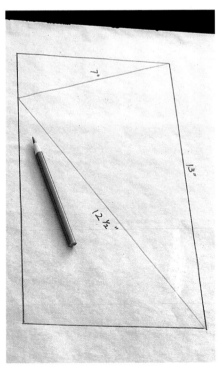

3) Draw 31¼" (79.1 cm) dotted line, connecting upper end of 2½" (6.5 cm) line and upper end of bias foldline. Draw cutting line, ¾" (2 cm) from dotted line, to allow for wing spar casing. This pattern is for sail of kite.

4) Draw 6⅝" × 13" (16.5 × 33 cm) rectangle on paper.

5) Mark a point 2½" (6.5 cm) from corner, on 13" (33 cm) side. Draw lines from this point to corners on opposite side of rectangle, to make a triangular pattern for keel, 7" × 12½" × 13" (18 × 31.8 × 33 cm).

How to Make a Fringed Delta Kite

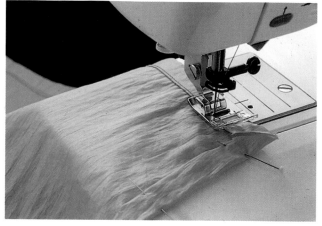

1) **Make** casings for the wing spars by turning under ¼" (6 mm), then ½" (1.3 cm) on 31¼" (79.1 cm) wing edges.

2) **Stitch** the keel pieces together along 7" and 12½" (18 and 31.8 cm) sides, stitching ½" (1.3 cm) seams. Trim corners; turn keel right side out. Topstitch ¼" (6 mm) from seamed edges, to reinforce.

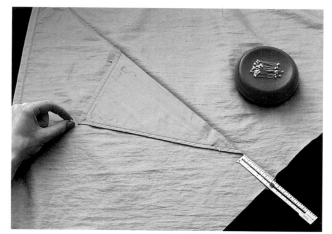

3) **Fold** sail in half on foldline; press. Align raw edge of keel to pressed fold, with narrow point of keel 2½" (6.5 cm) from lower edge of sail; pin in place.

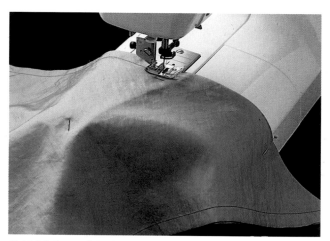

4) **Fold** the sail in half, matching the wing edges and enclosing keel; secure keel by pinning along foldline. Stitch from lower edge of sail to nose tip, ½" (1.3 cm) from foldline, to make casing for spine.

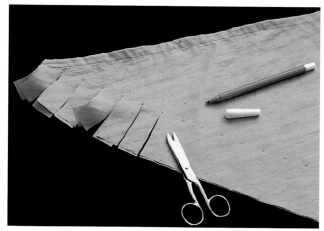

5) **Place** straightedge 2½" (6.5 cm) from lower edge; Mark dots at 1" (2.5 cm) intervals. Cut the fringe by slashing the sail from lower edge to marked dots.

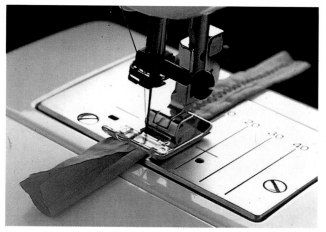

6) **Fold** 1¼" × 6" (3.8 × 15 cm) fabric strip as shown, overlapping edges ¼" (6 mm) at center; zigzag to secure lapped edges. Cut strip in half.

7) Apply glue around middle of pen cap. Wrap fabric strip around cap, over glue; hand-stitch close to cap. Fold ends of strip to inside, forming spreader tab. Repeat for remaining pen cap.

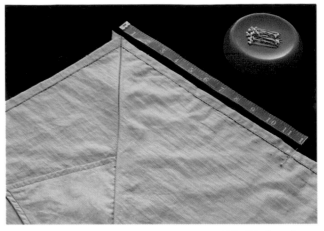

8) Mark points on each wing casing, 12" (30.5 cm) from nose tip, for placement of spreader tabs.

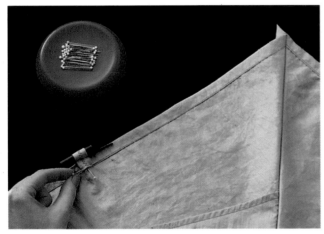

9) Pin the spreader tabs to the wings, with the tabs centered on marked points and with open ends of pen caps toward nose of kite. Stitch tabs to wings along stitching lines for casings.

10) Insert wing spars into wing casings. Insert spine in casing at center foldline. Stitch across casings at lower ends and nose tip.

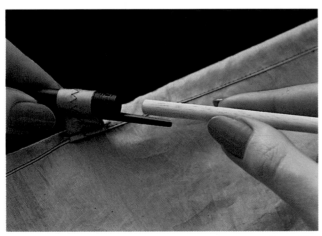

11) Insert ends of spreader into pen caps. Kite will hang loosely; spreader will not fall out.

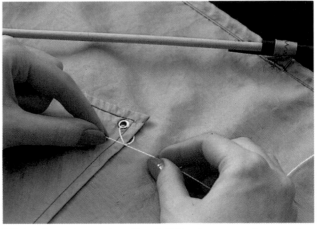

12) Apply eyelet to tip of keel, following manufacturer's directions, just inside topstitching. Tie line securely to the keel.

How to Make the Pattern for an Arch-top Flexible Kite

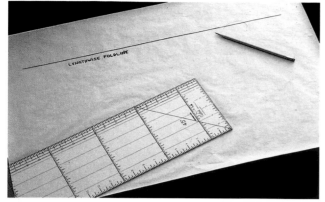

1) Draw 23½" (59.8 cm) line on paper, using pencil; label the line as the lengthwise foldline.

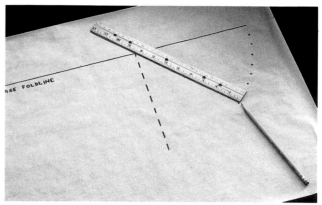

2) Mark a point on foldline, 8¼" (21.2 cm) from upper end. From this point, draw 8¼" (21.2 cm) dotted line, perpendicular to foldline. From same point, mark dotted line in 8¼" (21.2 cm) arc, using compass or straightedge, for upper portion of sail.

3) Draw 17½" (44.3 cm) dotted line, connecting end of 8¼" (21.2 cm) dotted line and the lower end of the foldline.

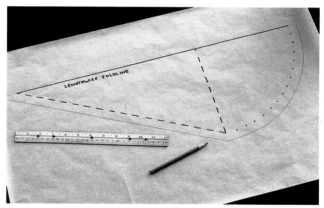

4) Draw cutting line, ¾" (2 cm) from dotted arc and straight line, for casing allowance.

How to Make an Arch-top Flexible Kite

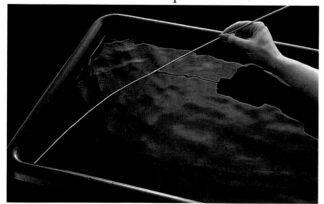

1) Place ⅛" (3 mm) dowel in warm water and allow to soak while following steps 2 to 4.

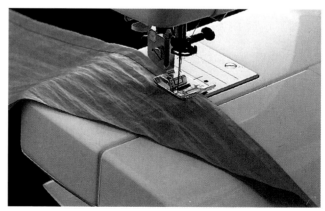

2) Fold the sail in half on foldline; press. Stitch ⅜" (1 cm) from foldline, to make casing for spine.

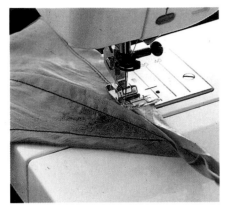

3) Hem the straight edges, turning under ¼" (6 mm), and then ½" (1.3 cm). Leave open at point, for inserting spine.

4) Make a casing on curved edge, pressing under ¼" (6 mm), then ½" (1.3 cm). Pin casing, placing pins close together. Stitch casing, stitching small pleats that form.

5) Remove dowel from water; wipe off. Bend dowel carefully, fastening one end to ironing board. Ease the dowel into the curved casing, while keeping dowel bent.

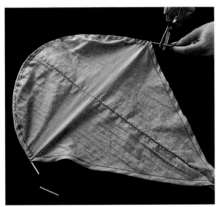

6) Cut ends of the dowel about 1" (2.5 cm) beyond the ends of the curved casing.

7) Insert the spine in center casing. Place two 5-ft. (1.58 m) tails at end of spine, one on each side, laying tails on sail. Secure tails, wrapping line tightly around end of spine. Turn tails down over end.

8) Fold 28" (71 cm) tail so that one end is 2" (5 cm) longer. Hand-stitch to gather tail at fold; secure to one end of curved dowel, taking several stitches into casing. Repeat for tail at opposite end of curved dowel.

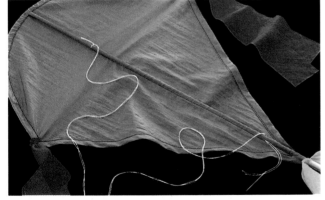

9) Mark points, 5½" (14 cm) and 19" (48.5 cm) from top of spine. Thread 96" (244 cm) line into needle. Stitch through kite, under spine, at points. Tie ends together securely next to spine, leaving 1" (2.5 cm) tails; this makes 47" (120 cm) double-strand bridle.

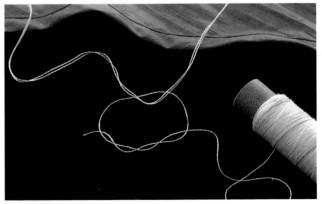

10) Attach line to bridle, tying a double overhand knot. The knot will self-adjust as the kite flies.

Teddy Bears

Although teddy bears can sometimes be time-consuming and difficult to make, this teddy with cut-on arms and legs is quick and easy to sew. Use the simplified pattern pieces on pages 304 and 305.

Select a wool flannel, textured wool, corduroy, velveteen, or robe velour. These fabrics are easier to work with than the usual fake fur and give a more old-fashioned quality to the bear. Hand-embroider the facial details to add to the old-fashioned appearance, or use the safety eyes and nose available at craft and fabric stores.

✄ Cutting Directions
Trace the partial pattern pieces (pages 304 and 305) and make full-size patterns as on page 302, step 1. Cut one back piece, placing the center back on a fold of the fabric. Cut two front pieces.

YOU WILL NEED

⅜ **yd. (0.35 m) fabric,** such as wool, corduroy, velveteen, or robe velour.

Embroidery floss.

Safety eyes and nose, optional.

Polyester fiberfill.

Pinking shears, optional.

Teddy bears can feature realistic safety eyes and nose or can be hand-embroidered for a more old-fashioned look.

How to Sew a Teddy Bear with an Embroidered Face

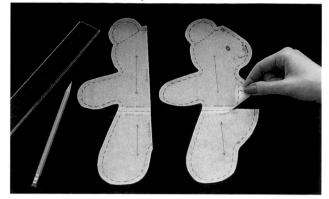

1) Trace partial patterns (pages 304 and 305) onto the tracing paper. Make full-size front pattern by taping front body and front leg pieces together, matching dotted lines. Make full-size back pattern, taping the back body and leg pieces together, matching dotted lines. Cut pieces from fabric as on page 301.

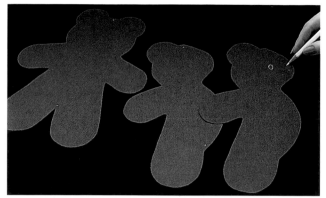

2) Transfer the dots at the top and bottom onto wrong sides of bear front and back pieces. Transfer pattern markings for eyes and dots at A, B, and C for nose and mouth, onto right side of bear front pieces.

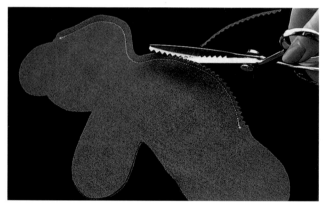

3) Stitch the center front seam from dot to dot. Notch curves with pinking shears, and clip inner corners with scissors. If pinking shears are not available, clip curves and corners with scissors.

4) Satin-stitch eyes at markings by stitching closely spaced parallel stitches, using three strands of embroidery floss.

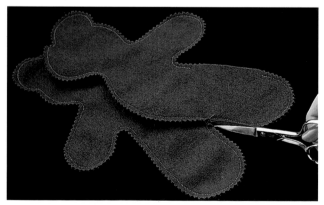

5) Pin front to back, right sides together, matching dots. Stitch around bear, leaving 3" (7.5 cm) opening on one side, along upper leg. Notch and clip the outer and inner curves as in step 3.

6) Turn the bear right side out. Stuff ears lightly with fiberfill. Using a zipper foot, stitch below the ears as indicated by dotted line on pattern.

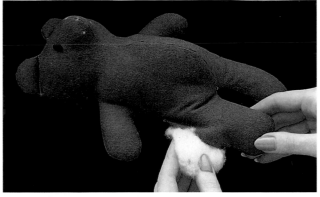

7) **Continue** stuffing bear with fiberfill until plump. Hand-stitch opening closed.

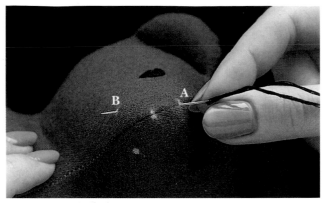

8) **Thread** needle with six strands of embroidery floss; knot ends together. Insert needle at Point A, bringing needle up at Point B on left side of mouth.

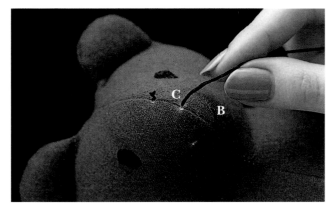

9) **Insert** needle at Point B on right side of mouth; bringing it up at Point C; to form curve of mouth, do not pull thread tight.

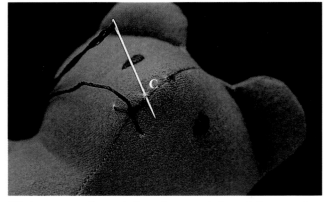

10) **Loop** needle and thread around thread for mouth; take small stitch at Point C, and do not cut threads. Satin-stitch nose vertically at shaded pattern area.

How to Sew a Teddy Bear with Safety Eyes and Nose

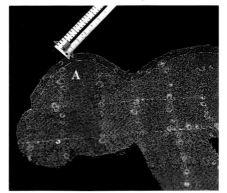

1) **Follow** steps 1 and 2, opposite. Stitch center front seam from dot at top of bear to Point A at the nose; secure stitching. Leaving ⅛" (3 mm) opening at nose, continue stitching seam to dot at bottom of bear; secure stitching.

2) **Notch** and clip center front seam allowances as in step 3, opposite. Stitch mouth as in steps 8 to 10, above; secure thread at Point C. Make small holes in bear front at markings for eyes, using awl. Insert shank of eye through hole.

3) **Place** locking washer over shank. Place bear face down on padded surface. Position thread spool over washer; tap gently in place, using hammer. Attach safety nose at the opening in center front seam. Finish bear as in steps 5 to 7, opposite.

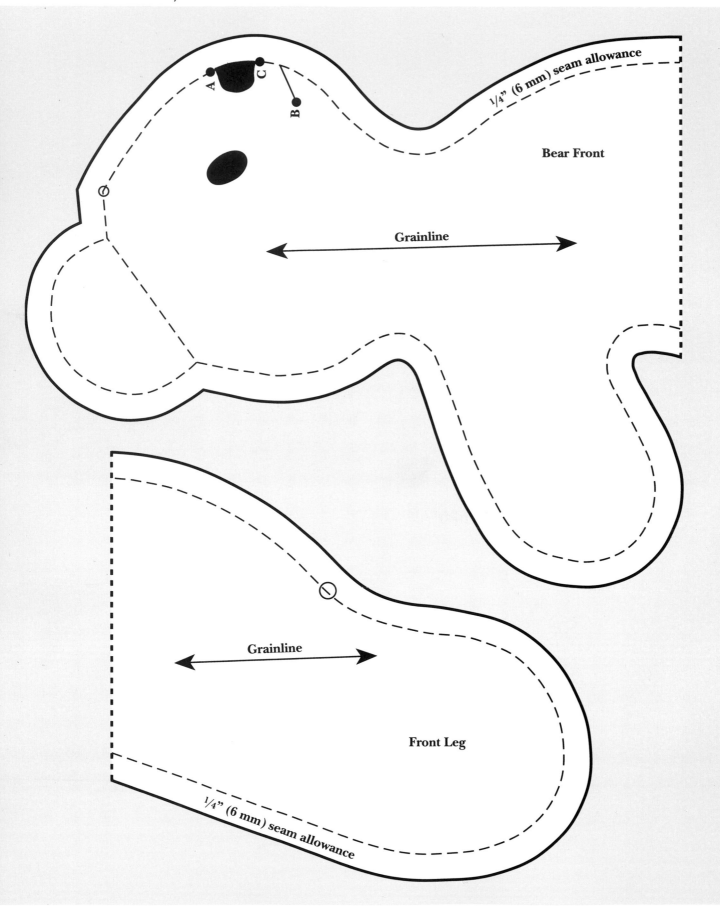

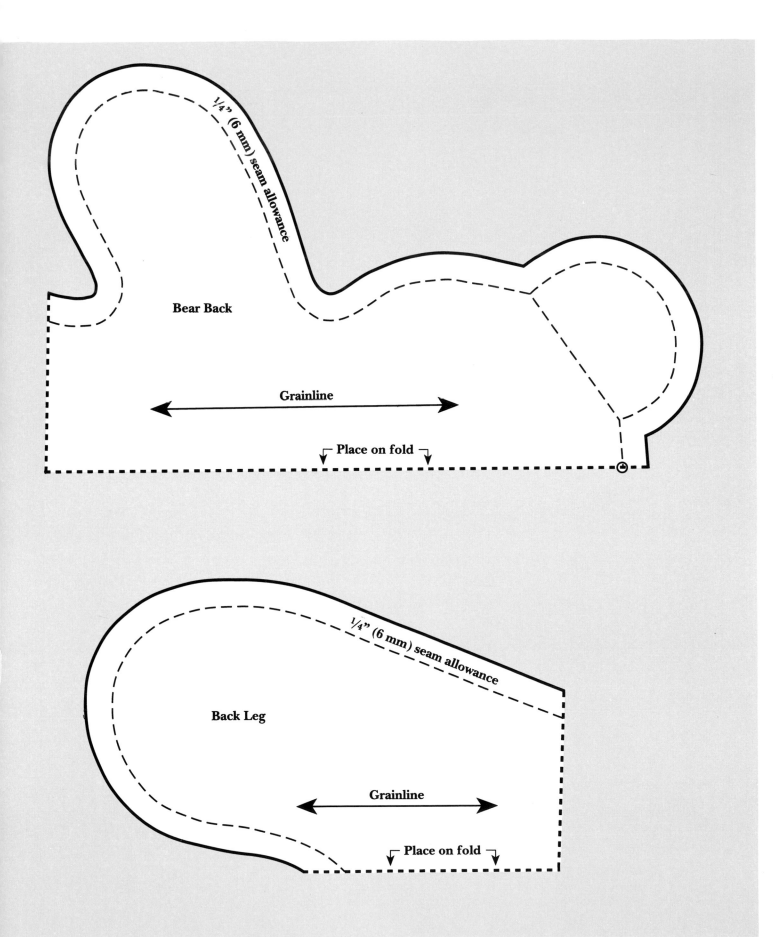

1/4" (6 mm) seam allowance

Bear Back

Grainline

Place on fold

1/4" (6 mm) seam allowance

Back Leg

Grainline

Place on fold

Hand Puppets

A ladybug and a daddy longlegs spider become hand puppets that are sure to delight any child. These crawling critters have gloves sized for a child's hand, allowing small fingers to become wiggly legs. Because both puppets have more legs than a child has fingers, the extra legs are stuffed to give them body. Made from two-way stretch fabric, such as swimwear fabric, these puppets can also be used comfortably by an adult.

✂ Cutting Directions

Prepare the puppet patterns, opposite. For each puppet, cut two bodies and two gloves from two-way stretch fabric; transfer the markings from the patterns. As in steps 4 and 5 on page 308, cut two eyes from felt or synthetic suede; for the ladybug puppet, also cut two wings from felt or synthetic suede, cutting out the dots on the wings.

YOU WILL NEED

½ yd. (0.5 m) two-way stretch fabric, for spider.

⅓ yd. (0.32 m) two-way stretch fabric, for ladybug.

Scraps of felt or synthetic suede, for eyes.

Scraps of felt or synthetic suede, for ladybug wings.

Polyester fiberfill, for stuffing.

Paper-backed fusible web.

How to Prepare the Hand Puppet Patterns

Ladybug. Trace ladybug patterns (pages 310 and 311) onto paper, tracing body, glove, and wing patterns once and tracing leg pattern three times. Tape three legs to curved edge of glove pattern.

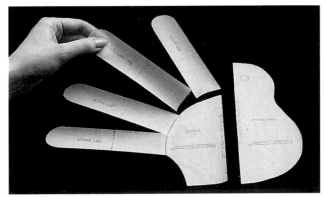

Spider. Trace spider patterns (pages 310 and 311) onto paper, tracing body and glove patterns once and tracing leg pattern four times. Tape four legs to curved edge of glove pattern, overlapping legs slightly.

1) Pin two glove pieces right sides together. Using short stitch length, stitch ¼" (6 mm) seam around legs; leave straight edge of glove unstitched. Clip seam allowances between legs.

2) Turn the glove right side out. Fold under ¼" (6 mm) on glove opening; stitch hem, using medium zigzag stitch.

3) Stuff one ladybug leg that will not be used for a finger when using the puppet.

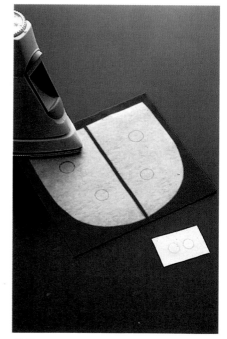

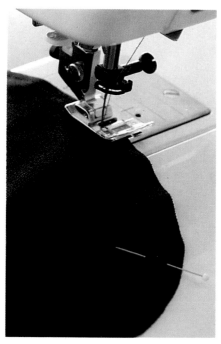

4) Trace eyes onto paper side of the paper-backed fusible web; cut. Fuse to the wrong side of synthetic suede or felt. Repeat for wings.

5) Cut out eyes and wings; fuse to upper body where indicated on pattern. Stitch around eyes, using short, narrow zigzag stitch. Stitch around wings, using straight stitch.

6) Cut 2" (5 cm) lengthwise slash in center of one body piece. Pin body pieces right sides together; stitch ¼" (6 mm) seam.

7) Turn body right side out through slash; stuff with fiberfill. Whipstitch slash closed.

8) Fold glove in half on foldline; position on underside of the body, matching markings, with foldline along the slashed line. Whipstitch glove to body along fold, taking care to catch only one layer of the glove in stitching.

9) Unfold glove; pin to the body at top of each leg. Slipstitch, using a double strand of thread; for the unstuffed legs, insert a finger into leg as you stitch, to catch only one layer of glove in stitching. For stuffed leg, catch both layers.

How to Sew a Spider Hand Puppet

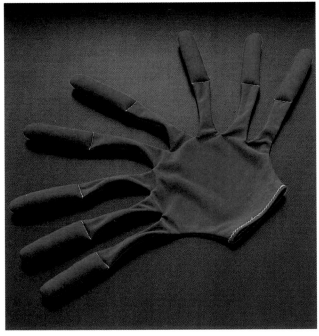

1) Follow steps 1 and 2, opposite. Stuff lower half of each spider leg with fiberfill; using zipper foot, machine-stitch across each leg at halfway point to form joint.

2) Stuff upper portion of three spider legs that will not be used for fingers. Complete the spider puppet, following steps 4 to 9, except omit wings.

Patterns for Ladybug and Spider Hand Puppets

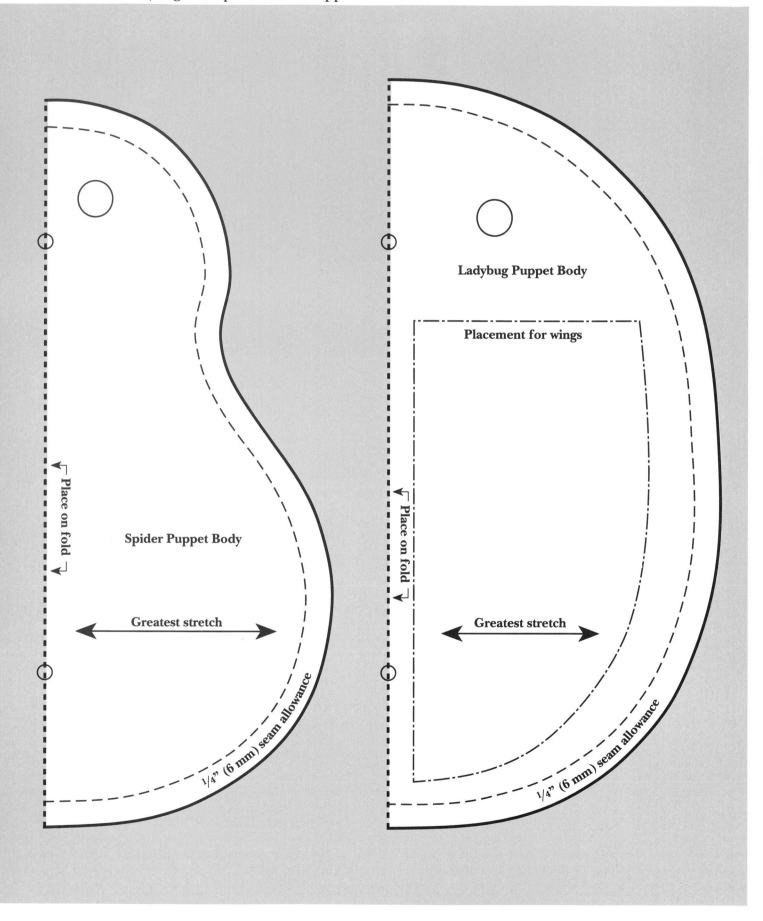

310

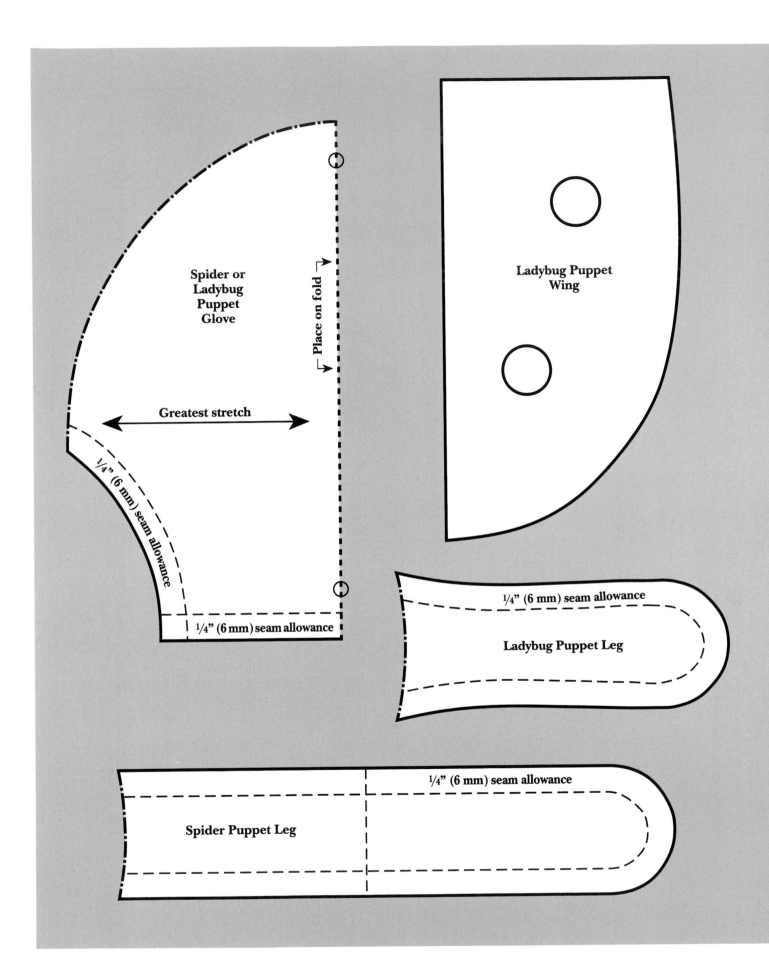

Spider or
Ladybug
Puppet
Glove

← Place on fold →

Greatest stretch

¹⁄₄" (6 mm) seam allowance

¹⁄₄" (6 mm) seam allowance

Ladybug Puppet
Wing

¹⁄₄" (6 mm) seam allowance

Ladybug Puppet Leg

¹⁄₄" (6 mm) seam allowance

Spider Puppet Leg

Playhouse Tents

This tent serves as either an indoor or outdoor playhouse. Supported by four ¾" (2 cm) PVC pipes, the tent can be erected quickly and easily by a child and stores compactly. The PVC pipe, available from hardware stores, is inexpensive, easy to cut, and very durable. A generous 54" (137 cm) on each side and 56" (142 cm) tall, the tent is large enough to share with friends.

For comfort, make the tent from cotton poplin or other mediumweight cotton fabric. Nylon fabric may also be used, but it will be hotter inside the tent. To add interest, select a bright-colored striped fabric for the casings.

✂ Cutting Directions

Cut three sides, one upper front, and two lower front sections, using the patterns on page 314, steps 1 to 3; for efficient use of the fabric, cut the pieces on the crosswise grain with the bottom of the pieces on the selvage. For the casings, cut 5" (12.5 cm) fabric strips on the crosswise grain; piece the strips together as necessary to make four 5" × 58" (12.5 × 147 cm) casing strips.

YOU WILL NEED

4½ **yd. (4.15 m) fabric**, 54" (137 cm) or wider, for the primary tent fabric.

⅞ **yd. (0.8 m) fabric**, 45" (115 cm) or wider, for the casing strips.

Four 68" (173 cm) lengths of ¾" (2 cm) PVC pipe.

Eight end caps for ¾" (2 cm) PVC pipe or for 1" (2.5 cm) chair legs.

One pair of shoelaces, 36" (91.5 cm) long.

Two squares of hook and loop tape.

Sandpaper.

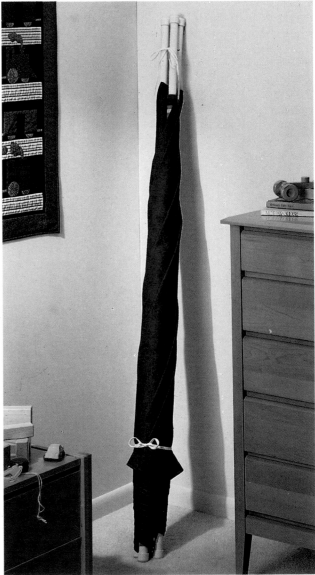

Collapse the tent for easy storage, wrapping it like an umbrella and securing it at the bottom with the attached shoelace.

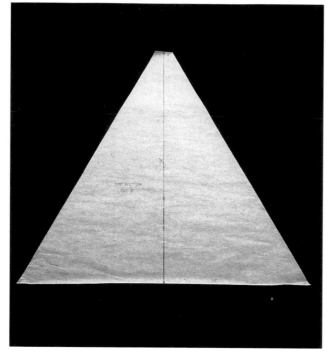

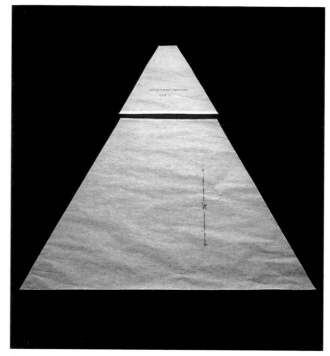

1) Draw 54" (137 cm) line for bottom of tent section. From center of this line, draw a perpendicular 54" (137 cm) line; draw 4" (10 cm) horizontal line, centered at end of this line. Connect ends of 4" (10 cm) line to ends of line at bottom. This trapezoid is the pattern for three sides of tent.

2) Draw a second trapezoid same size as in step 1; cut this trapezoid parallel to and 36" (91.5 cm) from bottom line. Add ½" (1.3 cm) seam allowance to edges where trapezoid was cut apart. Small trapezoid is pattern for upper front section.

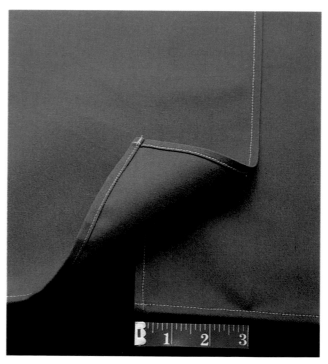

3) Fold bottom portion from step 2 in half lengthwise. Unfold, and draw a line, parallel to and 2" (5 cm) from fold; cut on line, and discard smaller piece. Larger piece is pattern for lower front sections. Cut fabric for tent (page 313).

4) Press under ¼" (6 mm) twice on vertical side of two lower fronts; stitch to make double-fold hems. Repeat for hems on lower edges. Overlap the two lower fronts 3" (7.5 cm); pin.

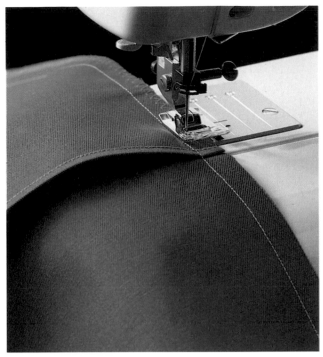

5) Align top edge of lapped lower front sections to bottom edge of upper front section, with pieces right sides together. Stitch ½" (1.3 cm) seam; finish the seam, using zigzag stitch.

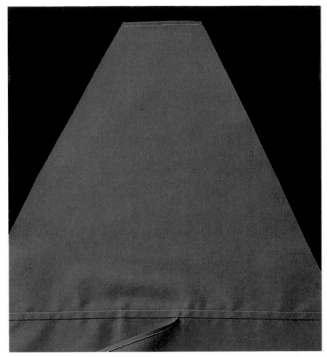

6) Press seam toward upper front section. Topstitch ⅜" (1.5 cm) from seam. Press and stitch ¼" (6 mm) double-fold hem on upper edge of front section.

7) Position squares of hook and loop tape at center of lower front opening (**a**) and near lower edge (**b**). Stitch in place.

8) Press and stitch ¼" (6 mm) double-fold hems on top and bottom edges of all remaining tent sections and on short ends of casing strips.

(Continued on next page)

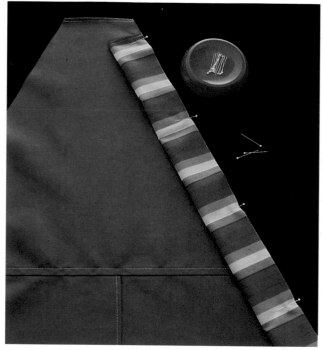

9) Fold a casing strip in half lengthwise, *wrong* sides together. Center folded casing strip on one diagonal edge of front section, with right sides together and raw edges even; pin.

10) Lay one side section of tent over the front section, right sides together, matching diagonal edges. Repin through all layers of tent and casing. Stitch ½" (1.3 cm) seam; finish seam, using zigzag stitch.

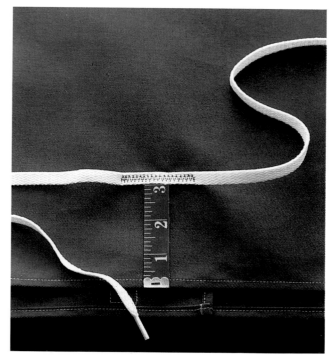

11) Apply remaining casings and stitch remaining diagonal seams of tent as in steps 9 and 10.

12) Pin one shoelace to outside of tent back section, centering it 3" (7.5 cm) from the lower edge. Stitch through the center of the shoelace for 2" (5 cm), using multizigzag stitch.

13) Drill hole completely through each PVC pipe, 4" (10 cm) from upper end, using 3/16" drill bit.

14) Remove any labeling or other markings from the upper 15" (38 cm) of PVC pipes, using sandpaper.

15) Slide PVC pipes into casings, with holes at top of tent; apply end caps to top and bottom of each pipe.

16) Thread remaining shoelace through holes in the PVC pipes as shown. To erect tent, spread the pipes apart at bottom of tent and arrange them as shown on page 92.

Index

Cy DeCosse Incorporated offers a variety of how-to books. For information write:
  Cy DeCosse Subscriber Books
  5900 Green Oak Drive
  Minnetonka, MN 55343